APOLOGIES TO THE IROQUOIS

Laurence M. Hauptman, Series Editor

Apologies
to the Iroquois

BY EDMUND WILSON

With a study of
THE MOHAWKS IN HIGH STEEL
BY JOSEPH MITCHELL

and with a new introduction
BY WILLIAM N. FENTON

SYRACUSE UNIVERSITY PRESS

Syracuse University Press Edition 1992
93 94 95 96 97 98 99   6 5 4 3 2

Publication of this book is through arrangement with Farrar, Straus &
Giroux, Inc.

" 'Apologies to the Iroquois': 1957–1965," from *Letters on Literature and
Politics: 1912–1972*, edited by Elena Wilson, reprinted by arrangement
with Farrar, Straus & Giroux.

Most of the material in this book, including "The Mohawks in High
Steel" in its entirety, appeared originally in *The New Yorker* in somewhat different form.

This book is published with the assistance of a grant from the John
Ben Snow Foundation.

The paper used in this publication meets the minimum requirements
of American National Standard for Information Sciences—Permanence of Paper for Printed Library Materials, ANSI Z39.48-1984. ∞™

Library of Congress Cataloging-in-Publication Data
Wilson, Edmund, 1895–1972.
    Apologies to the Iroquois/by Edmund Wilson. With a study of
The Mohawks in high steel/by Joseph Mitchell; and with a new
introduction by William N. Fenton.
    p.   cm.—(The Iroquois and their neighbors)
    Originally published: New York: Farrar, Straus, and Giroux,
1959. ISBN 0-8156-2564-2
    1. Iroquois Indians. I. Mitchell, Joseph, 1908– Mohawks in
high steel. II. Title. III. Series.
E99.I7W56   1992
305.897'5—dc20   91-46543

Manufactured in the United States of America

CONTENTS

ILLUSTRATIONS

Edmund Wilson, one of America's finest critics and essayists, served as associate editor of *The New Republic* and then book editor on *The New Yorker*. He is author of numerous books, among them *Axel's Castle*, a study of the Symbolist movement that established his standing as a literary critic; *To the Finland Station;* and *Upstate: Records and Recollections of Northern New York* (Syracuse University Press).

Joseph Mitchell is the author of *McSorley's Wonderful Saloon*, *Old Mr. Flood*, and *The Bottom of the Harbor*.

William N. Fenton is Distinguished Professor Emeritus of Anthropology at the State University of New York at Albany. He is the author of *The False Face of the Iroquois*, *The Role Call of the Iroquois*, *The Iroquois Eagle Dance* (Syracuse University Press), and editor of *Parker on the Iroquois* (Syracuse University Press).

FOREWORD

The greater part of the material contained in this book
—though in an abridged and somewhat different form
—originally appeared in the *New Yorker*, as did the
whole of Mr. Mitchell's study, and we are both of us
indebted to that magazine for making our trips among
the Indians possible. I am also much indebted to
the Iroquois leaders about whom I have written
here for their kindness and hospitality in receiving
me and for their patience in supplying me with
information; to the lawyers who have been representing the Iroquois in their suits—Mr. Arthur Lazarus,
Jr., Mr. William H. Quimby, Jr., Mr. Stanley Grossman, Mr. Edward E. O'Neill and Mr. Malcolm Montgomery—who have gone to a good deal of trouble to
set me right about legal procedure; and to the non-
Indian experts in Iroquois matters, such as Mr. Merle H.
Deardorff, Mr. Anthony F. C. Wallace and Mr. David
Landy, for advising me and for sending me their papers on special aspects of Iroquois history. I am also
grateful to Mr. Hugh Donlon of the Amsterdam *Recorder*, who wrote the first reports on Standing Arrow, and to Mr. John B. Johnson of the Watertown
Daily Times, both of whom gave me helpful briefings
as to what was going on in the Iroquois world. My

immense debt to Dr. William N. Fenton is partly explained in the course of what follows. If it had not been for his generosity in lending me books and papers and telling me where to look for information, in answering my questions and criticizing my manuscript, in sponsoring me among the Senecas and arranging for me to attend their ceremonies, I should never, in the two years I have worked on this book, have been able to see so much of the Iroquois world or even—in however imperfect a way—got so comprehensive a sense of its history. To his son, Mr. John Fenton, I am indebted for letting me read his detailed and graphic narrative of the adventure of the Seneca boy with the bear, which, written soon after the incident occurred, has enabled me to correct the much sketchier account that I had put together from conversations.

Mr. Wallace L. Chafe of the Smithsonian Institution —who has also been helpful in other ways—has supplied me with the correct pronunciation of Iroquois proper nouns as they are sounded in the Seneca dialect. I have given this pronunciation the first time that a word appears, but have afterwards only written it in a conventionalized English form. The names of the Six Nations are accented as follows: Móhawks, Sénecas, Onondágas, Oneídas, Cayúgas, Tuscaróras.

E.W.

"APOLOGIES" TO
EDMUND WILSON

by WILLIAM N. FENTON

By all odds the greatest man of letters to confront the vast Iroquois literature and to observe and interview their living descendants in the field was Edmund Wilson (1895–1972), America's foremost critic and essayist in this century. Because other writers have treated his career and assessed his *oeuvre* copiously, I shall confine my remarks to the Iroquois adventures that I shared with him and to the reading of the manuscript to "Apologies" and our subsequent discussions. During the fifteen years that I knew him until his passing, he "lifted up my mind," as the Iroquois would say, from the sloth of administration, convinced me that I should and could write prose free of anthropological jargon, and persuaded me that I should give up my job as a museum director and seek a research professorship where I could discharge my obligations to scholarship. Our meeting had a profound effect upon my life that I could have in no way anticipated.*

* After my article, "The Iroquois in the Grand Tradition of American Letters: The Works of Walter D. Edmonds, Carl Carmer, and

Wilson sought me out in late October of 1957. I was then Assistant Commissioner for the New York State Museum and Science Service—in effect, director of the State Museum in Albany. October 28 must have been a busy day, for there are no entries in my diary. By mid-afternoon affairs had slacked off, when my secretary ushered in an unexpected caller—a not infrequent occurrence in the life of a public official. The visitor was "close-coupled," on the pudgy side, and florid-faced. He wore a brown Brooks Brothers' suit of comfortable cut and carried a brown wide-brimmed felt hat. As he sat down in the chair across the desk, he wheezed a bit and then stammered as he commenced to speak. "All the paths lead here," he said. "Everywhere I have been among the Iroquois people, I have been told that I must see Fenton." I asked him where he had been; and he related his visits among the Mohawks of St. Regis and Caughnawaga, where Lincoln White, a Mohawk school-man in the village of West Leyden near Wilson's summer home in Talcottville, had introduced him.

As I listened, I came to realize that this man was no pretender and that he was Edmund Wilson, as he had introduced himself. The flow of his well-structured sentences and his pertinent questions moved me to dig out a bibliography and to suggest that we both watch the ascent of the Pleiades, or the "Dancing Boys" of Seneca thought, and mark the first full moon after the winter solstice so as to be ready to visit the Senecas at the Indian

Edmund Wilson," *American Indian Culture and Research Journal* 5, no. 4 (1981), pp. 21–39. By permission of the publisher. See also Richard Hauer Costa's foreword to Wilson's *Upstate* (Syracuse University Press).

New Year twenty days later. Wilson departed for a plane to Boston and wrote me next day from Wellfleet that he would be ready.*

I thought little about this interview for several months; but as the time approached when one could count twenty days to the fifth night of the next new moon, I sent Wilson a wire. If he were still interested, he should show up in Albany on or about January 22. Again I was preoccupied with other things. On that day the then state archeologist, the learned William A. Ritchie, was scheduled to report at our monthly seminar on his first season's work under a National Science Foundation grant. Ritchie was well into his presentation when Wilson wheezed in, hobbling with a cane, and announced: "I am here, but I have the gout. I am ready to start when you are." The taxi driver who followed him put down his heavy bags, and Wilson sat down to hear the rest of Ritchie's presentation. I introduced Wilson to the seminar, and he proceeded to ask Ritchie several pointed questions.

While the discussion continued, my secretary, Eileen Wood, ordered up a state car for what I had resolved should be an official visit to the Senecas. It was the first of several such trips during the next two years that Wilson and I made together, which facilitated much good talk as we drove and enabled me to share fieldwork with him.

After a late start, toward evening as it began to snow,

* Wilson to Fenton, October 29, 1957, from *Letters on Literature and Politics: 1912–1972*, Elena Wilson, ed. (New York: Farrar, Straus & Giroux, 1977), p. 553; and *The Fifties: From Notebooks and Diaries of the Period*, Leon Edel, ed. (Farrar, Straus & Giroux), p. 456.

we stopped at Geneva to have dinner and to spend the night at the Hotel Seneca. Edmund wrote to his wife, Elena, that I talked a blue streak all the way, but much to the point. I wanted Edmund to see Canandaigua, the site of the Pickering Treaty of 1794, in daylight and possibly to view the document itself in the Ontario County Historical Society, because at the time that treaty was thought to be crucial to the Kinzua Dam controversy, which was then at its height. The Allegany Reservation of the Seneca Nation of Indians, where we were going to witness the Midwinter Festival,* was the area immediately threatened; and the Coldspring Long-house settlement was at the center of the proposed lake. I had the feeling that the ceremonies that I first studied in 1933 would never be the same again. Moreover, though my sympathies were with the Senecas, as a public official just then I could not take a position on the issue. I hoped that Edmund would be moved to discuss the matter in print.

Our journey that morning took us beyond Batavia, the legendary place of the giant mosquito, and the earthwork enclosure at Oakfield, *Skenda:di* (Beyond the Meadows) to the Tonawanda Senecas, and on into the reservation at Basom. Crossing the creek and heading "down below" to the Longhouse district, we met two Seneca matrons about to go shopping for the Longhouse who affirmed that tomorrow was indeed the Indian New Year, the same day as at Cattaraugus and Allegany. This coinci-

---

* Midwinter Festival, or the "Indian New Year," is descended from the Feast of Dreams of the seventeenth-century Jesuit writers.

dence was worth noting given the variations in the lunar calendar and how the old people set the date. (Sometimes the local faithkeepers select a different moon and the celebrations fall a month apart, which leads other faith-keepers to question the wisdom of their counterparts.) That year all of the Seneca faithkeepers had confirmed my own predictions of the date, which afforded me that day to introduce Edmund to Nick (Nicodemus) and Edna Bailey (originally Billy), a Tonawanda Seneca cou-ple I had known since my Indian Service days, and to see how Edmund conducted an interview.

I asked Nick to tell Edmund about the people who had built the fort at Oakfield and originally inhabited Tona-wanda village. I gloss these details from my diary noting my first opportunity to watch Edmund at work. The old labor journalist, who had investigated Voodoo in Haiti and described the *Shalako* ceremonies at Zuni Pueblo, listened well and asked a few precise and apt questions on which Nick expanded. Wilson took no notes, al-though I wrote down for him the Seneca names of three earlier peoples on the Niagara frontier. The following day in Salamanca Wilson discharged his memory of the interview in a letter to his wife.*

As an ethnologist for some twenty-five years myself, and having observed Edmund during his first interview of a Seneca, in which he established rapport almost im-mediately, I asked him how he as a journalist went about it. Indeed, I had never seen anyone get into the confi-

---

* Edmund Wilson to Elena Wilson, January 24, 1958, in *Letters*, pp. 553–4, and in *Apologies*, 185–9, 198–9.

dence of informants as rapidly; and this was to be repeated in the days that followed. He told me that he
habitually kept a journal in which he wrote, as time
afforded, first-draft accounts of events that he had observed together with his own impressions as soon as possible after the event or interview, that he had schooled
himself to retain whole conversations and to recall situations sometimes several days afterward. He also wrote
letters of varying length to his wife, to his publisher, and
to friends, the first being more substantive, which Elena
kept until his return. These were the sources that he
mined later in his writing. Wilson's method may be
suited to the kind of critical journalism of which he was
master, and I have employed it in situations where notebook and pencil or tape recorder offends other partici-
pants in the situation; but I know of no substitute for
taking texts then or afterwards, nor does Wilson's
method have the precision of getting informants who
know the culture to recall afterward the significant parts
of an event or ceremony that is patterned in their unconscious. An outsider's observations include much accidental behavior that may not be significant; and until the
observer learns the pattern that governs such events, he
may miss much that is important.

Wilson had prepared himself for the field by reading
widely in the literature that I had called to his attention.
He commented on my ability to operate in the native
language, which I control, but imperfectly, and which
he thought he ought to learn, just as he had learned
Russian and studied Hebrew previously; and he kept
asking me for study materials. Wallace Chafe's *Seneca*

Morphology and Dictionary (1967) was then in the formative stages, and the *Handbook of the Seneca Language* (1963) was several years away; but Wilson's demands inspired me to get the State Museum to finance the fieldwork that launched both undertakings. He kept saying that the want of such materials handicapped him greatly.

From Tonawanda we crossed the flatlands to Gowanda, some thirty miles southwest of Buffalo, where Cattaraugus Creek, of the "smelly banks," dissects the Allegheny Plateau. We kept a dinner date with the attorney for the Seneca Nation, picked up pills for Edmund's gout, and stayed over hoping to catch the round of the Bigheads, who herald the Feast of Dreams, or Indian New Year, next morning at the Newtown Longhouse.

After a late start we first called on Cornelius Seneca, sometime president of the Seneca Nation, so that Edmund might hear his views on the Kinzua affair.* At noon when we reached Newtown the Bigheads were making the second of three rounds of the houses stirring ashes and urging the householders to reveal new dreams and renew old obligations. The Longhouse officials greeted us cordially just as the heralds entered by the opposite door, bumping their corn pounders and chanting indistinctly, apparently unsure of their lines. One herald wore a bear skin, the other an old blanket; both trailed cornhusk anklets, but they wore no other cornhusk decoration, which seemed a somewhat inadequate wardrobe for the role. At least Edmund got to see and

* *Apologies*, pp. 183–5; future page references are parenthetically cited in text.

hear the Feast of Dreams announced, albeit through a poor performance.

To the Senecas, going over the hills to Allegany Reservation is "to the other side," or to *Ohi:yo?*. That evening we visited Franklin and Mary John at Quaker Bridge, which is now inundated. Mary, matron of the Beaver Clan, which had adopted my wife and children, insisted that we stay for supper, enabling Edmund to share in Seneca hospitality and listen to Franklin foretell the gloomy future of his people. Franklin too had served often as president of the Seneca Nation, although he was then Allegany's lone working farmer. He commanded a vigorous style of address, both in Seneca and in English, that recalled the great Cornplanter. Although I had known him for years, I never heard him in better form than in response to Edmund's questions. The two men hit it off.

There was a blizzard in the night so we stayed in Salamanca next morning until noon. Over a leisurely breakfast Edmund urged me to write an Iroquois classic, and we discussed alternate plans for such a work. He would speak to his publishers. My tutor pronounced: "I have read your papers and you do not use the anthropological jargon. What the book needs is a clear style from one steeped in it—an authority." We estimated that such a writing project would take two years, that a sabbatical might break the back of it. "Could you get a year off from your job," he asked? With two of our youngsters in college just then, this prospect seemed impracticable. (I did manage a leave of absence two years later, which proved all too short.) Chapters written for the great work that never came off have appeared in various journals, and their publication recalls the folkloristic motif of magic flight—hindrances thrown off to the pursuing monsters. I never delivered the manuscript but returned the advance, which Roger Straus wrote me was "un-American!" Perhaps Edmund would have been satisfied with the publication, many years later, of *The False Faces of the Iroquois.**

There is no point now in comparing my diary entries on the ceremonies that winter with the account that Edmund printed in *Apologies* (pp, 202–51). At the time, I read the pertinent chapters in typescript and made corrections when the events were fresh in mind. What impressed me then as now on rereading the book was Edmund's willingness to accept criticism and to rewrite even in galley proof to get it right. He told me that with him six or seven drafts were not unusual, although I would settle for his second or third.

Edmund's gout proved something of an asset with the old men of Coldspring Longhouse. Jake Logan, who had known my father and always treated me as a neophyte, immediately came to Edmund's assistance with prescriptions of herbal remedies. Albert Jones, a great singer and speaker who had befriended me early on, joined the consultation along with Ed Coury, who though mostly white had understudied with Chauncey Johnny John, my erstwhile informant. They all wanted to help Edmund. Jake, then eighty-three, volunteered that the

---

* William N. Fenton, *The False Faces of the Iroquois* (Norman: University of Oklahoma Press, 1987).

present longhouse was built when he was a boy of perhaps ten, which would date its erection to about 1886. "The old longhouse," he said, "stood out near the road toward the river; it was built of logs and plank-sided up and down."

Having settled in among the old men at the north stove, we listened as the speeches flowed and the ceremony progressed. Indians have a great capacity for boredom. In the long intervals, however, small boys grow restless, although their antics seem not to bother the speakers. They were soon quieted with watching Edmund perform feats of magic, which even the elders seemed to enjoy: manipulating coins to appear and disappear, a handkerchief mouse that kept emerging from his coat sleeve—all done in low key.

Whether it was the gout pills, Jake Logan's advice, or fulfilling the Seneca aphorism—"perhaps all he needs is a little dance"—within a day or two Edmund improved sufficiently to walk around the singers' bench in Feather Dance, an act that endeared him to the Longhouse leaders, for whom participation is the essence of respect and the key to acceptance.

Two things about Wilson's fieldwork impressed me at the time and struck me again on rereading his book. The first was his uncanny ability to perceive the character of the persons he interviewed and then to enliven them for his readers. The second was his perspective, shaped by years as a reviewer of theatrical performances ranging from vaudeville, movies, and plays to musical events, that he brought to describing the ceremonies that we witnessed together.

Of the first, he sized up Standing Arrow, whom I knew slightly, as typical of Iroquois speakers and myth-makers, contrasting his folk version of the starved False Face breaking the glass in the State Museum with the carpenter's aide who inadvertently stepped on top of a standing glass case displaying the masks during my re-gime as director. In either version a traditionalist might say, "neglect of the masks caused it."

In the portrait of Philip Cook's attempts to fulfill his role at St. Regis, Wilson perceived a fundamental truth underlying Iroquois attitudes toward Euro-American culture and its bearers. "This resentment is always there, although buried; subdued beneath a taciturn sur-face, it at moments unexpectedly snaps its teeth" (p. 119).

I find the sketch of Mad Bear, the Tuscarora oppor-tunist, less convincing. I fear that Edmund was taken in. The allegory of the serpents attributed to the peace prophet is straight out of Seth Newhouse's "Prediction" with elaborations.* That the Iroquois are prophet-prone is undeniable.

Of the second attribute, as many times as I have sat through celebrations of the Dark Dance for the "Little People," in which a chorus of women dancers respond to the male drummer and assistant singers, it never oc-curred to me that it was an "oratorio" (p. 203).

And Wilson's account of the all-night sing to renew

* Seth Newhouse (1842–1921), "Prediction of De-ka-na-wi-dah." MS. 9 pp. Newberry Library, Chicago. #628 in Ruth Lapham Butler, *A Check List of Manuscripts in the Edward E. Ayer Collection* (Chicago: The Newberry Library, 1937).

the Little Water Medicine at Tonawanda, despite the controversy that ensued, I regard as one of the finest pieces in the Iroquois literature.

Indeed, people who live in the oral tradition are sensitive about writing. The Senecas since Red Jacket's day have reason to believe that they have been done in by "all that pen and paper business." While they wish to maintain their tradition and want their children to learn the lore and keep up the ceremonies in the native language, they are reluctant to see their rituals described explicitly. They often used to ask me, "are we really like that?" And they suspect that writers of books make money off their religion. In a sense that is true. But, in my experience, they avidly snap up and cherish the monographs and papers of ethnologists. I have seen woefully dog-eared copies of Lewis H. Morgan's *League of the Iroquois* (1851) circulating on the reserves; copies of my own studies have been used up and reprinted. This ambivalence raises some questions of ethics.

What does the ethnologist, having enjoyed the confidence of traditional people, participated in their "doings," and striven to learn and get things right, do with his field notes? He has an obligation to himself, he has invested time in a profession, he owes a debt to the academicians who trained him, and his colleagues expect that he will write up his notes and share them. This means publishing. How should he treat materials that are sensitive? In the half-century of my contacts with the Iroquois people, subjects that the old people did not classify as off limits have since been added to the list of tabu topics. Those members of a new generation who have only recently discovered their cultural roots resent persons who applied themselves to learning their culture but are never part of it. Topics once discussed openly with folklorists and ethnologists a century ago became part of the published literature. Versions of the origin legend of the Little Water Medicine Society began appearing in the *Journal of American Folk-Lore* in the 1880s, and Arthur Parker described the medicine societies in 1909. Although sacred to this day among traditional people, the subject was in the public domain when Edmund Wilson discovered Iroquoia. Here was a subject that he wanted to explore.

Readers may want to know how this argument is relevant to Wilson and myself. When he first applied for permission to attend the all-night sing to renew the strength of the medicine, which I had been going to for years, word came back that he would be admitted if I came too and if he promised not to write anything about it (Fenton, Diary, January 7, 1959). The invitation came through. That June we went up to Tonawanda together on the appointed day. We arrived in the late afternoon at the home of Chief Corbett Sundown, whose wife, Priscilla, insisted that we take supper with them. "It would be a long night," she warned us. I remember distinctly Edmund's explaining to Chief Sundown that he was a writer and that he planned to write an account of our visit. Perhaps Sundown did not get the point, or he was too polite to make an issue of it. Chapter nine of *Apologies* represents our combined observations on that occasion. I sat with the singers; Edmund sat apart. Although I wrote nothing at the time or afterward, I did read and correct Edmund's manuscript. This chapter has no peer in the Iroquois literature, and we are lucky to have it from so competent a writer.

Our parting at daybreak was most cordial, just as Wilson describes at the end of his book. On reaching home, I wrote to Chief Sundown thanking him for his hospitality and for the privilege of sitting with the singers.

The *New Yorker* ran much of Wilson's material before the book appeared, toward the close of 1959. For me the collaboration was a great learning experience. But it did not end as I then expected. No Seneca objected to what Edmund wrote until a certain self-appointed protector of Tonawanda tradition went up to the reservation with a copy of the *New Yorker* in hand and confronted Chief Sundown. This person also called on Nick Bailey and questioned the propriety of his having demonstrated the music on his flute, an instrument on which Nick was a virtuoso performer. Naturally Nick was upset. I relate this incident because it is an example of the way that white people sometimes patronize Indians, and it illustrates how adept Indians are at manipulating white people. I had observed this process at work during my tenure as Community Worker at Tonawanda during the New Deal. Whatever the fuss at the time, the irony of it was that the next time Chief Sundown was in my State Museum office, he left saying, "We are having it again. You had better come."

I do not know how many contemporary Iroquois have read Wilson's book. For a while it was on the proscribed list at the Seneca Iroquois National Museum shop. It is the one book that lifted up the cause of Iroquois cultural autonomy to the realm of *belle lettres*. It generated support for the Seneca case against the U.S. Corps of Army Engineers during the Kinzua crisis. President Kennedy read it, and it was discussed in the White House by Arthur Schlesinger and others, although it failed to avert the Kinzua Dam. Wilson later received a presidential medal.

In sum, Wilson perceived the Iroquois world view intuitively and overcame any obstacle to get at the truth. Indeed, he frequently proclaimed that he made his own version, one that I came to respect. Men of his ilk walk the earth, but seldom; and I am glad to have shared the path with him for a few brief years.

If I may put a patch on my speech, as Red Jacket once said, let me add a note on Joseph Mitchell's "Mohawks in High Steel," which Wilson reprinted from the *New Yorker* (1949) and which may have set him off on his quest. It is a seamless piece of writing. The sketch of Caughnawaga fits nicely with what I found a decade earlier in a brief quest for Iroquois medicines. In the 1950s the State Museum and Science Service awarded Morris Freilich a graduate student honorarium to follow up Mitchell's lead among the Mohawk steelworkers of Brooklyn. His report, "Cultural Persistence among the Modern Iroquois,"* has escaped readers beyond the pale of professional anthropology. Quite recently, Rick Hill, a native Tuscarora, artist, photographer, and museum director, has related his own rearing in a family of steelworkers on the Niagara Frontier in book and article for-

* *Anthropos* (Fribourg, Switzerland) 53 (1958).

mat.* A whole crop of native Indian writers has come to the fore. Edmund Wilson would have approved.

Keene Valley, New York
July 4, 1991

* *Northeast Indian Quarterly* (1990).

THE MOHAWKS IN
HIGH STEEL

by JOSEPH MITCHELL

The most footloose Indians in North America are a band of mixed-blood Mohawks whose home, the Caughnawaga Reservation, is on the St. Lawrence River in Quebec. They are generally called the Caughnawagas. In times past, they were called the Christian Mohawks or the Praying Mohawks. There are three thousand of them, at least six hundred and fifty of whom spend more time in cities and towns all over the United States than they do on the reservation. Some are as restless as gypsies. It is not unusual for a family to lock up its house, leave the key with a neighbor, get into an automobile, and go away for years. There are colonies of Caughnawagas in Brooklyn, Buffalo, and Detroit. The biggest colony is in Brooklyn, out in the North Gowanus neighborhood. It was started in the late twenties, there are approximately four hundred men, women, and children in it, it is growing, and it shows signs of permanence. A few families have bought houses. The pastor of one of the churches in the neighborhood, the Cuyler Presbyterian, has learned the Mohawk dialect of the Iroquois language and holds a service in it once a month, and the church has elected a Caughnawaga to its board of deacons. There have been marriages between Caughnawagas and members

3

of other groups in the neighborhood. The Caughnawaga women once had trouble in finding a brand
of corn meal (Quaker White Enriched and Degerm-
inated) that they like to use in making *ka-na-ta-rok*,
or Indian boiled bread; all the grocery stores in North
Gowanus, even the little Italian ones, now carry it.
One saloon, the Nevins Bar & Grill, has become a
Caughnawaga hangout and is referred to in the neighborhood as the Indian Bank; on weekend nights, two-
thirds of its customers are Caughnawagas; to encourage their patronage, it stocks one Montreal ale and
two Montreal beers. A saying in the band is that
Brooklyn is the downtown of Caughnawaga.

Caughnawaga Reservation is on the south shore of
the St. Lawrence, just above Lachine Rapids. It is nine
miles upriver from Montreal, which is on the north
shore. By bus, it is half an hour from Dominion Square,
the center of Montreal. It is a small reservation. It is a
tract of farmland, swamp, and scrub timber that is
shaped like a half-moon; it parallels the river for eight
miles and is four miles wide at its widest point. On the
river side, about midway, there is a sprawled-out village, also named Caughnawaga. Only a few of the
Caughnawagas are farmers. The majority live in the
village and rent their farmland to French Canadians
and speak of the rest of the reservation as "the bush."
The Montreal-to-Malone, New York, highway goes
through Caughnawaga village. It is the main street.
On it are about fifty commonplace frame dwellings,
the office of the Agent of the Indian Affairs Branch
of the Canadian government, the Protestant church (it

is of the United Church of Canada denomination),
the Protestant school, and several Indian-owned grocery stores and filling stations. The stores are the
gathering places of the old men of the village. In each
store is a cluster of chairs, boxes, and nail kegs on
which old men sit throughout the day, smoking and
playing blackjack and eating candy bars and mum-
bling a few words now and then, usually in Mohawk.
In the front yards of half a dozen of the dwellings are
ramshackly booths displaying souvenirs—papoose dolls,
moccasins, sweet-grass baskets, beadwork handbags,
beadwork belts, beadwork wristwatch straps, and pin-
cushions on which beads spell out "Mother Dear,"
"Home Sweet Home," "I Love U," and similar
legends. In one yard, between two totem poles, is a
huge, elm-bark tepee with a sign on it that reads,
"Stop! & Pow Wow With Me. Chief White Eagle.
Indian Medicine Man. *Herbages Indiens*." Except on
ceremonial occasions and for show purposes, when
they put on fringed and beaded buckskins and feather
headdresses of the 'Plains Indian type, Caughnawagas
dress as other Canadians do, and if it were not for
these front-yard establishments, most motorists would
be unaware that they were passing through an Indian
village. A scattering of Caughnawagas look as Indian
as can be; they have high cheekbones and jut noses,
their eyes are sad, shrewd, and dark brown, their hair
is straight and coal black, their skin is smooth and
coppery, and they have the same beautiful, erect,
chin-lifted, haughty walk that gypsies have. White
blood, however, has blurred the Indianness of the

majority; some look dimly but unmistakably Indian, some look Indian only after one has searched their faces for Indian characteristics, and some do not look Indian at all. They run to two physical types; one type, the commoner, is thickset, fleshy, and broad-faced, and the other is tall, bony, and longheaded. Some of the younger Caughnawagas have studied a little of the Indian past in school and they disapprove of the front-yard establishments. They particularly disapprove of Chief White Eagle's establishment; they feel that it gives visitors a highly erroneous impression of Caughnawaga right off the bat. First of all, the old Mohawks did not live in tepees but in log-and-bark communal houses called longhouses, and they did not make totem poles. Also, there haven't been any chiefs in Caughnawaga, except self-appointed ones, since 1890. Furthermore, while all Caughnawagas have Indian names, some much fancier than White Eagle, few go under them outside their own circles, and those who do almost invariably run them together and preface them with a white given name; John Goodleaf, Tom Tworivers, and Dominick Twoax are examples. Caughnawagas discovered long ago that whites are inclined to look upon Indian names, translated or untranslated, as humorous. In dealing with whites, ninety-five per cent of them go under white names, and have for many generations. Most of these names are ordinary English, Scotch, Irish, or French ones, a number of which date back to intermarriages with early settlers. The names of the oldest and biggest Caughnawaga families are Jacobs, Williams, Rice, Mc-

Comber, Tarbell, Stacey, Diabo (originally D'Aille-boust), Montour, De Lisle, Beauvais, and Lahache. The most frequent given names are Joe, John, and Angus, and Mary, Annie, and Josie.

On each side of the highway there is a labyrinth of lanes, some dirt, some gravel, and some paved. Some are straight and some are snaky. The dwellings on them are much older than those on the highway, and they range from log cabins to big field-stone houses with frame wings and lean-tos; members of three and even four generations of a family may live in one house. In the yards are gardens and apple trees and sugar-maple trees and piles of automobile junk and groups of outbuildings, usually a garage, a privy, a chicken coop, and a stable. Large families keep a cow or two and a plug horse; the French Canadians who rent the reservation farmland sell all their worn-out horses to the villagers. The dwellings in Caughnawaga are wired for electricity, just about every family has a radio and a few have telephones, but there is no waterworks system. Water for drinking and cooking is obtained from public pumps—the old-fashioned boxed-up, long-handled kind—situated here and there on the lanes. Water for washing clothes and for bathing is carted up from the river in barrels, and the horses are used for this. They are also used for carting firewood, and the children ride them. Most mornings, the cows and horses are driven to unfenced pastures on the skirts of the village. A few always mosey back during the day and wander at will.

The busiest of the lanes is one that runs beside the

river. On it are the reservation post office, the Catholic church, the Catholic schools, a parish hall named Kateri Hall, and a small Catholic hospital. The post office occupies the parlor in the home of Frank Mc-Donald Jacobs, the patriarch of the band. A daughter of his, Veronica Jacobs, is postmistress. The church, St. Francis Xavier's, is the biggest building in the village. It is a hundred years old, it is made of cut stone of a multiplicity of shades of silver and gray, and the cross on its steeple is surmounted by a gilded weathercock. It is a Jesuit mission church; at its altar, by an old privilege, masses are said in Mohawk. In the summer, sightseeing buses from Montreal stop regularly at St. Francis Xavier's and a Jesuit scholastic guides the sightseers through it and shows them its treasures, the most precious of which are some of the bones of Kateri Tekakwitha, an Indian virgin called the Lily of the Mohawks who died at Caughnawaga in 1680. The old bones lie on a watered-silk cushion in a glass-topped chest. Sick and afflicted people make pilgrimages to the church and pray before them. In a booklet put out by the church, it is claimed that sufferers from many diseases, including cancer, have been healed through Kateri's intercession. Kateri is venerated because of the bitter penances she imposed upon herself; according to the memoirs of missionaries who knew her, she wore iron chains, lay upon thorns, whipped herself until she bled, plunged into icy water, went about barefoot on the snow, and fasted almost continuously.

On a hill in the southern part of the village are two

weedy graveyards. One is for Catholics, and it is by far the bigger. The other is for Protestants and pagans. At one time, all the Caughnawagas were Catholics. Since the early twenties, a few have gone over to other faiths every year. Now, according to a Canadian government census, 2,682 are Catholics, 251 belong to Protestant denominations, and 77 are pagans. The so-called pagans—they do not like the term and prefer to be known as the longhouse people—belong to an Indian religion called the Old Way or the Handsome Lake Revelation. Their prophet, Handsome Lake, was a Seneca who in 1799, after many years of drunkenness, had a vision in which the spirits up above spoke to him. He reformed and spent his last fifteen years as a roving preacher in Indian villages in upstate New York. In his sermons, he recited some stories and warnings and precepts that he said the spirits had revealed to him. Many of these have been handed down by word of mouth and they constitute the gospel of the religion; a few men in each generation —they are called "the good-message-keepers"—memorize them. The precepts are simply stated. An example is a brief one from a series concerning the sins of parents: "It often happens that parents hold angry disputes in the hearing of their infant child. The infant hears and comprehends their angry words. It feels lost and lonely. It can see for itself no happiness in prospect. This is a great sin." During the nineteenth century, Handsome Lake's religion spread to every Iroquois reservation in the United States and Canada except Caughnawaga. It reached Caughnawaga right after the First World War and, despite the opposition of Catholics and Protestants, began to be practiced openly in 1927. Handsome Lake's followers meet in ceremonial structures that they call longhouses. The Caughnawaga longhouse is on the graveyard hill. It resembles a country schoolhouse. It is a plain, one-room, frame building surrounded by a barbed-wire fence. Several times a year, on dates determined by the phases of the moon or the rising of sap in the sugar maples or the ripening of fruits and vegetables, the longhouse people get together and hold thanksgiving festivals, among which are a Midwinter Festival, a Thanks-to-the-Maple Festival, a Strawberry Festival, and a String Bean Festival. In the course of the festivals, they burn little heaps of sacred tobacco leaves, eat a dish called corn soup, make public confessions of their sins, and chant and dance to the music of rattles and drums. The smoke from the tobacco fires is supposed to ascend to the spirits. The sacred tobacco is not store-bought. It is a kind of tobacco known as Red Rose, an intensely acrid species that grows wild in parts of the United States and Canada. The longhouse people grow it in their gardens from wild seed and cure the leaves in the sun. The longhouse rattles are gourds or snapping-turtle shells with kernels of corn inside them, and the drums are wooden pails that barn paint came in with rawhide or old inner tubes stretched over their mouths. The Catholics and Protestants complain that for several days after a longhouse festival everyone on the reservation is moody.

The Caughnawagas are among the oldest reservation

Indians. The band had its origin in the latter half of the seventeenth century, when French Jesuit missionaries converted somewhere between fifty and a hundred Iroquois families in a dozen longhouse villages in what is now western and northern New York and persuaded them to go up to Quebec and settle in a mission outpost. This outpost was on the St. Lawrence, down below Lachine Rapids. The converts began arriving there in 1668. Among them were members of all the tribes in the Iroquois Confederacy—Mohawks, Oneidas, Onondagas, Cayugas, and Senecas. There were also a few Hurons, Eries, and Ottawas who had been captured and adopted by the Iroquois and had been living with them in the longhouse villages. Mohawks greatly predominated, and Mohawk customs and the Mohawk dialect of Iroquois eventually became the customs and speech of the whole group. In 1676, accompanied by two Jesuits, they left the outpost and went up the river to the foot of the rapids and staked out a village of their own, naming it Ka-na-wá-ke, which is Mohawk for "at the rapids;" Caughnawaga is a latter-day spelling. They moved the village three times, a few miles at a time and always upriver. With each move, they added to their lands. The final move, to the present site of Caughnawaga village, was made in 1719. Until 1830, the Caughnawaga lands were mission lands. In that year, the Canadian government took control of the bulk of them and turned them into a tax-free reservation, parcelling out a homestead to each family and setting aside other pieces, called the Commons, for the use of future generations.

Through the years, grants of Commons land have grown smaller and smaller; there are only about five hundred acres of it left; according to present policy, a male member of the band, after reaching his eighteenth birthday, may be granted exactly one-fourth of an acre if he promises to build upon it. A Caughnawaga is allowed to rent his land to anybody, but he may sell or give it only to another member of the band. Unlike many reservation Indians, the Caughnawagas have always had considerable say-so in their own affairs, at first through chiefs, each representing several families, who would go to the Indian Agent with requests or grievances, and then through an annually elected tribal council. The council has twelve members, it meets once a month in the parish hall, and it considers such matters as the granting of Commons land, the relief of the needy, and the upkeep of lanes and pumps. Its decisions, when approved by the Indian Affairs Branch in Ottawa, are automatically carried out by the Agent.

In the early years at Caughnawaga, the men clung to their old, aboriginal Iroquois ways of making a living. The Jesuits tried to get them to become farmers, but they would not. In the summer, while the women farmed, they fished. In the fall and winter, they hunted in a body in woods all over Quebec, returning to the village now and then with canoeloads of smoked deer meat, moose meat, and bear meat. Then, around 1700, a few of the youths of the first generation born at Caughnawaga went down to Montreal and took jobs in the French fur trade. They became canoemen in the great fleets of canoes that carried trading goods to remote depots on the St. Lawrence and its tributaries and brought back bales of furs. They liked this work—it was hard but hazardous—and they recruited others. Thereafter, for almost a century and a half, practically every youth in the band took a job in a freight canoe as soon as he got his strength, usually around the age of seventeen. In the eighteen-thirties, forties, and fifties, as the fur trade declined in Lower Canada, the Caughnawaga men were forced to find other things to do. Some switched to the St. Lawrence timber-rafting industry and became famous on the river for their skill in running immense rafts of oak and pine over Lachine Rapids. Some broke down and became farmers. Some made moccasins and snowshoes and sold them to jobbers in Montreal. A few who were still good at the old Mohawk dances came down to the United States and travelled with circuses; Caughnawagas were among the first circus Indians. A few bought horses and buggies and went from farmhouse to farmhouse in New England in the summer, peddling medicines—tonics, purges, liniments, and remedies for female ills—that the old women brewed from herbs and roots and seeds. A good many became depressed and shiftless; these hung out in Montreal and did odd jobs and drank cheap brandy.

In 1886, the life at Caughnawaga changed abruptly. In the spring of that year, the Dominion Bridge Company began the construction of a cantilever railroad bridge across the St. Lawrence for the Canadian

Pacific Railroad, crossing from the French-Canadian village of Lachine on the north shore to a point just below Caughnawaga village on the south shore. The D.B.C. is the biggest erector of iron and steel structures in Canada; it corresponds to the Bethlehem Steel Company in the United States. In obtaining the right to use reservation land for the bridge abutment, the Canadian Pacific and the D.B.C. promised that Caughnawagas would be employed on the job wherever possible.

"The records of the company for this bridge show that it was our understanding that we would employ these Indians as ordinary day laborers unloading materials," an official of the D.B.C. wrote recently in a letter. "They were dissatisfied with this arrangement and would come out on the bridge itself every chance they got. It was quite impossible to keep them off. As the work progressed, it became apparent to all concerned that these Indians were very odd in that they did not have any fear of heights. If not watched, they would climb up into the spans and walk around up there as cool and collected as the toughest of our riveters, most of whom at that period were old sailing-ship men especially picked for their experience in working aloft. These Indians were as agile as goats. They would walk a narrow beam high up in the air with nothing below them but the river, which is rough there and ugly to look down on, and it wouldn't mean any more to them than walking on the solid ground. They seemed immune to the noise of the riveting, which goes right through you and is often enough in itself to make newcomers to construction feel sick and dizzy. They were inquisitive about the riveting and were continually bothering our foremen by requesting that they be allowed to take a crack at it. This happens to be the most dangerous work in all construction, and the highest-paid. Men who want to do it are rare and men who can do it are even rarer, and in good construction years there are sometimes not enough of them to go around. We decided it would be mutually advantageous to see what these Indians could do, so we picked out some and gave them a little training, and it turned out that putting riveting tools in their hands was like putting ham with eggs. In other words, they were natural-born bridge-men. Our records do not show how many we trained on this bridge. There is a tradition in the company that we trained twelve, or enough to form three riveting gangs."

In the erection of steel structures, whether bridge or building, there are three main divisions of workers—raising gangs, fitting-up gangs, and riveting gangs. The steel comes to a job already cut and built up into various kinds of columns and beams and girders; the columns are the perpendicular pieces and the beams and girders are the horizontal ones. Each piece has two or more groups of holes bored through it to receive bolts and rivets, and each piece has a code mark chalked or painted on it, indicating where it should go in the structure. Using a crane or a derrick, the men in the raising gang hoist the pieces up and set them in position and join them by running bolts through a few of the holes in them; these bolts are temporary. Then the men in the fitting-up gang come along; they are divided into plumbers and bolters. The plumbers tighten up the pieces with guy wires and turnbuckles and make sure that they are in plumb. The bolters put in some more temporary bolts. Then the riveting gangs come along; one raising gang and one fitting-up gang will keep several riveting gangs busy. There are four men in a riveting gang—a heater, a sticker-in, a bucker-up, and a riveter. The heater lays some wooden planks across a couple of beams, making a platform for the portable, coal-burning forge in which he heats the rivets. The three other men hang a plank scaffold by ropes from the steel on which they are going to work. There are usually six two-by-ten planks in a scaffold, three on each side of the steel, affording just room enough to work; one false step and it's goodbye Charlie. The three men climb down with their tools and take their positions on the scaffold; most often the sticker-in and the bucker-up stand on one side and the riveter stands or kneels on the other. The heater, on his platform, picks a red-hot rivet off the coals in his forge with tongs and tosses it to the sticker-in, who catches it in a metal can. At this stage, the rivet is shaped like a mushroom; it has a buttonhead and a stem. Meanwhile, the bucker-up has unscrewed and pulled out one of the temporary bolts joining two pieces of steel, leaving the hole empty. The sticker-in picks the rivet out of his can with tongs and sticks it in the hole and pushes it in until the buttonhead is flush with the steel on his side and the stem protrudes from the other side, the riveter's side. The sticker-in steps out of the way. The bucker-up fits a tool called a dolly bar over the button-head and holds it there, bracing the rivet. Then the riveter presses the cupped head of his pneumatic hammer against the protruding stem end of the rivet, which is still red-hot and malleable, and turns on the power and forms a buttonhead on it. This operation is repeated until every hole that can be got at from the scaffold is riveted up. Then the scaffold is moved. The heater's platform stays in one place until all the work within a rivet-tossing radius of thirty to forty feet is completed. The men on the scaffold know each other's jobs and are interchangeable; the riveter's job is bone-shaking and nerve-racking, and every so often one of the others swaps with him for a while. In the days before pneumatic hammers, the riveter used two tools, a cupped die and an iron maul; he placed the die over the stem end of the red-hot rivet and beat on it with the maul until he squashed the stem end into a buttonhead.

After the D.B.C. completed the Canadian Pacific Bridge, it began work on a jackknife bridge now known as the Soo Bridge, which crosses two canals and a river and connects the twin cities of Sault Ste. Marie, Ontario, and Sault Ste. Marie, Michigan. This job took two years. Old Mr. Jacobs, the patriarch of the band, says that the Caughnawaga riveting gangs went straight from the Canadian Pacific job to the Soo job and that each gang took along an apprentice. Mr. Jacobs is in his eighties. In his youth, he was a member of a riveting gang; in his middle age, he was, successively, a commercial traveller for a wholesale grocer in Montreal, a schoolteacher on the reservation, and a campaigner for compulsory education for Indians. "The Indian boys turned the Soo Bridge into a college for themselves," he says. "The way they worked it, as soon as one apprentice was trained, they'd send back to the reservation for another one. By and by, there'd be enough men for a new Indian gang. When the new gang was organized, there'd be a shuffle-up—a couple of men from the old gangs would go into the new gang and a couple of the new men would go into the old gangs; the old would balance the new." This proliferation continued on subsequent jobs, and by 1907 there were over seventy skilled bridgemen in the Caughnawaga band. On August 29, 1907, during the erection of the Quebec Bridge, which crosses the St. Lawrence nine miles above Quebec City, a span collapsed, killing ninety-six men, of whom thirty-five were Caughnawagas. In the band, this is always spoken of as "the disaster."

"People thought the disaster would scare the Indians away from high steel for good," Mr. Jacobs says. "Instead of which, the general effect it had, it made high steel much more interesting to them. It made them take pride in themselves that they could do such dangerous work. Up to then, the majority of them, they didn't consider it any more dangerous than timber-rafting. Also, it made them the most looked-up-to men on the reservation. The little boys in Caughnawaga used to look up to the men that went out with circuses in the summer and danced and war-whooped all over the States and came back to the reservation in the winter and holed up and sat by the stove and drank whiskey and bragged. That's what they wanted to do. Either that, or work on the timber rafts. After the disaster, they changed their minds—they all wanted to go into high steel. The disaster was a terrible blow to the women. The first thing they did, they got together a sum of money for a life-size crucifix to hang over the main altar in St. Francis Xavier's. They did that to show their Christian resignation. The next thing they did, they got in behind the men and made them split up and scatter out. That is, they wouldn't allow all the gangs to work together on one bridge any more, which, if something went wrong, it might widow half the young women on the reservation. A few gangs would go to this bridge and a few would go to that. Pretty soon, there weren't enough bridge jobs, and the gangs began working on all types of high steel—factories, office buildings, department stores, hospitals, hotels, apartment houses, schools, breweries, distilleries, powerhouses, piers, railroad stations, grain elevators, anything and everything. In a few years, every steel structure of any size that went up in Canada, there were Indians on it. Then Canada got too small and they began crossing the border. They began going down to Buffalo and Cleveland and Detroit."

Sometime in 1915 or 1916, a Caughnawaga bridgeman named John Diabo came down to New York City and got a job on Hell Gate Bridge. He was a curiosity and was called Indian Joe; two old foremen still remember him. After he had worked for some months as bucker-up in an Irish gang, three other Caughnawagas joined him and they formed a gang of their own. They had worked together only a few weeks when Diabo stepped off a scaffold and dropped into the river and was drowned. He was highly skilled and his misstep was freakish; recently, in trying to explain it, a Caughnawaga said, "It must've been one of those cases, he got in the way of himself." The other Caughnawagas went back to the reservation with his body and did not return. As well as the old men in the band can recollect, no other Caughnawagas worked here until the twenties. In 1926, attracted by the building boom, three or four Caughnawaga gangs came down. The old men say that these gangs worked first on the Fred F. French Building, the Graybar Building, and One Fifth Avenue. In 1928, three more gangs came down. They worked first on the George Washington Bridge. In the thirties, when Rockefeller Center was the biggest steel job in the country, at least seven additional Caughnawaga gangs came down. Upon arriving here, the men in all these gangs enrolled in the Brooklyn local of the high-steel union, the International Association of Bridge, Structural, and Ornamental Iron Workers, American Federation of Labor. Why they enrolled in the Brooklyn instead of the Manhattan local, no one now seems able to remember. The hall of the Brooklyn local is on Atlantic Avenue, in the block between Times Plaza and Third Avenue, and the Caughnawagas got lodgings in furnished-room houses and cheap hotels in the North Gowanus neighborhood, a couple of blocks up Atlantic from the hall. In the early thirties, they began sending for their families and moving into tenements and apartment houses in the same neighborhood. During the war, Caughnawagas continued to come down. Many of these enrolled in the Manhattan local, but all of them settled in North Gowanus.

At present, there are eighty-three Caughnawagas in the Brooklyn local and forty-two in the Manhattan local. Less than a third of them work steadily in the city. The others keep their families in North Gowanus and work here intermittently but spend much of their time in other cities. They roam from coast to coast, usually by automobile, seeking rush jobs that offer unlimited overtime work at double pay; in New York City, the steel-erecting companies use as little overtime as possible. A gang may work in half a dozen widely separated cities in a single year. Occasionally, between jobs, they return to Brooklyn to see their families. Now and then, after long jobs, they pick up their families and go up to the reservation for a vacation; some go up every summer. A few men sometimes take their families along on trips to jobs and send them back to Brooklyn by bus or train. Several foremen who have had years of experience with Caughnawagas believe that they roam because they can't help doing so, it is a passion, and that their search for overtime is only an excuse. A veteran foreman for the American Bridge Company says he has seen Caughnawagas leave jobs that offered all the overtime they could handle. When they are making up their minds to move on, he says, they become erratic. "Everything will be going along fine on a job," he says. "Good working conditions. Plenty of overtime. A nice city. Then the news will come over the grapevine about some big new job opening up somewhere; it might be a thousand miles away. That kind of news always causes a lot of talk, what we call water-bucket talk, but the Indians don't talk; they know what's in each other's mind. For a couple of days, they're tensed up and edgy. They look a little wild in the eyes. They've heard the call. Then, all of a sudden, they turn in their tools, and they're gone. Can't wait another minute. They'll quit at lunchtime, in the middle of the week. They won't even wait for their pay. Some other gang will collect their money and hold it until a postcard comes back telling where to send it." George C. Lane, manager of erections in the New York district for the Bethlehem Steel Company, once said that the movements of a Caughnawaga gang are as impossible to foresee as the movements of a flock of sparrows. "In the summer of 1936," Mr. Lane said, "we finished a job here in the city and the very next day we were starting in on a job exactly three blocks away. I heard one of our foremen trying his best to persuade an Indian gang to go on the new job. They had got word about a job in Hartford and wanted to go up there. The foreman told them the rate of pay was the same; there wouldn't be any more overtime up there than here; their families were here; they'd have travelling expenses; they'd have to root around Hartford for lodgings. Oh, no; it was Hartford or nothing. A year or so later I ran into this gang on a job in Newark, and I asked the heater how they made out in Hartford that time. He said they didn't go to Hartford. 'We went to San Francisco, California,' he said. 'We went out and worked on the Golden Gate Bridge.'"

In New York City, the Caughnawagas work mostly for the big companies—Bethlehem, American Bridge, the Lehigh Structural Steel Company, and the Harris Structural Steel Company. Among the structures in and around the city on which they worked in numbers are the R.C.A. Building, the Cities Service Building, the Empire State Building, the Daily News Building, the Chanin Building, the Bank of the Manhattan Company Building, the City Bank Farmers Trust Building, the George Washington Bridge, the Bayonne Bridge, the Passaic River Bridge, the Triborough Bridge, the Henry Hudson Bridge, the Little Hell Gate Bridge, the Bronx-Whitestone Bridge, the Marine Parkway Bridge, the Pulaski Skyway, the West Side Highway, the Waldorf-Astoria, London Terrace, and Knickerbocker Village.

North Gowanus is an old, sleepy, shabby neighborhood that lies between the head of the Gowanus Canal and the Borough Hall shopping district. There are factories in it, and coal tipples and junk yards, but it is primarily residential, and red-brick tenements and brownstone apartment houses are most numerous. The Caughnawagas all live within ten blocks of each other, in an area bounded by Court Street on the west,

Schermerhorn Street on the north, Fourth Avenue on the east, and Warren Street on the south. They live in the best houses on the best blocks. As a rule, Caughnawaga women are good housekeepers and keep their apartments Dutch-clean. Most of them decorate a mantel or a wall with heirlooms brought down from the reservation—a drum, a set of rattles, a mask, a cradleboard. Otherwise, their apartments look much the same as those of their white neighbors. A typical family group consists of husband and wife and a couple of children and a female relative or two. After they get through school on the reservation, many Caughnawaga girls come down to North Gowanus and work in factories. Some work for the Fred Goat Company, a metal-stamping factory in the neighborhood, and some work for the Gem Safety Razor Corporation, whose factory is within walking distance. Quite a few of these girls have married whites; several have broken all ties with the band and the reservation. In the last ten years, Caughnawaga girls have married Filipinos, Germans, Italians, Jews, Norwegians, and Puerto Ricans. Many North Gowanus families often have relatives visiting them for long periods; when there is a new baby in a family, a grandmother or an aunt almost always comes down from the reservation and helps out. Caughnawagas are allowed to cross the border freely. However, each is required to carry a card, to which a photograph is attached, certifying that he or she is a member of the band. These cards are issued by the Indian Affairs Branch; the Caughnawagas refer to them as "passports." More than half of the North Gowanus housewives spend their spare time making souvenirs. They make a lot of them. They specialize in dolls, handbags, and belts, which they ornament with colored beads, using variations of ancient Iroquois designs such as the sky dome, the night sun, the day sun, the fern head, the ever-growing tree, the world turtle, and the council fire. Every fall, a few of the most Indian-looking of the men take vacations from structural steel for a month or so and go out with automobile loads of these souvenirs and sell them on the midways of state, county, and community fairs in New York, Connecticut, New Jersey, and Pennsylvania. The men wear buckskins and feathers on these trips and sleep in canvas tepees pitched on fairgrounds. Occasionally, on midways, to attract attention, they let out self-conscious wahoos and do fragments of the Duel Dance, the Dove Dance, the Falseface Dance, and other old half-forgotten Mohawk dances. The women obtain the raw materials for souvenirs from the Plume Trading & Sales Company, at 155 Lexington Avenue, in Manhattan, a concern that sells beads, deerskin, imitation eagle feathers, and similar merchandise to Indian handicraftsmen all over the United States and Canada. There are approximately fifty children of school age in the colony. Two-thirds go to Public School 47, on Pacific Street, and the others go to parochial schools— St. Paul's, St. Agnes's, and St. Charles Borromeo's. Caughnawaga children read comic books, listen to the radio while doing their homework, sit twice through double features, and play stick ball in vacant lots the same as the other children in the neighborhood; teachers say that they differ from the others mainly in that they are more reserved and polite. They have unusual manual dexterity; by the age of three, most of them are able to tie their shoelaces. The adult Caughnawagas are multilingual; all speak Mohawk, all speak English, and all speak or understand at least a little French. In homes where both parents are Caughnawagas, Mohawk is spoken almost exclusively, and the children pick it up. In homes where the mother is non-Indian and the father is away a good deal, a situation that is becoming more and more frequent, the children sometimes fail to learn the language, and this causes much sadness.

The Caughnawagas are churchgoers. The majority of the Catholics go to St. Paul's Church, at Court and Congress Streets, and the majority of the Protestants go to Cuyler Presbyterian Church, on Pacific Street. Dr. David Munroe Cory, the pastor at Cuyler, is a man of incongruous interests. He is an amateur wrestler; he is vice-president of the Iceberg Athletic Club, a group that swims in the ocean at Coney Island throughout the winter; he once ran for Borough President of Brooklyn on the Socialist ticket; he is an authority on Faustus Socinus, the sixteenth-century Italian religious thinker; he studies languages for pleasure and knows eight, among them Hebrew, Greek, and Gaelic. A few Caughnawagas started turning up at Cuyler Church in the middle thirties, and Dr. Cory decided to learn Mohawk and see if he could attract more of them. He has not achieved fluency in Mohawk, but Caughnawagas say that he

speaks it better than other white men, mostly anthropologists and priests, who have studied it. He holds a
complete service in Mohawk the first Sunday evening
in each month, after the English service, and twenty
or thirty Caughnawagas usually attend. Twenty-five
have joined the church. Michael Diabo, a retired
riveter, was recently elected a deacon. Steven M.
Schmidt, an Austrian-American who is married to
Mrs. Josephine Skye Schmidt, a Caughnawaga woman,
is an elder. Mr. Schmidt works in the compensation-
claim department of an insurance company. Under Dr.
Cory's guidance, two Caughnawaga women, Mrs.
Schmidt and Mrs. Margaret Lahache, translated a
group of hymns into Mohawk and compiled a hymnal,
The Caughnawaga Hymnal, which is used in Cuyler
and in the Protestant church on the reservation. Dr.
Cory himself translated the Gospel According to Luke
into Mohawk. Dr. Cory is quiet and serious, his sermons are free of cant, he has an intuitive understanding of Indian conversational taboos, and he is the only
white person who is liked and trusted by the whole
colony. Caughnawagas who are not members of his
congregation, even some Catholics and longhouse people, go to him for advice.

Occasionally, in a saloon or at a wedding or a
wake, Caughnawagas become vivacious and talkative.
Ordinarily, however, they are rather dour and don't
talk much. There is only one person in the North
Gowanus colony who has a reputation for garrulity.
He is a man of fifty-four whose white name is Orvis

Diabo and whose Indian name is O-ron-ia-ke-te, or He
Carries the Sky. Mr. Diabo is squat and barrel-chested.
He has small, sharp eyes and a round, swarthy, double-
chinned, piratical face. Unlike most other Caughnawagas, he does not deny or even minimize his white
blood. "My mother was half Scotch and half Indian,"
he says. "My grandmother on my father's side was
Scotch-Irish. Somewhere along the line, I forget just
where, some French immigrant and some full Irish
crept in. If you were to take my blood and strain it,
God only knows what you'd find." He was born a
Catholic; in young manhood, he became a Presbyterian; he now thinks of himself as "a kind of a free-
thinker." Mr. Diabo started working in riveting gangs
when he was nineteen and quit a year and a half ago.
He had to quit because of crippling attacks of arthritis.
He was a heater and worked on bridges and buildings
in seventeen states. "I heated a million rivets," he says.
"When they talk about the men that built this country,
one of the men they mean is me." Mr. Diabo owns a
house and thirty-three acres of farmland on the reservation. He inherited the farmland and rents it to a
French Canadian. Soon after he quit work, his wife,
who had lived in North Gowanus off and on for almost twenty years but had never liked it, went back
to the reservation. She tried to get him to go along,
but he decided to stay on awhile and rented a room
in the apartment of a cousin. "I enjoy New York," he
says. "The people are as high-strung as rats and the
air is too gritty, but I enjoy it." Mr. Diabo reads a lot.
Some years ago, in a Western magazine, he came

across an advertisement of the Haldeman-Julius Company, a mail-order publishing house in Girard, Kansas, that puts out over eighteen hundred paperbound books, most of them dealing with religion, health, sex, history, or popular science. They are called Little Blue Books and cost a dime apiece. "I sent away for a dollar's worth of Little Blue Books," Mr. Diabo says, "and they opened my eyes to what an ignorant man I was. Ignorant and superstitious. Didn't know beans from back up. Since then, I've become a great reader. I've read dozens upon dozens of Little Blue Books, and I've improved my mind to the extent that I'm far beyond most of the people I associate with. When you come right down to it, I'm an educated man." Mr. Diabo has five favorite Little Blue Books—*Absurdities of the Bible*, by Clarence Darrow; *Seven Infidel U.S. Presidents*, by Joseph McCabe; *Queer Facts About Lost Civilizations*, by Charles J. Finger; *Why I Do Not Fear Death*, by E. Haldeman-Julius; and *Is Our Civilization Over-Sexed?*, by Theodore Dreiser. He carries them around in his pockets and reads them over and over. Mr. Diabo stays in bed until noon. Then, using a cane, he hobbles over to a neighborhood saloon, the Nevins Bar & Grill, at 75 Nevins Street, and sits in a booth. If there is someone around who will sit still and listen, he talks. If not, he reads a Little Blue Book. The Nevins is the social center of the Caughnawaga colony. The men in the gangs that work in the city customarily stop there for an hour or so on the way home. On weekend nights, they go there with their wives and drink Montreal ale and look at the television. When gangs come in from out-of-town jobs, they go on sprees there. When a Caughnawaga high-steel man is killed on the job, a collection is taken up in the Nevins for the immediate expenses of his family; these collections rarely run less than two hundred dollars; pasted on the bar mirror are several notes of thanks from widows. The Nevins is small and snug and plain and old. It is one of the oldest saloons in Brooklyn. It was opened in 1888, when North Gowanus was an Irishtown, and it was originally called Connelly's Abbey. Irish customers still call it the Abbey. Its present owners are Artie Rose and Bunny Davis. Davis is married to a Caughnawaga girl, the former Mavis Rice.

One afternoon a while back, I sat down with Mr. Diabo in his booth in the Nevins. He almost always drinks ale. This day he was drinking gin.

"I feel very low in my mind," he said. "I've got to go back to the reservation. I've run out of excuses and I can't put it off much longer. I got a letter from my wife today and she's disgusted with me. 'I'm sick and tired of begging you to come home,' she said. 'You can sit in Brooklyn until your tail takes root.' The trouble is, I don't want to go. That is, I do and I don't. I'll try to explain what I mean. An Indian high-steel man, when he first leaves the reservation to work in the States, the homesickness just about kills him. The first few years, he goes back as often as he can. Every time he finishes a job, unless he's thousands of miles away, he goes back. If he's working in New York, he drives up weekends, and it's a twelve-hour

drive. After a while, he gets married and brings his
wife down and starts a family, and he doesn't go back
so often. Oh, he most likely takes the wife and children
up for the summer, but he doesn't stay with them.
After three or four days, the reservation gets on his
nerves and he highballs it back to the States. He gets
used to the States. The years go by. He gets to be my
age, maybe a little older, maybe a little younger, and
one fine morning he comes to the conclusion he's a
little too damned stiff in the joints to be walking a
naked beam five hundred feet in the air. Either that,
or some foreman notices he hasn't got a sure step any
longer and takes him aside and tells him a few home
truths. He gives up high-steel work and he packs his
belongings and he takes his money out of the bank
or the postal savings, what little he's been able to
squirrel away, and he goes on back to the reservation
for good. And it's hard on him. He's used to danger,
and reservation life is very slow; the biggest thing that
ever happens is a funeral. He's used to jumping
around from job to job, and reservation life boxes him
in. He's used to having a drink, and it's against the law
to traffic in liquor on the reservation; he has to buy a
bottle in some French-Canadian town across the river
and smuggle it in like a high-school boy, and that
annoys the hell out of him.

"There's not much he can do to occupy the time.
He can sit on the highway and watch the cars go by,
or he can sit on the riverbank and fish for eels and
watch the boats go by, or he can weed the garden,
or he can go to church, or he can congregate in the

grocery stores with the other old retired high-steel men and play cards and talk. That is, if he can stand it. You'd think those old men would talk about the cities they worked in, the sprees they went on, the girls that follow construction all over the country that they knew, the skyscrapers and bridges they put up—only they don't. After they been sitting around the reservation five years, six years, seven years, they seem to turn against their high-steel days. Some of them, they get to be as Indian as all hell; they won't even speak English any more; they make out they can't understand it. And some of them, they get to be soreheads, the kind of old men that can chew nails and spit rust. When they do talk, they talk gloomy. They like to talk about family fights. There's families on the reservation that got on the outs with each other generations ago and they're still on the outs; maybe it started with a land dispute, maybe it started with a mixed-marriage dispute, maybe it started when some woman accused another woman of meeting her husband in the bushes in the graveyard. Even down here in Brooklyn, there's certain Indians that won't work in gangs with certain other Indians because of bad blood between their families; their wives, when they meet on Atlantic Avenue, they look right through each other. The old men like to bring up such matters and refresh their recollections on some of the details. Also, they like to talk about religion. A miraculous cure they heard about, something the priest said—they'll harp on it for weeks. They're all amateur priests, or preachers. They've all got some religious notion lurking around in their minds.

"And they like to talk about reservation matters. The last time I was home, I sat down with the bunch in a store and I tried to tell them about something I'd been studying up on that interested me very much—Mongolian spots. They're dark-purple spots that occur on the skin on the backs of Japanese and other Mongolians. Every now and then, a full-blood American Indian is born with them. The old men didn't want to hear about Mongolian spots. They were too busy discussing the matter of street names for Caughnawaga village. The electric-light company that supplies the village had been trying and trying to get the Indians to name the streets and lanes. The meter-readers are always getting balled up, and the company had offered to put up street signs and house numbers free of charge. The old men didn't want street names; they were raising holy hell about it. It wouldn't be Indian. And they were discussing the pros and cons of a waterworks system. They're eternally discussing that. Some want a waterworks, but the majority don't. The majority of them, they'd a whole lot rather get behind a poor old horse that his next step might be his last and cart their water up from the river by the barrel. It's more Indian. Sometimes, the way an Indian reasons, there's no rhyme or reason to it. Electric lights are all right and the biggest second-hand car they can find, and radios that the only time they turn them off is when they're changing the tubes, and seventy-five-dollar baby carriages, and four-hundred-dollar coffins, but street names and tap water—oh, Jesus, no! That's going entirely too damned far.

"On the other hand, there's things I look forward to. I look forward to eating real Indian grub again. Such as *o-nen-sto*, or corn soup. That's the Mohawk national dish. Some of the women make it down here in Brooklyn, but they use Quaker corn meal. The good old women up on the reservation, they make it the hard way, the way the Mohawks were making it five hundred years ago. They shell some corn, and they put it in a pot with a handful of maple ashes and boil it. The lye in the ashes skins the hulls off the kernels, and the kernels swell up into big fat pearls. Then they wash off the lye. Then they put in some red kidney beans. Then they put in a pig's head; in the old days, it was a bear's head. Then they cook it until it's as thick as mud. And when it's cooking, it smells so good. If you were breathing your last, if you had the rattle in your throat, and the wind blew you a faint suggestion of a smell of it, you'd rise and walk. And I look forward to eating some Indian bread that's made with the same kind of corn. Down here, the women always use Quaker meal. Indian bread is boiled, and it's shaped like a hamburger, and it's got kidney beans sprinkled through it. On the reservation, according to an old-time custom, we have steak for breakfast every Sunday morning, whether we can afford it or not, and we pour the steak gravy on the Indian bread.

"And another thing I look forward to, if I can manage it—I want to attend a longhouse festival. If I have to join to do so, I'll join. One night, the last time I was home, the longhousers were having a festival. I decided I'd go up to the Catholic graveyard that's right below the longhouse and hide in the bushes and listen to the music. So I snuck up there and waded through the thistles and the twitch grass and the Queen Anne's lace, and I sat down on a flat stone on the grave of an uncle of mine, Miles Diabo, who was a warwhooper with the Miller Brothers 101 Ranch Wild West Show and died with the pneumonia in Wheeling, West Virginia, in 1916. Uncle Miles was one of the last of the Caughnawaga circus Indians. My mother is in that graveyard, and my father, old Nazareth Diabo that I hardly even knew. They called him Nazzry. He was a pioneer high-steel Indian. He was away from home the majority of the time, and he was killed in the disaster—when the Quebec Bridge went down. There's hundreds of high-steel men buried in there. The ones that were killed on the job, they don't have stones; their graves are marked with lengths of steel girders made into crosses. There's a forest of girder crosses in there. So I was sitting on Uncle Miles's stone, thinking of the way things go in life, and suddenly the people in the longhouse began to sing and dance and drum on their drums. They were singing Mohawk chants that came down from the old, old red-Indian times. I could hear men's voices and women's voices and children's voices. The Mohawk language, when it's sung, it's beautiful to hear. Oh, it takes your breath away. A feeling ran through me that made me tremble; I had to take a deep breath to quiet my heart, it was beating so fast. I felt very sad; at the same time, I felt very peaceful. I thought I was all alone in the graveyard, and then who loomed up out of the dark and sat down beside me but an old high-steel man I had been talking with in a store that afternoon, one of the soreheads, an old man that fights every improvement that's suggested on the reservation, whatever it is, on the grounds it isn't Indian—this isn't Indian, that isn't Indian. So he said to me, 'You're not alone up here. Look over there.' I looked where he pointed, and I saw a white shirt in among the bushes. And he said, 'Look over there,' and I saw a cigarette gleaming in the dark. 'The bushes are full of Catholics and Protestants,' he said. 'Every night there's a longhouse festival, they creep up here and listen to the singing. It draws them like flies.' So I said, 'The longhouse music is beautiful to hear, isn't it?' And he remarked it ought to be, it was the old Indian music. So I said the longhouse religion appealed to me. 'One of these days,' I said, 'I might possibly join.' I asked him how he felt about it. He said he was a Catholic and it was out of the question. 'If I was to join the longhouse,' he said, 'I'd be excommunicated, and I couldn't be buried in holy ground, and I'd burn in Hell.' I said to him, 'Hell isn't Indian.' It was the wrong thing to say. He didn't reply to me. He sat there awhile—I guess he was thinking it over—and then he got up and walked away."

1949

APOLOGIES TO THE IROQUOIS

1. STANDING ARROW

In the summer of 1957, a young English writer came to visit me in the little town in upstate New York in which I have since childhood spent many of my summers. As we were driving back one day from the county fair, I retailed to him, with an air of authority, a scrap of information which I had only lately acquired: that the name Adirondack meant, "They eat bark," and had been applied by certain Indians to other Indians that lived in the mountains which were visible, as we drove, in the distance. My visitor asked me what had become of the Indians, and I replied that there were only a few of them left, scattered in reservations. He inquired about the Mohicans, and I told him they were the same as the Mohawks.

Later on—in the middle of August—I discovered in the New York *Times* what seemed to me a very queer story. A band of Mohawk Indians, under the leadership of a chief called Standing Arrow, had moved in on some land on Schoharie Creek, a little river that flows into the Mohawk not far from Amsterdam, New York, and established a settlement there. Their claim was that the land they were occupying had been assigned them by the United States in a

treaty of 1784. The *Times* ran a map of the tract
which had at that time been recognized by our government as the territory of the Iroquois people, who
included the Mohawks, the Senecas, the Onondagas,
the Oneidas, the Cayugas and the Tuscaroras, and
were known as the Six Nations. The tract was sixty
miles wide, and it extended almost from Buffalo to
Albany.

I had already known about this agreement as the
Treaty of Fort Stanwix (now Rome, New York),
which had first made it possible for white people to
settle in upper New York State without danger of
molestation by its original inhabitants; but I had not
known what the terms of this treaty were, and I was
surprised to discover that my property, acquired at
the end of the eighteenth century by the family from
which it had come to me, seemed to lie either inside
or just outside the northern boundary. Having thus
been brought to realize my ignorance of our local relations with the Indians and continuing to read in the
papers of the insistence of Standing Arrow that the
Mohawks had some legal right to the land on which
they were camping, I paid a visit, in the middle of
October, to their village on Schoharie Creek. I had
learned in the offices of the Amsterdam *Recorder* and
from talking with the county archivist that this settlement had had as its nucleus a group of Mohawk steelworkers from Brooklyn, who had been working on
the nearby bridge that was a part of the new state
Thruway. The Mohawks who spend their winters in
`Brooklyn have had often also summer homes in a reser-

vation at Caughnawaga, just south of Montreal, and
some have been deprived of these homes by the construction of the St. Lawrence Seaway, which has been
put right through the reservation. There were some of
these among Standing Arrow's followers, as well as
a family from another reservation, St. Regis on the St.
Lawrence, in which some other Mohawks had been
losing their land as a result of the straightening of the
river's channel. It was not very clear how or when the
crew who were working on the bridge had come to be
associated with Standing Arrow, a former chief from
St. Regis, but he had certainly brought with him adherents who had been dispossessed of their land.

On the road that ran past the settlement, he had put
up a sign "Indian Village," and during the summer
they had sold souvenirs to tourists. When the catwalk
was completed at the end of the summer, most of the
workers on it had gone back to Brooklyn, leaving
Standing Arrow and a handful of followers living in
shacks and an old city bus. The farmers on whose land
they were squatting complained that their children
were damaging the crops, but were expecting to be
rid of the Indians when the now tiny handful of dwellings should be flooded by the river in the winter rains.

Standing Arrow was not at home when I first attempted to see him. I inquired of two men who were
chopping wood, and—as often happens with Indians
—they did not answer my question till I had asked it
again, when, following some further silence, they replied, "His wife is over there." I knocked at the indicated shack, where two little children were playing.

When I said "Hello" to these children, they did not respond with a "Hi." The only being whose attitude was friendly was a little mongrel dog, brown with a stripe down his back, who jumped up on me and ran around madly. At last a woman appeared, not emerging but standing in the half-open door. She was handsome and had considerable presence; in spite of blue eyes and pale skin, she seemed to me a true Indian type. She told me that her husband would be back in the evening. Did she mean night or late afternoon? Should I come back about five? Silence; then, "You do that." I asked whether they expected to spend the winter there. She looked at me again in silence with an expression that was almost fierce. "We're aimin' to," she finally said.

At five Standing Arrow had still not returned, and she suggested my coming next morning at nine. When I arrived, I was greeted by the dog, who again ran around in circles, but I failed, as before, to get any information from one of the children, who was playing in the creek. My knocking at the door brought no answer. I had just got into the car and was starting back when Standing Arrow appeared and waved to me. It was characteristic of an Indian that, not being up and dressed, he should not shout that he would be out in a minute but should wait till he could present himself with dignity. He was a short fattish man with a round face, who received me very pleasantly. I explained that I had been sent as a reporter, and said that I could not see the justice of their claims to the land they were occupying: the archivist had shown me a photostat of a document, dating from the late eighteenth century and signed by the Indian Joseph Brant, by which the Mohawks surrendered this region to the whites. "Will you let me show you something?" he asked, and disappeared into the cabin. I waited for some time. I stood looking at the little river. I knew that Schoharie was a Mohawk name—the English of which was Floodwood. The Mohawk Trail had crossed this creek, and at its mouth had stood one of the principal Mohawk villages, which had been sacked and destroyed by the French in 1665. I tried to imagine how this landscape had looked to the Mohawks themselves. There was a light morning mist, and the water was black, with a patch of bright blinding flashes near the stones on the hither bank; beyond it, the yellowing trees rose on a sheltering slope. But what was to me autumn scenery, gazed upon from my car when I left the hotel, had been the Indians' world in which they lived.

Standing Arrow at last reappeared and invited me into the house. He had stowed away the rest of his family in a little crate of an annex, knocked together against the original shack, where at first they had all lived in one room. This room was not, however, ill-kept. On the wall hung a landscape of a lake, a feathered headdress and a large rattle made out of a snapping-turtle's shell. Standing Arrow now read me a long printed statement, prepared in 1924, which was described as an "excerpt from evidence" submitted by the "Hon. E. A. Everett to a commission appointed by the State Legislature of New York to determine the status of the Six Nations Indians" vis-à-vis the United States. (I was to encounter this statement again and again. It seems to be the only opinion formulated by a public official and sponsored by a white legal firm which supports the maximum claims of the Iroquois.) This Confederacy or League of the Iroquois, originally the *Five* Nations—is supposed to have been founded about 1570. It constitutes, so far as is known, the only enduring achievement on the part of the American Indians of the East in unifying their scattered branches and imposing on them an overall government. Their social groups had previously multiplied by fission. The usual practice had been, when a locality showed signs of being hunted out and the fertility of its soil exhausted, or when a group became split into factions, for a leader to form a new band, detach himself from the parent community and move on to another locality, in which language and habits and rites would eventually diverge from the parent ones. In the case, however, of the Iroquois group—at a time when this divergence had not gone too far for a common understanding to be possible—the situation is supposed to have been taken in hand by two peace-loving constructive statesmen: Deganawida (Day-ga-na-weé-da) and Hiawatha (Ha-yó-went'ha). (The real Hiawatha should not be confused with the hero of Longfellow's poem. Longfellow, who depended on the pioneering studies of Henry R. Schoolcraft, assumed that the legendary heroes of the Indians were more or less interchangeable and substituted the name Hiawatha—as his edi-

tor says, "more euphonic"—for that of an Ojibway
hero. The exploits of Longfellow's Ojibway have very
little in common with those of the Iroquois Hayówent'ha.) When the Europeans arrived in North
America, they thus found the Confederacy already in
being and saw it grow, owing to stimuli originally produced by themselves, into a formidable Indian empire,
which subjugated or absorbed other tribes. The stronghold and core of the Iroquois was roughly that part of
the state of New York between Lake Erie and the Hudson River, but in course of the seventeenth and eighteenth centuries their conquests came to extend from
the Mississippi through New England and from the
St. Lawrence to the Tennessee. The impact of their
power may be gauged by their relations with their
neighbors the Delawares. The Iroquois first reduced
these to the status of a tributary nation; then, when the
latter betrayed them by attacking another nation at
that time under Iroquois protection, the Iroquois
punished them with permanent captivity, putting
corn-pounders in the hands of the men, dressing them
in the skirts of squaws and forbidding them to engage
in war. When, however, the Tuscaroras—who belonged, as the Delawares did not, to the Iroquois linguistic group—were driven out of the South by the
whites, the Iroquois took them into the League and
made them their sixth nation. It seems clear that the
strength and cohesion of the League were reënforced
after the arrival of the whites—in the period between
1600 and 1800—by their peculiar geographical position between Albany, the headquarters of the fur

market, and a hinterland north and west from which most of the pelts were supplied at a time when the territory of the Iroquois was almost completely hunted out (it is said that by the end of the seventeenth century there was not a beaver left in the area). This fierce and effective group seems to have taken that trade away, first, from their cousins the Hurons; then, from the alien Algonquins, who had at one time formed a sketchier confederacy but had declined as the Iroquois prospered and were to lose almost everything of their traditional culture while the Iroquois kept and developed theirs. The Six Nations became the great middlemen. Dependent on their trade with the English and Dutch, they made common cause with them against the French, and they probably turned the balance of our early history.

"The Iroquois Confederacy was so powerful"—so Standing Arrow's document continued—"and their social order and system of government [were] so far ahead of anything, in theory and practice, that the European had ever known, that the immigrants to the new world reported to their respective governments a mighty nation existed here. And soon you find England, Holland and France sending ambassadors to the Confederate League. These ambassadors came with authority to purchase land in the new world, but found they could purchase no land from subject tribes; all lands had to be purchased from the Six Nations Government. . . . The Iroquois Confederacy was the only nation of Indians on the new continent which was never conquered and the only one recog-

nized as a sovereign government in whom the fee
simple was vested." Standing Arrow now told me—
quite truthfully, though I did not remember to have
heard it—that Benjamin Franklin had been influenced
by the example of the Iroquois Confederacy in his
project for uniting the American colonies. It has always, I found, been the boast of the Iroquois that our
written constitution, with its federal authority bal-
anced against states' rights, was derived from their
unwritten one, with its six semi-autonomous units and
its high council on which they were all represented.
At the time of our Revolution, this high council of
the Confederacy announced its neutrality: the individual nations were to support whichever side they
pleased. The majority fought for the British, but a
few—the Oneidas, notably, and a part of the Tuscaroras—gave support to the revolted colonies [the statement read by Standing Arrow minimized the importance of the former group and failed to mention
that most of the Mohawks had been on the side of the
British]; but after the war was over the Continental
Congress had agreed to dismiss any grievance against
Iroquois who had worked for England and by the
treaty mentioned above—of which Standing Arrow
produced a facsimile—had "recognized the two nations as equals," had "recognized the sovereign title of
the Confederacy to their title forever, and agreed to
protect them in the same as against any encroachment
whatsoever 'as long as grass grows and water runs' "—
a phrase, as I afterwards found, well remembered and
much quoted by the Indians. It followed from this.

said the statement, that no part of the land then assigned to the Iroquois Confederacy could be sold except through the government of the Six Nations and with the consent of the government of the United States. In spite of this, "the State of New York has purchased millions of acres of land from the individual states of the Confederacy, in no instance purchasing it through the Six Nations Government, never even asking the consent of the U.S. government, and buying it over the written protest of the U.S. government. This outrage has continued until there remain today only 78,000 acres of the original eighteen million." The agreement which the archivist had shown me was therefore, said Standing Arrow, not valid. It had been signed by the Mohawk Joseph Brant—supposed to have had white blood—who had held a commission in the British army, had fought against the colonists at Oriskany, had gone to Canada when the British were defeated, and had possessed no authority whatever to dispose of the land on Schoharie Creek. Standing Arrow referred to Brant as "an Englishman." Brant's son had indeed gone to Oxford.

Standing Arrow commenced our interview by getting a little tough—understandably in view of the fact that on first meeting him I had challenged him rather sharply; but he soon began exerting charm. Though he had a slight cast in one eye, his features were rather fine and reminded me of portraits of the youthful Napoleon. He had also, as I could see, some of the qualities of the Mussolinian spellbinder. He used gestures, as he spoke, of a kind that rather surprised me on the part of an Indian, gestures which I thought might perhaps have been picked up from the Canadian French and which seemed to show experience in public speaking. When I talked later to another Mohawk—not one of Standing Arrow's followers—of the leader's persuasive powers, he answered, "He's got a touch of the hypnotist. People go to him prejudiced against him and come away completely convinced." Another Mohawk, who disapproved of him, told me that his eloquence in English—of which his command was imperfect—was nothing to his eloquence in Mohawk: "When he talks to me, as long as he's there, I can't disagree with anything he says." I felt something of this myself. I had heard about Standing Arrow some unfavorable things yet I found myself won over in contact with him. He appealed to the imagination.

While Standing Arrow was reading the statement, another Indian entered the shack. I had noticed him, on my arrival, fast asleep in the back seat of a car, which he filled with a compact lump. He was dark, broad-shouldered and stocky, somewhat formidable-looking with his strongly cut features that recalled the cigar-store Indian but seemed rather made of iron than of wood, and his piercing eyes open on a crack. He shook hands with me, then sat down and listened. Soon he said to me, "I will talk to him in my own language." They spoke Mohawk for a minute or two, then Standing Arrow turned to me: "You say you're a magazine writer. Can you show me your credentials?" I had not provided myself with any, but I managed to reassure them. The dark man became quite friendly—I was to see him twice after that. I found he had a sly Indian deadpan humor. He was a worker in high steel, and he told me with pride that not only had he worked on the Empire State Building but that he had even helped to put up the tower. A good many of these Iroquois Indians, if not the majority of them, are steel- and ironworkers. They are equipped with what one Mohawk described to me as "an uncanny sense of balance" and an astonishing coolness in working at heights, which evidently derive from their earlier life, from threading forests and scaling mountains, from canoeing in streams rough with rapids. A very important factor is undoubtedly their habit, in walking, of putting one foot in front of the other, instead of straddling as, when they see our tracks, we seem to them to do. They do not need to make an effort in walking a narrow beam. That this aptitude of the Iroquois was well developed before modern engineering was known is shown by a passage in an early English book, John Lawson's *History of Carolina*, published in 1709; "They will walk over deep brooks and creeks," he writes of the Tuscaroras, "on the smallest poles, and that without any fear or concern. Nay, an *Indian* will walk on the ridge of a barn or house and look down the gable-end, and spit upon the ground, as unconcerned, as if he was walking on *terra firma*." And today—it is a proof of the persistence of their strength—they have found in the construction of bridges, high buildings and power-line towers an incongruous opportunity for exercising their traditional self-control, their muscular coördination, and their indifference to physical danger. The story of the Iroquois's development as experts in this occupation has been told here by Mr. Mitchell in his study of the Mohawks in high steel.

Standing Arrow now explained to me the clan system which has played such an important rôle in the cohesion of the Iroquois people. I was to read a more complete account of it in Lewis H. Morgan's pioneering book *The League of the Iroquois*, which, published in 1851, explained for the first time in a systematic way the structure of a society, many centuries old, so alien to that of the whites that they had never more than vaguely understood it. This structure, though now dissolved among certain of the Christianized groups, has endured in an impressive way, and the whites, except for experts in Indian affairs, are still hardly aware of its existence. The essential point to grasp is that, although the Six Nations are the *political* units of the League, the fundamental *social* unit is the clan. These clans are all named after totems: mammals, turtles, birds, even plants. They are common to all the Six Nations, though every nation does not have them all. You are free to marry a woman from your own or from another nation, but you may not marry a woman from your own clan. Your children all belong to the clan of your wife—"I'm a Turtle," Standing Arrow told me, "but my children are Wolf because my wife is a Wolf." The wife's brothers, who belong to her clan, are responsible for her children, and her husband is responsible for the children of his sisters. Lewis Morgan believed—and his opinion is shared by certain of the early Jesuit missionaries— that this system, which he also found among other primitive peoples, had arisen from the difficulty, at an earlier stage, of their knowing who any child's father was. I was told by one Mohawk that the Indians had given their women a dominant position because, in observing the animals—who were so much closer to them than they are to us: almost like other races of men—they had noted that the maintenance of the animal family depended entirely on the mother. The society of the Iroquois Indians is, in any case, matrilineal. The senior woman of the clan, known as the "clan mother," names the chief or chiefs for her clan, and, as Standing Arrow explained to me, a wife whose husband is drunken or otherwise undesirable may first have him reprimanded, then, if the offense is repeated, put him out of the house, which belongs to her. In the early days, it seems, the husband did not always even live in the house of his wife, who might live with other members of her own clan. The women then did all the work at home while the men went out fighting and hunting. It was even believed that the earth would not bear unless cultivated by women, and the Iroquois, who had always used hoes, were a long time in taking up ploughs because working with them was too heavy for women. This dominance of the female, no doubt, has made for a certain conservatism, hence guaranteed a certain stability. The ban against marriage inside the clan would act as a brake on inbreeding. The marriages between the six nations would help to bind them together.

As soon as Standing Arrow was satisfied that I was genuinely interested in what he was saying, he set out to put on a show for me. He took down and demonstrated the snapping-turtle rattle. I asked whether the headdress was his. "No," he answered. "It's his"—referring to the swarthy steelworker. "But I wear it around when the tourists are here. They don't think you're a real Indian, you know, unless you wear one of those things." He brought out a cloth bag, gathered with a string at the top, like the bags in which table silver is carried, and produced from it a red wooden mask with a curiously twisted mouth and its nose squashed against one cheek—not unlike a Picasso, I thought. "At night," he said, "he makes a terrible noise." "What kind of a noise?" I asked. "You wouldn't sleep afterwards!" he answered. I knew that some of their masks were supposed to whistle, and turned it around to see if there were any device for this purpose. "Don't put it on!" he warned me. "We feed him," he went on. "We had to help Dr. Fenton out the other day." I had already heard of William N. Fenton as a leading authority on the Iroquois and the director of the Albany State Museum. "They've got one of these at the museum in a glass case—that's another thing we don't like." (He had previously been complaining of the digging up of Indian graves.) "And one night the night watchman heard a smash. He went into the room and found the glass case broken. He [the mask] was lying on the floor. They put him back and put in new glass, and the same thing happened again. Then Dr. Fenton sent for us to come and feed him, and after that he was quiet." I was eventually, as will later appear, to have a chance to hear this "terrible noise" and to find out why the features of the mask were awry. I was also to discover that there was this much of truth in the story that Standing Arrow had told me. It was true that these masks were periodically fed with tobacco and sunflower oil, which were smeared around their mouths, and Fenton, who had never seen the ceremony, had invited some Indians he knew to perform it with the specimens on display in the museum. This project had, however, not been carried out. Another part of the story had evidently been suggested by the news which had reached the Indians that a carpenter's assistant who was working on a wall had put his foot through the case that contained the masks. These incidents had soon been combined to create the legend of the leaping mask. The Indians, Dr. Fenton tells me, are likely to worry about objects of theirs exhibited in white men's museums. They have a feeling of alienation and are haunted by the notion that such things as masks are imprisoned and unhappy there. They have even sometimes made attempts to recover the wampum belts that their predecessors have given away or sold.

There was to take place, the two Indians told me, only a few days from then at the Onondaga reservation, a big council of the Six Nations League. Standing Arrow invited me to it. It would help me to get an

A mask somewhat similar to the one that was shown me by Standing Arrow. The face is painted red; the hair is made of white horsetail, and the eyes are of sheet copper. This mask was carved in 1937 on the Tonawanda Reservation by Elon Webster, an Onondaga, and is now in the Cranbrook Institute of Science, Bloomfield Hills, Michigan. *Photograph by William N. Fenton.*

idea of what was now going on in the Iroquois world. His moving in at Schoharie Creek, he had given me to understand, was no isolated personal exploit.

I had promised to bring my daughter, if possible, a pair of Indian moccasins, and when I asked whether they had any from their stock of the summer, the steelworker produced a few pairs from his car, as well as some little beadwork dolls.

I felt that I had visited a world as different from the United States as any foreign country, and I began to see upstate New York, all my life so familiar to me, in a new and larger perspective. My old New York State was taking its place in a backward extension of history: it was no longer, in fact, so old. The Valley of the Mohawk River was now full of autumn color: hillsides of crimson and orange, with lemony wisps of birch; and on the hills among which Utica lies the foliage was sometimes still golden. But a little farther north I found that the leaves had fallen in the last few days. I had never seen the landscape so stripped. The widely scattered farms of that countryside, in the summer concealed by greenery, could now look across at one another, and the black and white cattle seemed poorer for the poverty of the dry paling pastures. The Adirondack Mountains beyond, blue in summer and dimly romantic, now showed forbidding and black. I could better now imagine how that country had looked to the earliest settlers, and I tried to imagine how the Iroquois had got through its paralyzing winters. They had lived not in wigwams—being more advanced than most of the Eastern Indians—but in "long-houses" constructed of a frame of poles, on which were lashed lengths of dried bark. Later on, when the use of the ax had been learned, the houses—like the white man's—were built of logs. There would be four or five families in a house, with a separate hearth for each and for each a section of berths on shelves that ran along the walls. There was a vent in the roof for the smoke—though the accounts of the early Jesuits show that the inmates of the longhouse were in winter sometimes nearly suffocated and had to hug the ground in order to breathe. The ears of corn to be eaten in winter were suspended from the cross-beams in strings; cured venison and charred corn were buried in watertight bark-lined pits. Their utensils, their weapons and their clothing were hung up all over the house. And so they had passed their winters before the invaders arrived. When later, after my visit to the Onondagas, which had brought me closer to the Iroquois world, I approached the old family house in which I spent my summers, one of the first built by white settlers there, it now seemed—no longer screened by the vines or the trees—a little blocked mound of gray limestone, looking out with glittering windows from the eminence on which it was lodged, facing squarely, with the courage of those pioneer New Englanders, the dense forests and the darkened mountains; a mere adequate human shelter, hardly stouter than those vanished bark houses, almost a hut like Standing Arrow's, knocked together in that northern wilderness which the Iroquois had first surveyed with their sharpening expanding minds and where our wide roads still follow their narrow trails.

2. ONONDAGA

The high council to which I had been invited was
held for the inauguration of the new ranking chief of
the Six Nations League, whose title is Ta-do-dá-ho
and who must always be an Onondaga because the
original Tadodáho was one. The legendary Tadodáho
is supposed to have been at the peak of his power
toward the end of the sixteenth century at the time
when the League was formed. He is said to have
defeated in war the Senecas and the Cayugas, and
in his arrogance, to have held out against joining
the League, which at that time consisted only of
the Cayugas, the Oneidas and the Mohawks. According to one authority, the name Tadodáho means "He
Obstinately Refused to Acquiesce," but in a translation of the legend from the Onondaga I find it given
as "He Whose House Blocks the Path." In any case,
he was bitterly obstructive, and, when finally persuaded, he laid it down as a condition of his allying
himself with the other three nations that the Senecas
be also brought in, and he dictated the stiffest possible
terms to make sure of Onondaga hegemony. In their
representation on the federal council, the Onondagas
were to have fourteen chiefs, though none of the other
nations had more than ten; the Tadodáho was to be

supreme—he only was to have the right to summon
the then Five Nations Council, and no act of the
council should be valid unless ratified by the Onondagas. Onondaga thus remains to this day the capital
of the Six Nations. The Onondagas have the rôle of
Firekeepers—that is, they preside over the council fire;
and they are also the Keepers of the Wampum, a belt
made of shells strung like beads, into which the laws
of the League have been "talked"—that is, written in
the form of symbols—so that it constitutes a permanent record of Iroquois procedure and Iroquois
treaties. Their village was the site of the Peace Tree,
under which the federation was founded. According
to the Iroquois legend, the tallest pine there was up-
rooted; all the weapons of the covenanting parties
were thrown into the pit which this made; then the
tree was planted again. Since the Onondaga speak of
this tree as if it were still standing, I said that I should
like to see it, and was told, "The tree is imaginary."

It was strange, after driving among the factories and
passing through the standardized business streets of
industrial Syracuse, to turn off a suburban road lined
with old-fashioned corner drugstores and newly built
shopping centers and to find, as it were in a pocket,
the Onondagas still inhabiting their pretty little valley.
Though an airfield encroached at the entrance, Onondaga looked quite cozy and peaceful, pillowed by its
low round hills—Onondaga means "on the hills"—
yellow-brown with their close growth of trees that
covered them like the nap of a carpet. These hills are

supposed to have been formed in the days of the great
Stone Giants, who preyed on the Iroquois in ancient
times and ate up so many of their people that the
Creator had to come to their rescue. The Holder-up
of the Heavens, disguised as one of these ogres, was
sent to go among them and trick them. Pretending to
lead them against mankind and promising them a
sumptuous feast, the Holder-up of the Heavens brought
the giants to the foot of the mountains on which the
Onondagas had built their stockade, and told them to
hide in caves till, at the first light of dawn the following day, the moment for attack arrived. He then went
up on the mountain and gave the whole landscape
such a shaking-up that a new configuration of the
hills was formed and, trapped in their hiding places,
the Giants were crushed to death—with a single exception, who got away and who lived to become, as
will later appear, the father of that race of strange
spirits of one of which Standing Arrow had shown
me a contorted mask.

Onondaga, though the capital of the League, is by
no means the most populous or flourishing of the
Iroquois reservations. There are hardly nine hundred
people living on its sixty-one hundred acres, in buildings that range from crude shacks to dwellings the
size of small farmhouses. These are likely to be unpainted, like the Iroquois's original houses of bark,
and their yards are sometimes cluttered with chicken-
coops, old car-parts and other junk. But a few of the
places are well kept up, and it was in one of the
most attractive of these that I found the man with

whom Standing Arrow had told me to get in touch:
a small white suburban-type residence, with a glass
and aluminum door in which a big aluminum "P"
stood for Papineau, the name of the owner. Though
married to an Onondaga, who has brought him into
her own community, Louis Papineau is himself a
Mohawk. The descendants of the Mohawks who fled
to Quebec at the end of our Revolution have often
taken such French names. The steelworker I had
met at Schoharie Creek was representative of Ontario as well as Quebec in combining a Scottish first
name with a French family name. This steelworker
together with Standing Arrow I found at Louis
Papineau's house. Our host was a man of forty-one,
of the characteristic chunky Mohawk build, with
white teeth and a straight candid gaze. Before I had
talked to him long, I realized that I was dealing with
nothing less than an Iroquois nationalist movement—
not unlike Scottish nationalism or even the "ingather-
ing" of modern Israel—in which he was one of the
most zealous workers. I shall later discuss the causes
and the aims of this movement, but in the meantime
must explain that Louis Papineau was representative
of its most serious elements. (It is worth noting that
a Louis Papineau led a last revolt of the French against
British domination in Canada.) It may be that all such
nationalist movements are activated by the two contrasting types of the Papineaus and the Standing Arrows: the dedicated workers and the fancy talkers.
Louis Papineau is upright, sincere and capable, and
has a very strong conviction of his people's rights. A

tree surgeon, busy at his trade all day, he reads up on their history at night. He has some difficulty expressing himself in English and does not always know the pronunciation of English words which he has only seen in books, calling *lineage*, for example, "line-age." On the other hand, he is quite proficient in the various Iroquois dialects and is in demand at such inter-nation councils as the one I had come to attend, where communication is sometimes imperfect. He told me that the old Tadodáho had died and that he was now being succeeded by his son. When I asked whether the Tadodáho had tenure of office for life, his answer contained a phrase which I took to be "if he heirs," but which turned out to be "if he errs": if he misbehaves, he can be deposed. (One has, however, heard this word mispronounced by whites.) But his English was a good deal better than that of another supporter of the movement—also a dedicated man—with whom I afterwards talked at St. Regis and with whom I often found myself at cross-purposes, he misunderstanding my questions and I misunderstanding his answers. My experience with the Iroquois has reënforced an already well-developed sense of the difficulty of transmitting from one language to another the meaning of traditional social customs, the formulas and symbols of religion, and even the concepts of politics. One is well enough aware of this difficulty in regard to ourselves and the Soviet Union; but it is truly amazing to discover that, in the Iroquois communities of New York State and Canada, which comprise perhaps some twenty thousand people—that is, perhaps twice the

number estimated by Sir William Johnson in 1763—
there are many of the older generation who can
hardly speak English at all and many among the
younger who cannot speak it with any great fluency.
This means that there are a large number of Iroquois
who live still in the Indian world and for whom the
Great Spirit, the Tadodáho, Deganawída and Hayówent'ha are more real than the Christian Trinity, the
President of the United States, George Washington
and Thomas Jefferson.

When Standing Arrow presented me to Papineau,
he had explained, "I'm not the boss here. *He's* the
boss. He'll have to fix it up." Mr. Papineau said that
he would talk to the delegates and have them admit
me to the council. He had recognized my possible use
as a reporter of their cause to the outside world. At
that time the exploit of Standing Arrow was the only
event in connection with the movement which had
received any notice in the press, and such younger
men as Papineau were prepared to waive the secrecy
of the council, from which white men had always
been excluded, in the interest of "public relations."

But they had reckoned without their elders. These
cherished the traditional point of view and cared nothing about public relations.

Those ceremonies which involve the whole local
community—or, as in this case, the whole Confederacy—are held in what is called the Longhouse.
In the more primitive days, as has already been said,
all the Iroquois lived in longhouses; but today the

only "longhouse" is this: the temple, the center of the ancient religion, and the council chamber where practical decisions are made. The Longhouse is also a symbol of the unity of the Iroquois league, since the whole of the Six Nations territory, which was roughly contained in a rectangle, was originally imagined as "the Longhouse," the Senecas being the keepers of the western door that looked out upon Niagara and the Mohawks the keepers of the eastern door that looked out upon the Hudson. The present Longhouse, as far as my experience goes, is always a simple rectangular building, much like an old-fashioned school, which varies between one reservation and another in size, accommodations and neatness and which consists of a single room with windows and, as a rule, two doors, one for men, one for women, sometimes both at the front, sometimes at either side or end. The Longhouse at Onondaga, following the tradition of the house of the original Tadodáho, which was supposed to have "blocked the path," runs from the north to the south, instead of, like the others, from the east to the west.

I was told to be on hand at two, so went back to Syracuse and had lunch. When I returned, with a cousin from upstate who was driving me, Mr. Papineau had left for the Longhouse, but his wife showed us where it was and asked us to give a lift to an old Mohawk who had come down to the council from the St. Regis Reservation. He was very tall, straight and stiff, and, as I afterwards noted at the Longhouse, he was the only person present who was wearing the traditional headband with its single upstanding feather.

He maintained a solemn reserve. When I asked him if he spoke English, he answered, "Not very much." His skin, however, was pale, and his features seemed decidedly Nordic.

At the Longhouse I found my sponsor and—knowing, from past experience with the Indians of the Southwest, that these situations are sometimes delicate—I asked whether he was perfectly sure that I should be well-received at the council. He assured me that my admittance had been approved. He would sit next to me and explain the proceedings. They wanted me to be able to see that the Six Nations—all here represented—were still meeting and working together. But he did not actually take us in, and we stood for sometime near the door watching the company gather. There was a remarkable variety of physical types, sometimes in such violent contrast that one found them rather hard to account for as all offshoots from a parent stock. Some were round-faced and some were aquiline; some were powerful giants and others were chinless with birdlike beaks. I learned later that this variation was partly to be accounted for by the elements from the many widely scattered tribes that the Iroquois had long ago absorbed, and that the Indian blood itself had in almost every case been diluted from a medley of European strains, English, French, Dutch, Irish and German. Louis Papineau told me on a later occasion that there was probably not a full-blooded Iroquois in existence—a few of the Senecas, perhaps, came nearer to it than anyone else. (A study of Indian families on the Tonawanda Seneca reservation, in cases in which a genealogy was traceable, did not, I understand, succeed in discovering any stock that had less than a sixteenth of white blood.) Wasn't Standing Arrow's steelworker lieutenant a full-blooded Indian? I asked. "He has hair on his face!" was the answer. The Indians are supposed to have been beardless and to have had little hair on their bodies—thus, according to the anthropologists, proving their Mongolian origin. He added, in this connection, a remark which seemed to me of profound significance in connection with political issues in which questions of color are involved. "When you think about your white blood," he said, "you know that you've got to be a complete Indian!"

My sponsor had left us at the door to attend to some other business, and the rigid and laconic old Indian to whom we had given a lift, seeing us standing there, came up to us and admonished us in the formal British accent that survives among these once pro-British Mohawks. "You can't go in, you know!" I explained that we had been invited. "I'll ask," he said, and went inside. We waited a long time. I decided at last to look up our friend and ventured into the Longhouse. I found him in argument—speaking Mohawk— with the dignified old man who had forbidden us to enter, as well as, alternately, with another old man, a ninety-year-old giant, of whom I had been told when we saw him go in that he had once been a celebrated football player at the Carlisle Indian school. It was plain that Louis Papineau was doing his best to persuade them that they ought to admit us, and that the old men were utterly unyielding. Papineau with an hospitable but nervous gesture invited us to sit down on one of the benches, but at a moment when he was arguing with the giant, the Mohawk took a seat beside me, laid his hand on my arm and said quietly but sternly, "You go out." I got up and said to my friend that I did not want to embarrass him. He nodded, and my cousin and I went outside, where he joined us with regretful apologies. The old Mohawk then emerged, and he and Papineau continued the argument with evidently increasing heat. A young man in a lumberjack shirt and cap, broad of build, with a round face and lively black eyes, came up and introduced himself: "Wallace Anderson—I'm a Tuscarora." I was to meet him again months later. He was Mad Bear, who has since become famous. Not wanting to remain as a subject of contention, I asked whether they would mind if we waited outside and watched the arrival of the chiefs. Mr. Papineau, though shaken, approved, so we went to sit in the car. Another young man, who had been standing by listening to the conversation, and as to whom I had had no idea whether his attitude was friendly, indifferent or hostile, came up to the window of the car and said to us, "Old people they don't understand nothing!" and immediately walked away.

At some distance off, out of sight, beyond the turn of the road, the meeting of the Confederacy chiefs was taking place around the council fire. They were praying to the Great Spirit and burning pinches of tobacco. Louis Papineau had said he resented—as, I

found, did all non-Christian Iroquois—the tendency
of Christian whites to speak of the Indians as "pagans."
After all, they, too, he said, worshipped one God, and
the tobacco they offered up was no different from the
Catholics' incense. Eventually, he had explained to us,
the chiefs—usually pronounced by the Iroquois
"chieves," on the analogy of *thieves* and *leaves*—
would arrive in a formal procession, each accompanied
by his clan mother. The titles had been established, at
the time of the founding of the League, as hereditary
in certain families, but they did not go by primogeni-
ture: the men who were to bear them were nominated,
supposedly on merit, by the ranking matrons, each for
her own clan. This nomination had to be ratified, first
by the clan, then by the nation, and finally by the council of the League; but the head of the family, on her own
initiative, could afterwards depose her nominee if she
did not approve of his conduct. In this way, I learned,
Standing Arrow himself had just been deprived of his
title by his grandmother, the mother of the Turtle
Clan, who was living as far away as Troy. It was decreed by Deganawída at the time of the founding
of the League that the chiefs should wear headdresses
of antlers, and though actual antlers are no longer
worn, a chief who has been deposed is still said to have
been "dehorned."

But today the procession was three hours late. It was
a horrid afternoon of drizzle and chill, and those who
had to take part in it had been hoping, no doubt, that
the drizzle would cease. When they finally arrived,
they were not in costume; the chiefs wore no feather

crests. Some were tall, dark and lean, with insolent wide-brimmed hats; but in the rain they seemed a little pathetic, with the discrepancies of their mixed breeding and with their drab American clothes. The first part of this inauguration ceremony consists of mourning for the chiefs who are dead—the occasion is called a "Condolence"—and a singer in the front rank was chanting a lonely dirge. The new Tadodáho came last. He was the only chief accompanied by his clan mother—in this case, his actual mother. The original Tadodáho, in Iroquois legend, was a monster with seven kinks in his body, prodigious sexual organs and hands and feet that were great turtle-claws. When he heard that the Mohawks, the Oneidas and the Cayugas had made an alliance against him, he was so furious that he ran to the forest and chewed up the grass and leaves, and his evil thoughts came rocketing out of his head in the form of writhing vipers. When he finally joined the Confederacy, it was necessary to pull out his kinks, to trim his genitals down to normal and to comb the snakes out of his hair. This last service was performed by Hayówent'ha, whose name—according to one interpretation among several—signifies "He who combs." The present Tadodáho has no snakes in his hair. He wore glasses and was dressed in a business suit; dark-skinned, with a recessive chin, he seemed rather inbred, as if he might be the King of Siam. His mother, though her skin, too, was somewhat dark, might have been a New York State farmwife on a fairly well-to-do level. She was wearing stoutly made black shoes and a small black old lady's hat, and her white hair had evidently been "done" for the occasion. When the men had filed into the Longhouse, four or five cars drove up, and the rest of the clan mothers got out of them. They had decided among themselves, I supposed, that they were not going to take that long walk in the rain.

I was later to discover that the story of my ejection from the Onondaga Longhouse was known—through the returning delegates—in almost every reservation I visited. I was told that the stiff-necked old Mohawk had in general become such a nuisance that he was no longer allowed to attend the councils. When I last saw him at Onondaga—piqued, no doubt, by the contretemps in the Longhouse—he had definitely abandoned the assembly. He took off his Indian costume, packed it in a small suitcase and went to sleep in the back seat of a car. I learned later, however, that he had turned up again for the ceremonies of the evening and had himself got bodily expelled by a drunken young Onondaga, who, not recognizing the visitor from St. Regis, insisted that his Nordic appearance clearly showed him to be a white man. The young man, however, had not remained, and the old devotee had returned.

I was struck in this connection and others by the primitive democracy of the Iroquois. Though there is someone to initiate the ceremonies and though the clan mothers occasionally intervene, there does not seem to be anyone invested with the authority to see that order is kept. If the children are unruly, they are uncontrolled unless their parents control them, and a sufficiently vigorous protest against the admission of an alien, though counter to the general sentiment, may result in a brawl or expulsion in which nobody inter‑venes and to which—though the Indians notice every‑thing—nobody, at the time it is going on, appears to be paying attention.

3. ST. REGIS

A good deal more light was to be thrown for me on the Iroquois nationalist movement by a series of visits to St. Regis, the Mohawk Reservation near Hogansburg, New York—a tract of almost 39,000 acres along the St. Lawrence River, which lies partly in Canada and partly in the States.

To the stranger, the most obvious sign of Iroquois patriotism is the fashion of wearing "scalplocks" on the part of the boys and young men. In order to produce a scalplock, you have both sides of your head shaved bare, with a narrow strip left in the middle that runs from the forehead to the back of the neck, where the scalplock proper hangs down. The scalp could be ripped off by taking hold of this lock, and thus to simplify the problem for the enemy was an act of insolent defiance. When driving one day in the St. Regis reservation, we picked up two Mohawk boys who were thumbing a ride, and I saw that—though the hair was now growing back—one of them had been shaved for a scalplock. In the hope of finding out something about the nationalist movement I asked him how long they had been doing this. He answered sharply, "About three thousand years." (The practice of scalping, it seems, was originally confined to the Iroquois and their neighbors; it was not known in the West or New England.) This revival of the scalplock reminded me of the revival of the Confederate flag, which the Southern boys now sport on their cars and which I used to see a few years ago through the windows of Princeton dormitories. Both fashions, I am told, have been sometimes adopted by boys who are not Southerners or Iroquois Indians—in both cases as protests, I think, against the prevalent pressure toward acceptance of the mechanical uniformity imposed by industrial civilization.

But a more important symptom of the recent revival of the spirit of the ancient league is a new interest in the Iroquois religion. The ceremonies that center in the Longhouse have something in common with those of other North American Indian groups; but the Iroquois are apparently unique in possessing a body of doctrine, a code of manners and morals, which is inculcated by way of the Longhouse. At the end of the eighteenth century, a prophet and religious reformer appeared among the Senecas. Ganyo-die-yo (1735-1815), who is known in English as Handsome Lake, was the half-brother of the famous chief Cornplanter, who worked for the revolted colonies after the Revolution, acting as an intermediary between the whites and the Indians. Handsome Lake —who was somewhat at odds with his half-brother— attempted to solve in a different way the problem of coming to terms with the whites, of accepting some elements of their civilization without losing the traditions of his own.

It has been shown by Mr. Merle H. Deardorff, the author of a valuable paper on Handsome Lake,* that the Iroquois prophet had been influenced by the teaching of Quaker missionaries, who had been sent to the Seneca community on the Allegheny River in which Cornplanter and Handsome Lake lived. The Quakers approached the Indians in a less theological and aggressive way than the Catholics and the Protestants had. They had counselled them, in answer to questions as to how they should direct their lives—I quote from Mr. Deardorff: "Look inside. You have a light in there that will show you what is good and what is bad. When you know you have done wrong, repent and resolve to do better. Outward forms and books and guides are good; but they are made by men. The Great Spirit himself puts the inner light in every man. Look to it. Learn to read and write so that you may discern for yourself whether or not the white man's book is true." There is a legend that Handsome Lake would disappear for weeks down the Allegheny and that spies found him sitting in a mountain cabin and having the Bible read to him by an old man in a black coat. In any case, he soon had a revelation, a vision that came in a dream. (With the Iroquois, dreams, as we shall later see, play a sometimes cardinal rôle in the waking life.) He had been ill at his half-brother's house and seemed on the point of death. Now, Handsome Lake had been something of a wastrel, and as he lay looking up at the opening in the ceiling through which the smoke

* *The Religion of Handsome Lake: Its Origin and Development*, in Bulletin 149 of the Bureau of American Ethnology.

escaped—seeing the sunlight by day and the stars at night—he began to think about the Creator, and he thanked Him for these and for the song of birds, and wondered whether He might not help him to rise and "walk again in the world." The liquor which had been brought by the white man had evidently, in Handsome Lake's case, had a very deleterious effect on a character of exceptional quality. The whole code and training of the Iroquois had been based upon self-control. When captives were taken from a defeated tribe, some would be adopted by the captors, but others would be tortured systematically as a spectacle for the victors, and one was schooled to face the possibility of being subjected to this. It was a contest, a performance, a drama. The victim must remain impassive, continue to insult his tormentors, threatening them with the vengeance of his tribesmen, up to the moment of death. Their language—except in council, where eloquence was in order—was terse, undemonstrative, trenchant. There are almost no labials in the Iroquois languages, and they talked without moving their lips. They had had, before the white man arrived, no experience of alcohol, and had acquired no technique for resisting its effects. Their indulgence in it had proved disastrous. In the Allegany community, in which Handsome Lake lived, the sacred dances had been turning into orgies, and the demoralization there reached a climax when, in the spring of 1799, a group of Indians came back from Pittsburgh, where they had just sold their winter furs. With the whisky they had got in exchange, they embarked on a spree that went on for weeks. Several men were killed in brawls, and others, who had passed out on the ground, were allowed to die of exposure. The Quakers appealed to Cornplanter to call a council. He did so, and persuaded his people to put a ban on hard liquor and to appoint two young chiefs to enforce it. Those festivals that had been imitated from the whites and had become occasions for riot were henceforth to be abolished and only those of the traditional cult to be continued in their more austere original form.

On June 15 of that year, then, Handsome Lake, lying ill in Cornplanter's house and brooding on the errors of his life, had the first of a series of visions. He thought he heard someone calling him, and got up and went out of the house, and there he saw three men standing, each holding a bush that bore berries. They told him that he would live that summer to see the berries grow ripe again—berries are very important in the diet of the Iroquois—and he ate one from each bush. They told him that the Creator was much displeased at the drunkenness of his people, and that he, who had been a hard drinker himself, had been forced by his illness to abstain from drink and to think about the Creator. They announced that a fourth person would later arrive, and when, in a further dream, this fourth person did appear and declared to Handsome Lake that he pitied him and was going to take him away, he felt that he was talking with the Creator himself. On waking, he told his half-brother Cornplanter that he, Handsome Lake, was going to see his own son and Cornplanter's daughter, his niece—

both of whom were dead. Now Handsome Lake fell into a trance, which lasted for seven hours and in the course of which his arms and legs grew cold but during which, he afterwards reported, a guide, carrying bow and arrows and wearing clothes of "a clear sky color," led him away to his son and niece, the former of whom told him that he was greatly displeased with his own son, Handsome Lake's grandson, for not taking care of his grandfather when Handsome Lake was suffering so much, and the niece that she was greatly distressed to hear her father and brother on earth engaged in such angry arguments. The guide now admonished Handsome Lake to give up his drinking forever, and bade him look around at a river near the brink of which they were standing. When Handsome Lake looked, he saw many canoes loaded with kegs of whisky and accompanied by "an ugly fellow" —I quote a Quaker account—"going about very busy, doing and making all the noise and mischief he could." The guide said that this was the Devil.

Handsome Lake now recovered and declared that the four divine messengers had made him a revelation which he was ordered to preach to his people to save them from corruption and degradation. The process by which his visions were perpetuated and reduced to a moral code was not unlike that which produced the Koran. Like Mohammed, the Iroquois prophet simply repeated his message, he never wrote anything down; nor did his grandson and disciple Sos-háy-yo-wa (Big Burden Strap—he was known in English as James Johnson), who, however, established an oral text—

known as the Gúy-wee-yo, Good Message—which had currency almost everywhere in the Iroquois world and has survived to our own day. It is recited in the Longhouse every other year, in three or four instalments, which occupy successive mornings, and it has retained the authority of Scripture for those Indians who are seriously religious but who have not accepted Christianity. This text has undergone variations in the memories and on the lips of its various preachers, and sometime in the early sixties of the last century a council was appointed to reduce it to a reliable version in the Seneca language, written down according to a system invented by the Reverend Asher Wright, a pioneering Congregationalist missionary. This text was eventually lost, but a further attempt was made in 1903 to put on record the correct version of the Good Message. A translation of this by the Seneca scholar Arthur C. Parker was published in 1913 as a bulletin of the Education Department of the University of the State of New York, and in the meantime, half a century before, Lewis H. Morgan had included in his book on the League some selections from the code supplied him in translation by Brigadier General Ely S. Parker, a grandson of Soshéoa and a great-uncle of Arthur C. My knowledge of the Handsome Lake Code has been derived from these two sources and from the notes of Asher Wright. To the white reader the Good Message is impressive; it increases one's respect for the Iroquois. I want to give some account of it here since it helps to explain the basis for their striking moral self-dependence.

The Handsome Lake Code begins with the story of the prophet's visions and goes on to a denunciation of liquor. He had looked upon the poverty and debasement of his people and had seen, "as far as his vision reached . . . the increasing smoke of numberless distilleries arising, and shutting out the light of the sun"; he had seen "a costly home, made and furnished by the pale faces—a house of confinement, where were fetters, ropes and whips," to which the addicts of liquor were sent; he had seen the "dissensions and divisions" which were wrecking the traditional councils. "Now, some have said that there is no harm in partaking of fermented liquids. Then, let this plan be followed: let men gather in two parties, one having a feast of food, apples and corn, and the other have cider and whisky. Let the parties be equally divided and matched, and let them commence their feasting at the same time. When the feast is finished, you will see those who drank the fermented juices murder one of their party, but not so with those who ate food only." (There is a story of a very heavy drinker who was found, after a Handsome Lake preacher's death, to be the only man on the reservation who knew the code by heart. It devolved upon him, thus, to recite it at the annual ceremony. When asked whether he did not feel that this function was rather incongruous, he answered, "Not in the least. Who is better fitted then I am to bear witness to the evils of drink?")

The anxieties of Handsome Lake in connection with his own family are reflected in the Good Message.

"Children should obey their parents and guardians, and submit to them in all things. Disobedient children occasion great pain and misery. They wound their parents' feelings, and often drive them to desperation." But: "Talk slowly and kindly to children and never punish them unjustly." The Iroquois did not whip their children. The mother would sometimes blow water in the face of the naughty child. Handsome Lake advises the mother to take the children to "the water's edge" and threaten to put them in. "If they persist in disobedience, douse them." In regard to husband and wife: "The marriage obligations should generate good to all who have assumed them. [Marriage had by that time become partially regularized: most Indians had only one wife at a time.] Let the married be faithful to each other, that when they die it may be in peace." There are special admonitions to wives that they must not grow impatient and have lovers when their husbands are away on long hunting trips. But if the husband should go on a visit and "induce some agreeable woman to live with him, saying he is single," and then go back to his family, and his wife should find out about this, she should "behave as if no trouble had occurred. Now, we, the Messengers, say that the woman is good in the eyes of the Creator and has her place reserved for her in the heaven-world; but the man is on his way to the house of the Wicked One." In regard to parents and children: "Children should never permit their parents to suffer in their old age. . . . To abandon a wife or children is a great wrong, and produces many evils.

It is wrong for a father- or mother-in-law to vex a son- or daughter-in-law; but they should use them as if they were their own children. It often happens that parents hold angry disputes over their infant child. This is also a great sin. It [the child] feels badly and lonely. It can see for itself no happiness in prospect. It concludes to return to its Maker. It wants a happy home and dies. The parents then weep because their child has left them. You must put this evil practice from among you, if you would live happy." The wife must not leave her husband on account of becoming jealous of his love for his child.

The admonitions about manners are interesting. The men are told not to boast. If a man is unusually handsome or strong or a very swift runner, he must not talk to other people about it but simply give thanks to the Creator. If a woman pays a visit to another house, "she must help at the work in progress and talk pleasantly." If she tells funny stores, they must never be malicious, but always jokes on herself. If she speaks harshly of others, the woman of the house must say to her, "I remember the desires of our Creator. I cannot hear what you say." The women are particularly warned against telling *godiodiáse*, which are defined by Arthur Parker as "stories that augment by repetition." These are not, however, it seems, merely stories that become exaggerated but the devices by which a woman will deliberately provoke a quarrel between two other women, reporting first to one, then the other, that her neighbor has said horrible things about her. "Now great troubles arise

and soon a fight, and one woman causes it all. Therefore the Creator is very sad." If the mother of a
family who are just about to eat should look out and
see a visitor coming, "she must not hide the food to
save it till after the visitor leaves, but should offer
some to the guests, saying 'Sedékoni,' [come eat]."
In the course of my own recent visits to the Iroquois,
I was often invited to dinner or lunch. When I commented once at St. Regis on Iroquois hospitality, I was
told that I must never refuse it—"Even if you've just
eaten, ask for a glass of milk—they'll understand"—
otherwise they would take one for an enemy. This
point, too, I afterwards found embodied in the Handsome Lake code: "Now, it is not right to refuse what
is offered. The visitor must take two or three bits at
least and say 'Niawén' " ("Thank you"—the last syl-
lable is a nasal as in the French *bien*). The women are
told to feed the children of poor parents if they are
playing in the vicinity of her house, and if they should
see "an unfortunate girl who has neither parents nor
settled home," to "call her in and help her repair her
clothing, cleanse herself and comb her hair."

The prophet—having studied the religion of the
white man—provided the Iroquois with a Heaven
and a Hell. They had already had a kind of Devil—a
spirit called "The Evil-Minded," who was the ad-
versary of the Creator; but Handsome Lake gave him
horns, cloven hoofs and a tail; and he had seen in his
vision how this spirit would make the drunkard drink
a dipperful of red-hot liquid and then bid him "sing
and make himself merry, as was his want while on

earth"; how a wife-beater was presented with a red-hot statue of a woman and invited to let himself go, and how the sparks flew out and burnt off his arm; how a man who had sold his land (the land is regarded as a mother who has given birth to the Indians and cannot be sold) was condemned to remove grain by grain a heap of sand which never diminished; and other such appropriate punishments. But these punishments were not everlasting. When the sinners had paid for their sins, they would be admitted to Heaven.

This Heaven of Handsome Lake—which he called "The New World" because his people had not known about it before he revealed it to them—is not, as for some other Indians, a Happy Hunting Ground but a paradise of berry-picking. In Handsome Lake's vision, "the light was dazzling. Berries of every description grew in vast abundance. Their size and quality were such that a single berry was more than sufficient to appease the appetite. A sweet fragrance perfumed the air. Fruits of every kind met the eye. The inmates of this celestial abode spent their time in amusement and repose. No evil could enter there. None in Heaven ever transgresses again. Families were reunited and dwelt forever in harmony. They possessed a bodily form, the senses and the remembrance of the earthly life. But no white man ever entered there." No white man with one exception. This was the Destroyer of Villages, as the Iroquois called George Washington. (It has usually been assumed by both Indians and whites that this name was given to Washington in consequence of Sullivan's destructive raid of 1779, carried out by his orders in reprisal against damaging attacks by the Senecas, who were then in the service of the British; but it has now been established that he was designated by this title long before the Revolution, and there seems to be some reason for believing that it had originally been assigned to Washington's great-grandfather John. It has in any case been applied ever since to all the American Presidents.) He lived in a fort with an enclosure around it, just outside the gate of Heaven. Everyone who entered Heaven saw him "walking to and fro within the enclosure. His countenance indicated a great and good man. They said to Handsome Lake: 'The man you see is the only paleface who ever left the earth. He was kind to you when, on the settlement of the great difficulty between the Americans and the Great Crown, you were abandoned to the mercy of your enemies. The Crown told the great American, that as for his allies, the Indians, he might kill them if he liked. The great American judged that this would be cruel and unjust. He believed they were made by the Great Spirit and were entitled to the enjoyment of life. He was kind to you, and extended over you his protection. For this reason he has been allowed to leave the earth. But he is never permitted to go into the presence of the Great Spirit. Although alone, he is perfectly happy. All faithful Indians pass by him when they go to Heaven. They see him, and recognize him, but pass on in silence. No word ever passes his lips.'" I am quoting from Morgan here. In Parker's translation of the code, the account is somewhat different. The Messengers point to "a certain spot between the earth and the clouds," and the prophet sees a house suspended there, and on the veranda with a railing about it, a man walked and with him was a penny dog [?]." The followers of Cornplanter and Handsome Lake had also, however, good reason to be grateful to President Jefferson. Handsome Lake had visited the capital in 1802 and had brought back letters from Jefferson commending to the Seneca people both Handsome Lake and his half-brother Cornplanter. This, says Deardorff, was of great importance in strengthening the position of Handsome Lake against an opposing faction who were suspicious of the influence of the Quakers.

The impression made on Handsome Lake by the teaching of the Christians appears at several points in the code—in the doctrine, for example, that no one who repents can be damned even if repentance comes only at the end of a wicked life; and that "it is better to be poor on earth and rich in the sky-world than to have earth riches and no heaven." Jesus himself plays a curious rôle. Handsome Lake in one of his visions meets a man whose hands and feet and breast are wounded and smeared with fresh blood. "They slew me," he tells the prophet, "because of their independence and unbelief. So I have gone home to shut the doors of Heaven that they may not see me again until the earth passes away.... Now let me ask how your people receive your teachings." Handsome Lake replies that he thinks that "half my people are inclined to believe in me." "You are more successful than I," says the man, "for some believe in you but none in me. I am inclined to believe that in the end it will also be so with you. Now, it is rumored that you are but a talker with spirits. Now, it is true that I am a spirit and the one of him who was murdered. Now, tell your people that they will become lost when they follow the ways of the white man." The palefaces, says Asher Wright, because Jesus was divine and they had slain him, were required by God to weep and pray, but their "tears and prayers would be of no avail, for none of them could be received into Heaven; whereas the Indians, not having participated in his murder, would be received at once into Heaven, if they were faithful to observe the dances, and refrained from the vices he had forbidden." In regard to "the ways of the white man," the teaching of Handsome Lake ran directly counter to the white man's customs in two important respects. He advocated the killing of witches —always for the Indians a serious problem—who were punished in Handsome Lake's Hell by being alternately plunged into cauldrons filled with freezing and with boiling liquids; and he was opposed to having Indian children sent to white schools. He told his people that they were free to "grow cattle, and build yourselves warm and comfortable dwelling houses," but that this was "all they could safely adopt of the customs of the palefaces. You cannot live as they do."

This code has played a certain rôle in preserving the solidarity of the Iroquois League. The text of it, transmitted orally—in spite of the written version set down in 1903—differs somewhat in the different dialects and even from Longhouse to Longhouse; the language is sometimes archaic and no longer well understood, and passages are said to be garbled; but the Good Message of Handsome Lake has a scope and a coherence which have made it endure as has the teaching of no other Indian prophet, and it is accepted at the present time by at least half the Iroquois world as a source of moral guidance and religious inspiration. Instead of losing its hold and fading away, as anthropologists at one time expected, it has lately shown vigorous signs of revival. The prophet, who was born a Seneca, spent most of his life among his own nation, first on the Allegheny River, then, north of there, at Tonawanda. At the very end of his life, he was invited to Onondaga, and his Messengers told him to go. A further vision in the course of his journey seemed to show him a pathway of grass leading to the New World, and immediately on arriving at Onondaga Handsome Lake fell ill and died. His tomb, just across the road from the Longhouse at Onondaga, is marked by a large granite tombstone of the kind that was conventional in the cemeteries of the whites in the nineties and early nineteen hundreds.

The religion of Handsome Lake has thus been particularly identified with the Seneca and Onondaga reservations; but, as Parker wrote in 1913, "the force of Handsome Lake's teaching . . . is still felt and affects in some way all the New York reservations." He adds, "except perhaps the St. Regis." It is a sign of the prestige and tenacity of the gospel of Handsome

Lake as well as of the reawakening of the Iroquois nationalist self-consciousness that St. Regis should now be cultivating this gospel. This Mohawk reservation, which straddles the St. Lawrence so that it lies on both sides of the Canadian border and includes several islands in the river, has always been dominated by the Catholic Church, whose chief representative there is a Mohawk priest trained in Canada. But about thirty years ago a group of unconverted Indians—though, to protect themselves against Catholic pressure, they had at first to ally themselves with the Methodists—inaugurated a Longhouse there. Precisely what the strength of this religion is now it would be difficult to ascertain. It is hard to get accurate figures on even the population of an Iroquois reservation—since the Iroquois resist the census as they do other efforts on the part of the whites to study or check their communities; but I have been given an estimate for St. Regis of perhaps three hundred Longhouse members (and about the same number of Protestants) to about seventeen hundred Catholics, and it is believed that the Longhouse congregations are growing. A few years ago, I am told, there were only about half a dozen families affiliated with the Longhouse religion, and now there are about ninety. Many Indians who are nominally Catholics—though told that it is a mortal sin—are said now to attend the ceremonies. (A similar restoration of the Longhouse has taken place in the Mohawk reservation—also Catholic-dominated—at Caughnawaga in Canada. In the Catholic province of Quebec, the traditional religion of the

Iroquois is not merely frowned upon as it is in the part of St. Regis that lies on our side of the line: it is to all intents and purposes forbidden. A distinguished anthropologist, who was at one time connected with the Smithsonian Institution, has told me that he was somewhat embarrassed, in his semi-official position, to find that, in his capacity as a scientist, he was dealing in Quebec with a movement that was virtually underground.)

This nationalist self-consciousness of the Iroquois has been stimulated and much embittered, in the course of the last two years, by a whole set of white encroachments, incidental to various engineering projects, which have seemed to converge on them all at once, hitting one reservation after the other, and which have ended by causing the Indians to suspect a systematic persecution intended to drive them out of their lands and to disperse them as a troublesome minority that would better be out of the way. They remember that in the early nineteenth century, when upper and western New York State were first being opened to settlers, the state did adopt the policy of trying to get rid of the Iroquois in order to dispose of their lands. A Christianized Mohawk missionary, who was born at Caughnawaga and who died in St. Regis, the once well-known Eleazar Williams, who claimed later to be the lost dauphin but was acting then as agent for a land company, induced the majority of the Oneidas to emigrate to Green Bay, Wisconson, where they were given unimproved lands in exchange for the more comfortable ones on which they had been living in the county that had been named for their nation. (It is significant that the Wisconsin Oneidas, who had been converted before they left and who had completely lost touch with the Iroquois League, should lately have been recovering their history and making contact with their people in the East.) Now, it is hardly conceivable that the recent attempts on the part of the state and the federal governments to condemn Indian property for public works or to make it uninhabitable by flooding it are the results of a concerted policy. Yet these efforts have certainly been characterized by total ignorance of Iroquois civilization and a contemptuous disregard of those rights of the Six Nations Confederacy which were assumed to be guaranteed them by treaty. The Iroquois, invoking these treaties, regard themselves as a sovereign people at peace with the United States. They are supposed to own their property outright, with no obligations to the white authorities: they do not pay property tax, and they sell their own licenses to white men who want to hunt or fish on their lands. Though they have been given the right to vote by a Citizenship Act of 1924, which they themselves had never demanded, they have for the most part refused to exercise it. In the war of 1914-1919, they separately declared war on Germany, and in the second of the big white wars, a number of them either evaded the draft or resisted it and went to jail. (Those who did serve, however, take a good deal of pride in their records, as they do in all their dangerous enterprises, and are proud also of having been found useful, on account of their impenetrable languages, in the transmission of secret messages.)

The affairs of the St. Regis Mohawks, from the political as well as from the religious point of view, must, I should think, be the most confused in the whole American Indian world, where the question of legal status seems generally to be more or less obscure. I have mentioned the religious situation which has been caused by the dominance of the Catholic Church, but the influence of French Quebec has had also its disruptive consequences for the Iroquois social system. The Catholics have made an effort to liquidate the clans and the nations, and they have given the title "the Seventh Nation" to the Indians they seek to control, a name which the Indian resistance is in the habit of using ironically for the Church itself. But the splitting of the St. Regis reservation by the boundary line between Canada and the United States has created, also, other problems. The Indians on the Canadian side have been free to come over to ours and earn money by such occasional activities as selling souvenirs at county fairs, while the Indians who live on our side—on the assumption that they are American citizens—are forbidden by the Canadian government to work on the other side. An Indian from south of the line who did take a job in Canada was recently found murdered, and the Indians on our side are complaining of Canadian Indian families who have moved just over the line—which may mean simply renting the house next door—in order to be eligible for the industries which, as a result of the St. Lawrence Seaway and the great power plant connected with it, are now being drawn to that part of the world. In the meantime, those St. Regis Mohawks who are loyal to the Six Nations constitution do not want to admit a conflict between the interests of the two groups of Indians.

But for the Mohawks of the St. Regis reservation, even aside from the United States-Canadian problem, the matter of political responsibility is already sufficiently complicated. You have at St. Regis the regular chiefs, appointed by their clan mothers, who are supposed to be functioning in conformity with the provisions of the old constitution and upholding the claims of the Confederacy that derived from the original treaties. But you have also a board of three "state chiefs" or "elected" or "elective chiefs," as they are variously called, ostensibly chosen by popular vote but actually, according to the Confederacy chiefs, selected by the white authorities and subservient to white interests. The election of these chiefs took place in a Catholic Youth Center outside the reservation. Two candidates for each office were nominated, but there were only about twenty votes cast. These "chiefs" are, in any case, however, the representatives with whom the state deals. And there has also been a third group of chiefs—which is said to have ceased to be active—known as the Council of Twelve, who were originally set up by the French in the middle of the eighteenth century. This departed from the Iroquois system and followed that of the French nobility by making the rank of chief the inheritance of the eldest son in the patrilineal line. (The old families in which the rank was hereditary in the mother's line are called by the Mohawks *rodiyane*, and what is now called a chief was a *royane*, which the nobility-minded English translated "nobles" and "lord" but which, according to the great Seneca chief, Ely S. Parker, did not imply the same exalted station.) That lively expounder of Iroquois affairs, of mixed Mohawk and Irish blood, whose Irish name is Ray Fadden but who writes under the Mohawk name of Aren Akweks, tells us, in his *History of the St. Regis Akwesasne Mohawks*, in almost identical words at the end of each of the sections in which he describes these three factions, that "their chiefs sit in council and discuss problems of their nation. They claim to be the lawful chiefs."

There are problems, also, of legal jurisdiction. The Iroquois on our side of the boundary, except in the case of ten major crimes, were up to ten years ago supposed to have jurisdiction over their own affairs. Disputes at St. Regis were settled—depending on which of the two bodies the parties preferred to resort to—by either the Six Nations Council or the council of elective chiefs. If it was a question of one of the more serious crimes, the Iroquois claimed the privilege—since their treaties had been made with the United States—of dealing not with the state but with the federal government. The first important test case on this issue occurred in 1821. A Seneca at Buffalo Creek had been appointed by his council to execute a woman believed to be a witch and had carried out the order. This had horrified the neighboring whites, and they had had him indicted in a New York State court. But the famous Seneca orator Red Jacket defended the execution, and scored heavily when he addressed the jury: "What, do you denounce us as fools and bigots, because we still continue to believe that which you yourselves sedulously inculcated less than two centuries ago! Your black-coats have thundered their doctrine from the pulpits—your Judges have pronounced it from the bench—your Courts have sanctioned it with the formalities of the Law, and you would now punish an unfortunate brother for adhering to the opinion of his forefathers! Go to Salem! look at the records of your Government, and you will find hundreds executed there for the very crime which called forth the sentence of condemnation upon this woman and drew down the arm of vengeance upon her. What have we done more than the Rulers of your people have done? and what crime has this man committed by having executed in a summary way the Laws of his Country and the injunctions of his God?" It was decided that the state court had no jurisdiction over Indian crimes, and the man who had killed the witch was acquitted. It became in the long run, however, such a nuisance for the white authorities always to have to bring in a federal marshal to arrest an Indian for a major crime that jurisdiction by the state in such cases came to be greatly desired by most of those who had to deal with the Indians; and since the Indians in most reservations not infrequently applied for justice to the courts of the state instead of settling their difficulties among themselves, why not, asked some Indians as well as many whites, transfer all jurisdiction to the state? An intelligent Carlisle-trained Seneca, not a supporter of the nationalist movement, told me that he had served on a delegation that went to Washington to urge this transfer. He declared that in his locality the cases brought into court had been often held up by the defendant on grounds of improper jurisdiction and that so much time would be occupied in debating this ancient question that the case itself was never decided. That the state, however, was capable of acting in an insolent and unauthorized way in contempt of the decisions of a tribal council was shown in a recent case about which the St. Regis Mohawks are still extremely bitter. A Mohawk woman who had married a man of her own race and lived in the reservation found herself, after her mother's death, in possession of her mother's house and of such money as her mother had left. It was decided in a tribal council that the daughter should keep the property and offer to divide the money with her sisters, who had left the reservation. But the niece of one of these sisters, whose mother had married a white man and who lived in a nearby white town, brought an action through the state courts and had State Troopers sent to St. Regis to evict her aunt. The aunt was seventy-five and an invalid, but the Troopers broke down her door, moved her furniture out on the street and put the old lady in jail. A United States district attorney, not happy about the affair, had her removed after a few days; but the Troopers were sent in again. This time they found the doorway obstructed by an Indian of enormous girth, who invited them to shoot right through him, and documents were produced by the Mohawks to demonstrate that the bill, then pending, to transfer jurisdiction to the State of New York, had not yet been passed by Congress. The Troopers were persuaded to go away; but, as soon as the bill had been passed, the property was sold at auction and purchased by the suing niece, on condition that she pay off the other heirs, who got $235 apiece.

For in 1949 and '50—in the teeth of much Iroquois protest—a whole set of bills was put through Congress transferring to the various states jurisdiction over Indian reservations in both civil and criminal cases. I am inclined to believe that the impulse which has set off the present agitation was first given by the passage of these bills.

But the two most important matters which are agitating St. Regis today are the question of whether or not the state government has the right to make the Indians pay income tax, and the various problems arising from the taking of Indian property for the building of the St. Lawrence Seaway and the great power project connected with it. In regard to the first of these, the Iroquois contend that since they pay no tax on their land, they ought not to pay tax on their incomes (such taxes were of course unknown at the time of the original treaties); but many of the Indians have been working on the Seaway and in the aluminum factories at Massena, and—although a distinction has been made between money earned inside and outside the reservation—a federal tax has been withheld from their wages. In August, 1958, the state came down on the Mohawks and tried to collect back taxes. The Mohawks employed counsel to fight this demand on the ground that they were "wards of the government," and so not subject to taxation. Actually, this well-known phrase, which early appeared in the wording of federal legislation affecting the Indians, seems to have lost any precise legal meaning. It was ruled in the Franklin County Court that since the income of any infant is taxable, so also must be the income of any Indian, even though his relation to the United States resembles that of a ward to his guardian. More than a hundred St. Regis Indians were subpoenaed. The hereditary Confederacy chiefs appealed to President Eisenhower, and threatened, as the heads of a sovereign nation, to take their case to the United Nations. They insisted—despite an opinion which was formulated in 1943 by the then state attorney general to the effect that, since citizenship had been given to the Indians by the act of 1924, they were liable to all the obligations of citizens—that they had never consented to accept this act and that they did not then accept it. They are not living, they say, in the United States, so they cannot be made citizens of it.

It had, however, been actually the elective chiefs who had taken the step of retaining a lawyer and who would be responsible for paying him, and serious dissension followed between these and the reviving Confederacy. The elective chiefs attempted to banish from the New York State side of the line three nationalists from Canada who had crossed it. One of these was the Confederacy's war chief, who had been active in the Six Nations movement; the elective chiefs went to court and got an eviction notice against him. The nationalists, of course, claimed that there was no such thing as a Canadian or a New York State Iroquois: their country was Iroquoia. But there had to be some understanding between the two Indian factions as to paying the white lawyers who were fighting the case. A meeting was called by the elective chiefs, which the hereditary chiefs agreed to attend, accompanied by their clan mothers. At this meeting the presiding elective chief refused to answer the questions of the nationalists, and the latter raised a cry of "dictatorship." The meeting broke up in a turmoil. The elective chiefs have since announced that they will not try to appeal the court ruling, and have agreed to meet with representatives of the New York State Tax Commission. The nationalists have announced that they will continue to fight through the courts.

This conflict between the two Mohawk factions has been further exacerbated by the problems of compensation for the Indian property which has recently been taken by the state. The disputes about title involved are among the most perplexing of legal tangles. It has been facetiously said that a part of the difficulty of getting them untwisted has been due to their being in the hands of two groups who have an interest in keeping them tangled: the lawyers and the Indians.

But it may perhaps be worthwhile here to outline a couple of these cases as examples of the vexed uncertainly which characterizes so many aspects of the status, and hence the identity, of the Indian.

In the course of constructing the Seaway, its engineers found it necessary, in straightening out the channel of the river, to trim off a point of land—Racquette Point—which comprised about eighty-eight acres. This resulted in the displacement of four Indian families as well as taking the property of a few other Indians. The whole compensation offered was $100,000. The elective chiefs of St. Regis, who handled these negotiations, reserved their right for the future to make a claim that this sum had not been sufficient, but in the meantime they accepted an offer on the part of the federal agency for the Seaway to deposit with the court the arbitrary sum of $62,000, half of which was to be paid to the occupants to induce them to move off the land and the other half of which was to be put in the hands of the board of elective chiefs to be equitably divided by them among the people of the reservation. There had been, however, at Racquette Point, among the dispossessed families, some adherents of the Longhouse and the League, and these nationalists promptly gave notice to the office of the Assistant United States District Attorney that the three elective chiefs were not properly constituted officials and that they had been given no authority to act for the Confederacy. A list was supplied to the District Attorney of the genuine Six Nations chiefs, signed by the Tadodáho, and at a hearing in the United States

District Court for the Northern District of New York on May 6, 1958, a delegation of these chiefs appeared. The presiding judge, S. W. Brennan, made the objection that half of these were Canadian, and that these Canadian chiefs had had nothing whatever to do with distributing the money for compensation which had been paid on the Canadian side. The case was deferred to a later hearing, which took place on October 14. The court record shows general confusion, in which, however, one thing is clear: the firm determination of the judge to recognize the elective chiefs and to maintain that the title of the St. Regis lands was vested in the state of New York. He begins by complaining that the names of the chiefs who are now supposed to speak for the Confederacy are not always the same as at the previous hearing, and that between the "Conspiracy Chiefs"—as the record, no doubt unintentionally, makes it—"the Longhouse or Loghouse Chiefs, the Condolence Chiefs and Lifetime Chiefs," he cannot for the life of him make out who it is that are demanding to be recognized. My friend Louis Papineau of Onondaga, who was among the Six Nations representatives in court (and whose name is also garbled in the record), made an effort to explain to the judge that all of these are names for the same officials; but Judge Brennan either had not grasped or did not wish to waste time arguing the position of the Six Nations chiefs vis-à-vis the elective ones, and he implied that, since Mr. Papineau admittedly lived not in St. Regis but in Onondaga, he had no business to appear at all; he laid it down that the case was exclusively concerned with the Indians who lived in St. Regis. The delegates of the Six Nations Confederacy were seriously handicapped at this hearing through the difficulty they had had—on account of their slender means—even in securing counsel who would competently defend their case. They had got a new lawyer since the previous hearing, and they complain that he let them down; but he had only just been retained and explained to the court that he was badly prepared. The best that he could do was to cite a provision of a state law of 1794, which, in deference to the old treaties, forbade the purchase by the state of fee in land from the Indians. The lawyer for the "American Party"—the name adopted by the group that the elective chiefs represented—cited agreements of 1796 and 1797, according to which the Mohawks ceded all their lands to the State of New York except those now comprised in their reservation. "I don't think," asserted the judge, "that the constitution of the Six Nations organization can override the laws of the state of New York." He had already, he said, in 1943, handed down a decision in a St. Regis case in favor of the elective chiefs, and it turned out, in the argument that followed, that he was somewhat better informed about the whole situation than his earlier expressions of bewilderment might have led one at first to suppose. Mrs. Lulu G. Stillman of Troy was present at this second hearing. Mrs. Stillman is one of those rare white crusaders, of the race of John Collier and Helen Hunt Jackson, who have taken up the cause of the Indian. She pointed out that, at the time when the elective chiefs had been set up by New York State law, the state had not yet been invested with its recently acquired jurisdiction—to which Judge Brennan replied that he would take the law as he found it, and that if it turned out to be unconstitutional, some higher court could correct him. "Thank you, Your Honor," said Mrs. Stillman. "I shall stand corrected, also. That is fair enough." But the buried basic worrying problem now erupted with a dramatic force which throws into sharp relief at once both the grievances of the Indians and the difficulties of the judge. I quote from the court record:

MR. PAPINEAU. Can I ask a question?

THE COURT. Yes.

MR. PAPINEAU. Do you respect Federal treaties consummated by this nation and the Federal—well, the United States?

THE COURT. Well, your question, "Do I respect Federal treaties"—certainly I respect Federal treaties.

MR. PAPINEAU. I inserted that Treaty of 1794 as evidence to prove that these lands were founded to the Six Nations, including these lands in question.

THE COURT. Well, now, young man—

MR. PAPINEAU. And not the state of New York.

THE COURT. All right. We have had something similar to this before, and fifteen years ago I wrote eight or ten pages about it and went into all of those treaties, and I came to the conclusion that I guess the New York State law controlled. And that stood for twenty-five years unchallenged, and I am not going to change it now. I have had all those treaties before me before.

MR. PAPINEAU. Now, can I ask you a question?

THE COURT. Yes.

MR. PAPINEAU. If these treaties that are consummated between the two nations, the Iroquois Confederacy, an independent nation, and the United States—Continental Congress of the United States —do these treaties in law become law, supreme law of the land when they are made?

THE COURT. Well, I don't want to get into a rather deep discussion about that matter—

MR. PAPINEAU. Well, that is what we are here for.

THE COURT (*continuing*). —about treaties, but generally you can answer it this way, that treaties have the force of law.

MR. PAPINEAU. And in that treaty there is Article 4—they guarantee our rights to the land that we hold in possession. Now, those titles were vested solely in the Six Nations and never left the Six Nations.

THE COURT. You are getting back to argument that has long since gone. What you are arguing in substance is that the United States has no right to take the lands. To argue that, the time has long since gone by. The lands were taken and nobody objected.

MR. PAPINEAU. We are objecting now.

THE COURT. You are too late. Objections were all right long ago.

MR. PAPINEAU. They are still there. These treaties are still binding.

THE COURT. But the lands have been taken, and that is foreclosed. There is no use our arguing that now. I can't do anything about it and neither can you. The only thing we are talking about is compensation for the lands taken.

MR. PAPINEAU. That is the Federal law.

THE COURT. What is the Federal law?

MR. PAPINEAU. When this treaty is enacted, it becomes the supreme law of the United States, and how can New York State supersede the Federal law.

THE COURT. This has been gone over many times. I won't argue with you. You can make any statements you want but I am going to take the law as I see it and you can take it from there. I am not infallible and I make mistakes, but I can't do anything for you in that regard. Your argument is getting back to the power of the United States to condemn. In my opinion, you are too late for that. What we are talking about now is who gets compensated, not the power at all. That has gone by.

All right, gentlemen, now I think I will turn to the individual owners. . . .

The claimants to compensation were now checked and their claims approved. They have been paid $31,000. The remaining $69,000—partly as a result, no doubt, of the nationalists' opposition to turning it over to the elective chiefs—has never been paid at all.

There are two points involved in the argument

above. One, whether the United States is not obligated, under its treaties, to deal with the chiefs of the Confederacy; the other, whether the state of New York has the right to intervene at all in the disposal of Indian lands. This latter question has caused much confusion, and the policies adopted at various times are so contradictory or equivocal that the writer cannot but be grateful to Professor Gerald Gunther of the Columbia School of Law, who, as a member of the Inter-Law School Committee of Constitutional Simplification, has prepared a report on this subject which appears in the *Buffalo Law Review* of Autumn, 1958, and which has done more to unravel its complicated history and to clarify its legal aspects than anything else the writer has seen.

It is, of course, true, as contended in court by Mr. Papineau, that the Indians' rights to their lands were guaranteed by the federal government and could not, according to the original treaties, be alienated without the permission of that government; but it is also true that the state of New York, before the first treaty with the Indians was signed, "anxious to remove hostile tribes"—I quote from Professor Gunther—had claimed the right to deal separately with the Indians, as it had done when it was one of the colonies, had "obstructed the central government's negotiations and indeed arrested some of the national agents"; and that there has always been a tendency in New York State to assume that the state authorities have the right to deal directly with the Indians. In the last years of the eighteenth century, the state, without consulting the federal government, which had apparently become indifferent, acquired, through its own treaties, a good deal of land from the Indians. In 1802, the situation was regularized by a federal Indian Intercourse Act, which required that Indian titles could be extinguished only by treaty, but empowered the state to negotiate for them if a United States Commissioner were present. "By the 1830's," says Mr. Gunther, ". . . state Indian legislation was fairly comprehensive and state control over Indian affairs was generally unquestioned." But a crisis in the relations of the whites with the Senecas, which will later be explained in its place, had the result, in a treaty of 1842, of returning to the federal government the duty of protecting the Indians. New York State, however, in 1888, attempted to resume control. In a report of a special committee (the Whipple Committee) appointed "to investigate the 'Indian Problem,' " it was assumed, without any mention of "a possible overriding federal authority, that the state could eliminate tribal property holdings." This report is a classical statement of the domineering Yankee attitude, self-interested and hence self-righteous, which attempts to ride roughshod over Indian rights and to liquidate Indian society. It blamed, says Mr. Gunther, "the defects in Indian education, health and morals on the persistence of a large degree of tribal self-government. Indian Peacemakers' courts, applying tribal customs, were described as 'inefficient and often corrupt.' " "The 'invariable' answer discovered" by the members of the Whipple Committee "in its search for a solution of the 'Indian problem' " was: "Exterminate the tribe and preserve the individual; make citizens of them and divide their land in severalty." The committee was well aware that the Indians would oppose this policy, yet concluded, as it said, "bluntly" that Indian consent "should no longer be asked." But the New Yorkers did not quite dare to do such things, were not quite sure they had the right to do them. The recommendations of the Whipple Report had no result in legislation. The claims of the state, however, were to assert themselves again, in 1896, in the case of the Seneca Nation vs. Christie, in which it was held that the colonies had succeeded to the title of the Crown to all ungranted lands, "with the exclusive right to extinguish by purchase the Indian title, and to regulate dealings with the Indian tribes. . . . The original States," this opinion continued, "before and after the adoption of the federal Constitution, assumed the right of entering into treaties with the Indians, for acquiring title to their lands . . . independently of the government of the United States." This was said to be notably true of New York. It was no doubt some such precedent as this that Judge Brennan had in mind. We shall later see that further rulings were to be based on the assumption that such issues as this had to be settled with the federal government.

In the meantime, let us return to the other important case of Indian claims in connection with the St. Lawrence Seaway: the case of Barnhart Island. This island was regarded as necessary for the construction of the immense power dam—on a scale surpassed only

by those of Grand Coulee and Niagara—which has
been built between it and the mainland, and it was
taken over in 1954, under the right of eminent domain,
by Mr. Robert Moses, the chairman of the New York
Power Project. The three elective chiefs of St. Regis,
asserting that the title belonged to the Indians, at
once filed a suit against the State of New York for
$34,000,000 compensation. The history of the title to
Barnhart Island turned out, however, to be rather
baffling. The boundary line between Canada and the
United States was by a treaty of 1783 established just
south of this island, which at that time had been ceded
to the Indians. The Indians eventually leased it to a
British subject named Barnhart for $30 a year—a rent
which was raised later to $150. In 1822—when, by the
Treaty of Ghent, we had settled our affairs with the
English after the War of 1812—the joint commissioners under the treaty had the border run *north* of
the island, so that it now was included in the state
of New York. Let us remember at this point the
agreements that have been mentioned in connection
with the Racquette Point case, the agreements by
which the Mohawks at the end of the eighteenth
century—though, as it is now claimed by them, contrary to treaties made only a few years before—
cede to the state of New York all their lands except
those that now constitute their reservation. But they
had not, of course, ceded lands which were at that
time included in Canada, and the Treaty of Ghent
had provided that all "possessions, rights and privileges" which had been granted to the Indians in

Canada should be respected by the United States if, by the shifting of the old boundary, they should be transferred to our territory. This proviso was, however, not respected in the case of Barnhart Island. Without any consultation with the Indians, the island was in 1823 patented by the state of New York to the powerful Ogden family after whom Odgensburg is named, who first ejected the British Barnharts, then allowed them to return at the price of paying the Ogdens for the land and for their own, the Barnharts', improvements. The Indians got no more rentals. The Barnharts brought suit against the state of New York and eventually, though not before the fifties, succeeded in obtaining some damages. The Indians, too, pressed their claims, and in 1856 the Committee on Indian Affairs decided that New York State, by selling the island to the Ogdens, had "disregarded" the provisions of the Treaty of Ghent and the Indian title to Barnhart, and recommended an appropriation for damages. It was estimated that the annual rents from 1822 to 1856—plus interest—which should have been collected by the Indians amounted to $5,960, and specific directions were issued as to the procedure by which this sum should be withdrawn from the treasury, and how it should be distributed, but no record has been discovered that this distribution ever took place. There is some reason for believing that it disappeared between the New York politician who arranged for it and the Canadian government agent who was responsible for collecting the rent from the Barnharts and paying it over to the Indians. Between then and the taking of the island, with its value now so vastly increased, the Indians seem to have given up the struggle, but since their title has never been extinguished by any treaty, deed or "other conveyance," it is regarded by the Mohawks' lawyers as "still outstanding and concurrent."

The Indians' suit for $34,000,000 was brought in November, 1954, and in April of the following year the state requested of the Court of Claims that it invalidate the Indians' claim. This court, however, allowed it, but their verdict was reversed by the Appellate Division. An application by the plaintiff for reargument—on the basis of "certain recently discovered historical facts"—was denied by the New York Supreme Court in October of the following year, and a petition of certiorari, filed in January, 1959, has been denied by the Supreme Court of the United States.

It is interesting to note some of the judicial opinions which were cited by Mr. William H. Quimby, Jr., of Watertown in his brief for the suit of the Mohawks. A Chancellor John is cited as taking the view, in 1823, that it was "immaterial whether the Indians had their lands by immemorial possession, or by gift or grant by the whites, provided they had an acknowledged title. In either case, lands were of equal value to them, and required the same protection and exposed them to the same frauds. . . . After all this, who will hesitate to say, that it was worthy of the character of our own people, enjoying so great a superiority over the Indians in the cultivation of the mind, in the lights of science, the distinctions of property, and the arts of civilized life, to have made the protections of the property of the feeble and dependent remnants of the nations within our limits a fundamental article of the government? It is not less wise than it is just, to give to that article a benign and liberal interpretation, in favor of the beneficial end in view." This has the accent of the Jeffersonian age, the era of the welfare of humanity, the progress of the arts and sciences. In 1912, however, we find a New York State judge, in the case of Choate vs. Trapp, still wanting to give the Indians the benefit of the doubt: "In the government's dealings with the Indian . . . the construction, instead of being strict, is liberal; doubtful expressions, instead of being resolved in favor of the United States, are to be resolved in favor of the weak and defenseless people who are wards of the government and dependent wholly upon its protection and good faith. This rule of construction has been recognized, without exception, for more than a hundred years, and has been applied in tax cases." He quotes from an opinion of John Marshall's: "The language in treaties with the Indians shall never be construed to their prejudice if words be made use of which are susceptible of a more extended meaning."

Yet one finds among the St. Regis Mohawks, looming darkly in the background of these issues, a general apprehension lest they may lose their whole reservation. There has been clamped on them from the north, like a collar that chokes, the huge linkage of locks and dams that constitutes the St. Lawrence Seaway; and these facilities are now bringing industry to that once rather deserted region, so that the Indians have already, hemming them in to the west, one old and one brand new aluminum plant and a General Motors plant, which will cast the aluminum produced by the factories. These factories and the Seaway have caused to spring up in the neighboring town of Massena and other surrounding territory large encampments of permanent trailers, and—right up against the fretted woodwork and high dormers of the old brick houses of upstate New York—whole colonies of uni- or duo-cellular cottages, pink and yellow and gray and maroon, apple and olive green, of a dinky and neat uniformity that would not, I think, seem to most Mohawks appropriate habitations. The Indians are afraid that since so much of their land has already been taken from them by invoking a right of eminent domain which many of them do not recognize, the state government could easily go further and expropriate the reservation on the pretext of the necessity of "public works" in the shape of "housing projects" for the workers in the industries that are walling them in.* The paradox, central to the whole situation of the Iroquois in New York State, of a race of skilled machinists and workers in iron and steel, who earn their livings in ways that are removed by millennia from primitive handicrafts yet who belong to a cultural tradition that immeasurably antedates these and who de-

---

* Since the above was written, the state has announced its intention of running Route 37 through the St. Regis reservation. This has been resisted by the nationalists, who have been obstructing the movements of the surveyors and the claims adjusters.

sire to lead a life which has little in common with that
of the contrivers of the processes they serve, produces
a strange impression, and is likely to be quite unim-
aginable to their white neighbors who have never
looked into it. St. Regis is, on the surface, more modern since less rural than most Iroquois reservations,
and has been thought by our Indian Department to
be closer to its own ideal of ripeness for "integration"
(a subject to which we must later return); but any
external resemblance on the part of a Mohawk dwelling to one of those little toy cottages provided for
the flocking whites does not in the least imply that
you will find, if you go inside, the ambitions and ideas
of those whites or any feeling of solidarity with them.
In a shining and up-to-date kitchen, equipped with
the familiar canned goods, I talked—to some extent at
cross-purposes, due to cultural and language difficulties—with one of the most earnest of the nationalists.
When I left him, I wished him luck. "I don't expect
people to help us," he said, and pointed above his head.
"I only hope for help from the Creator. I thank Him
all the time for everything." He gestured toward the
modern kitchen sink: "I even thank Him for the water
from the tap!" He had said to me in speaking of the
money that was to be paid them in compensation:
"The earth is my mother. You cannot sell your
mother. You keep it for your children." This was not
at all dramatics, not an act for my benefit, but traditional ritual and doctrine, supported by the teaching
of Deganawída.

❖   ❖   ❖

I do not want to leave the St. Regis community without giving some account of one of its most remarkable members. There is at St. Regis a well-known family—able, influential and all-pervasive—who, having long since accepted Catholicism, have discarded their Indian names and adopted that of Cook. A member of this family, Philip Cook, who was formerly an ironworker in the old aluminum plant at Massena, has just been made general foreman of the structural ironworkers in the new one. At first meeting, he may give the impression of a striking example of assimilation to the materials in which one works. He is tall, straight and strong, with gray eyes and gray hair that stands up like wire. He is distinguished, so far as I can judge, by only one characteristic Iroquois feature: a modified form of the parrot-beaked nose. In discussing the aptitude of the Iroquois for working on high steel, he confessed that, though it usually meant nothing to him to walk on these vertiginous structures, he had sometimes had seizures of fright—it was bad when it was sleeting, he said—and he told me a terrible story which almost made my hair stand on end like his. He and one of his brothers had been painting on the skeleton of a big building in Rochester. They were standing on a twenty-inch purlin (a small beam laid across the rafters), ninety feet above the ground. A non-Indian, who was inexperienced but had undertaken the work on account of the high pay, looked down below and "froze." They spoke to him but he did not answer, and they knew that his situation was serious. Philip's brother, who was standing behind the man, hit him hard with his paintbrush on the back of the head, and Philip, who was standing in front of him, caught him in his arms as he fell. They had him tied with a rope and lowered, and when he found himself going down, he shrieked such a horrible shriek that Philip and his brother almost fell off their beam. On the ground, he was unconscious for a couple of hours. The Cooks were considerably shaken. What, however, makes Philip Cook exceptional is his strongly developed religious sense. One finds this among the Iroquois—Handsome Lake was the great exemplar— but rarely nowadays to such a degree. This foreman is also a preacher. This skilled mechanical worker has also a touch of the saint.

Philip Cook was born forty-five years ago, one of a family of fifteen children, on the St. Regis reservation; but his father—"a jack of all trades," he says— took the family all over the state, working at one thing and another. They had been Catholics since his grandmother's time, and did not now know what clan they belonged to. The Catholic Church, he says, has always done its best to prevent the Indians from learning anything about their traditions, and it was only from non-Catholic Indians whose acquaintance he made here and there in the course of the family's wanderings that he began to get some inkling of the Iroquois past. They returned to St. Regis when Philip was twenty. He could more or less understand Mohawk, but, due to his long absence, he had had no occasion to speak it and had thus become somewhat alienated from the aboriginal Mohawk world. Philip and one of his brothers accepted the office of elective chief. But in the spring of the following year (1948), a political crisis occurred. As a result of discontent with the elective chiefs and the pressure of the Six Nations party, a referendum was held to decide which of these factions should govern. Those who lived on the Canadian side and who had long had imposed upon them a system that corresponded with that of the "American Party," mostly voted for continuing the present arrangement, but of those on the United States side only eighty-three voted for the elective chiefs. In response to this, Philip and his brother and the other elective chief resigned, "acting," as they said in a statement, "in accordance with the wills of the majority of the adult residents of St. Regis." The bills for transferring jurisdiction from the federal government to the states were at that time before Congress, and Philip Cook and his brother had collaborated with Ray Fadden, the Irish Mohawk mentioned earlier, and the Tuscarora leader Mad Bear, in writing a leaflet opposed to these bills. The Cook contribution to this leaflet is headed "Does a Small Nation Have the Right to Exist?" and contains some caustic remarks on the behavior of the "so-called 'white father'" in his relations with the Six Nations Indians at a time when he is "pointing an accusing finger" at the behavior of Russia toward "its weaker neighbors."

Philip had thought it his duty, in his rôle of elective chief, to inform himself better about his people, and he set out to do some systematic reading in the history of the Six Nations. The French and English official documents create, he says, an impression that is very misleading. When the invaders wrote reports to their governments, they always referred to the Indians as "savages" or "pagans," primitive creatures to be kept at bay by force or conciliation; but in the personal letters and the diaries of the whites you can find a circumstantial day-by-day account of their actual dealings with the Indians which shows the respect that the latter inspired. He learned to be proud of his race, and when he realized how badly they had been treated by the whites, who had cheated them and double-crossed them, who had burned the Indian villages and massacred their populations, old and young, men, women and children, his whole point of view had changed. (I do not know whether Cook went so far afield as to look into John De Forest's *History of the Indians of Connecticut*, but even that cool Yankee, who is writing about Indian peoples a good deal less advanced than the Iroquois and who regards them as a hopelessly inferior breed, is aroused by the behavior of the whites, in certain episodes he is forced to record, to expressions of indignation and repugnance.) "There came a time," says Cook, "when I wasn't a human being. I didn't have a heart here—I had a piece of lead! When I'd see a white man on the reservation, my hair would stand up on my head."

He knew then that he must break with the Catholic Church. The French in the early days had treated the Indians the worst of all; they had driven them to side with the English. He had, besides, come to realize that whole races of men, including the great Indian civilizations of Central and South America, had flourished over periods of thousands of years and then become almost extinct before God had provided salvation through Christ—and what kind of a God was that? The next year he took his children out of the Catholic school, which is just across the street from his house, and this of course caused a fuss. Two nuns were sent to see him, and he was threatened, from the priest, with excommunication. He "hardly had a friend on the reservation"—though a sister who had married a Baptist and the brother who had contributed to the leaflet (he had graduated from Dartmouth) had also left the Catholic Church. But Philip maintained his position and began to investigate the Protestant sects— the Presbyterians, the Episcopalians, the Methodists and the Baptists, all of whom had congregations at St. Regis. He had at first liked the friendliness of the Protestant clergy, their willingness to receive him as a brother, which contrasted with the attitude of the Catholic priests. But, after all, the Anglicans in the early days had treated the Indians, he knew, almost as badly as the Catholics, and when he read up on the history of Protestantism, he found that he could not accept it, since all of these churches, if you traced them back, turned out to have sprung from the Catholic Church. Even allowing for the bitterness that one sometimes finds on the part of relapsed Catholics, his attitude seemed to me curious, and I asked him why this worried him so much, since the primary purpose of the Protestants had been to reform the old Church. He reflected, then said that he didn't know: the hostility he felt was "instinctive," and I now became aware that the explanation was something which I had already noticed, and was afterward sometimes to encounter in talking to other Indians, yet which I had not at first understood when I found it in this otherwise benevolent man: a harsh unforgiving strain which I took to be an atavistic resentment at the impotence of the ill-equipped red man in his one-sided struggle with the white. This resentment is always there, although buried; subdued beneath a taciturn surface, it at moments unexpectedly snaps its teeth. It is of interest, bearing this in mind, to follow the career of Cook and to see how, though still repudiating the Christian cult of the whites, he fulfilled a religious vocation which was deeply and strongly felt.

The first step was the discovery of Handsome Lake. The Longhouse, as I have said, was relatively recent at St. Regis, and though it had its devoted priests—called in English "Keepers of the Faith"—there was at that time nobody living in St. Regis who could recite the Handsome Lake code. In order to take part in this service, the Mohawks who were followers of Handsome Lake had to go to some other reservation (there are now two men at St. Regis who are able to recite the code). Philip Cook, however, now went to school to an expert in the Handsome Lake religion, who came to St. Regis to teach him, and he was moved by enthusiasm for its purity and wisdom. It was not true at all, he now realized, that the Iroquois, as the Christians asserted, were worshippers of the sun and the moon, the thunder, the winds and the corn. These were merely the "appointed ones," the deputies of the Creator. "Our older brother, the Sun," and "our grand-mother the Moon," and the other forces of nature, in the ceremonies by which they were celebrated, were merely thanked for their beneficent influence. Philip Cook, with his scholarly turn of mind, recognized the Christian influence in the Handsome Lake religion, but, in turning his back on the Church, he had not rejected Jesus, and this was primarily an Indian cult which had never been a cult of the white man. He set out to prepare himself to be a ministrant of the Longhouse religion; but since the services are conducted in the Iroquois languages, he discovered that he was seriously handicapped by the inadequacy of his Mohawk. He found, also, that he was up against a conservative element, a formalized version of the cult, of the kind that exists in every religion and that at St. Regis was then dominant in the Longhouse. Cook says that the dead-letter ritual which he found being practiced in St. Regis had nothing whatever in common with his conception of the Handsome Lake ideals. The ministrants, he says, had "crawled into a hole and pulled the hole in after them," and they did not want any new members. He thought that the code was encumbered with ancient and absurd superstitions, and my impression is that, if at this point he had been given a free hand in the Longhouse, he might well have been a successor to Handsome Lake, a reformer in his own right. I had learned from another source that Philip Cook had been driven out of the Long-house by the very same intransigent old man who had expelled me from the Onondaga Longhouse, and, more especially, by this old man's wife, who, in line with their gynocratic tradition, was the controlling Keeper of the Faith. The anguish of Cook in his desire to serve, when excluded by this pair from the Longhouse, had, I learned from someone else, been acute. There was a legend that he had spat blood. When I told him of my ejection at Onondaga by the same old fanatic who had kept him out, he buried his face in his hands. Later on, when I saw him again, he had inquired about the incident, and explained to me that the procedure at Onondaga had actually been irregular inasmuch as my admission to the Longhouse had not been approved by the council, but that the failure to welcome a friend as a brother was contrary to the Handsome Lake spirit.

At the time when Philip Cook had been made to feel that the door of the Longhouse was closed to him, he was visited by two Mormon missionaries. As soon as they began to deliver their message, he told them with some asperity that he did not care to hear it. He knew exactly what it was going to be: just another brand of Christian doctrine. But the Mormons stayed two weeks after that in St. Regis, going from house to house, and one day Philip Cook, who was driving in his car, saw them walking in the direction of Massena. They had evidently no "transportation." He does not like to let people walk without offering to pick them up, so he invited them into his car. They talked about the weather and baseball, and by the time they arrived in Massena, he had got quite a favorable

impression of them. He told them about the Handsome
Lake religion, and said that what was needed was a
faith that was founded upon the primary truths, such
as human brotherhood, and which did not allow itself
to be alienated from them. He asked them when the
Mormon religion had broken off from the Catholic
Church. They replied that it had never done so; that
the Mormons did possess the fundamental religion,
which had never been connected with the Catholic
Church; that the revelation from Heaven had come
direct to Joseph Smith at Palmyra right there in New
York State; that their holy book dealt with the Indians and showed how they had come from Jerusalem.
They didn't have completely at their fingerends all
the part about the Indians in the Book of Mormon,
but they would give him the answers later. In one of
his flashes of resentment, Cook told them he would
hold them to their word, and if they failed to prove
their assertions, he would have them run off the
reservation. "And I could have done it!" he said. "I
could have had them stoned by the people."

Now, the Mormons were here on very sure ground.
The imagination of Joseph Smith had been much excited in the eighteen-twenties by the discovery of
Indian burial mounds, which suggested at that time
that an early race had largely destroyed itself in a
series of tremendous battles, and by the theory then
current that the Indians were descendants of the lost
tribes of Israel. When he dictated the Book of Mormon, he put into it the story of the prophet Lehi,
who left Jerusalem in A.D. 600 and sailed to America

in a kind of ark. Lehi and his family were originally white, but some of them turned out so badly that God cursed them by making them red. The two races fought for a thousand years, and the whites were eventually exterminated, which accounts for the fact that the first Europeans found nobody in America but redskins. These missionaries from Utah, then, had a special message for the Indians from the prophet Lehi himself: the Indians and the whites were brothers, and the Mormons were attempting to guide the reds to what should have been their hereditary religion. Philip Cook thought at first that Smith must have been influenced by the Handsome Lake doctrine, through the Senecas of western New York, but then he concluded that no white man at that time could ever have had access to their ceremonies or understood what was said if he had. He visited Salt Lake City. His interest in Jesus was strengthened by learning that when Cortes had arrived in Mexico, he was taken at first for the "Fair God" whom the people had been awaiting, and from his contacts with the western Indians Philip Cook became convinced that in the Indian world a Savior had always been expected. And the news of the Christ had been brought to the Mormons without the intervention of any church. They called themselves the Church of Jesus Christ of Latter Day Saints. Philip Cook became an elder of the Mormon church in 1951. He was then the only Mormon on the St. Regis reservation. Today there is a congregation of a hundred and ten.

Thus Cook has managed at last to fulfill his religious

vocation. You feel that he is now a happy man, and that the spirit he diffuses is benign. He has married a handsome Armenian wife, who says that it is "exciting to be married to a Mohawk," and has three attractive daughters and two sons. One of his daughters has been studying Latin and French at the Albany State Teachers College, with the object of teaching the former, and one of the sons geology at Brigham Young University in Utah—though the family are inclined to believe that he is showing a strong bent toward philosophy. They have made of their extensive backyard, which a little while ago, says Cook, was a jungle of weeds, bushes and rubbish, a beautifully smooth lawn that, bordered on one side with bright flowers, the white and purple and yellow of iris and Johnny-jump-ups, with a cornpatch and a vegetable garden at the bottom, stretches down to the shining St. Regis river, where a small boat is moored under willows. Near the river are tables and chairs and a fireplace for out-of-door grilling, and here the Cooks entertain a variety of guests—Indian neighbors, new aluminum workers, visiting scholars and journalists—with the traditional hospitality which is such an attractive feature of Iroquois life. One feels in the family an atmosphere of affection, good discipline and mutual respect. There are grandchildren as well as children, and a cat with many kittens. The house, which is being enlarged, seems always to be full of lodgers. And Philip Cook, who had once, as he says, hardly a friend on the reservation, now occupies a position of authority which is purely a personal one and not due to official func-

Philip R. Cook, with Mrs. Cook and their daughters. Taken against the background of the Albany State Teachers College, where one of Mr. Cook's daughters was a student.

tion. One sees here all sorts of people coming to him for all sorts of favors: young men out of college who are looking for jobs, new arrivals who are looking for houses, students of Indian affairs looking for information. And he helps them in whatever way he can.

A young man just graduated from Hamilton whom I saw at the Cooks' in June I found, on a later visit, at a gas station on the edge of the reservation. Philip Cook, he said, had got him the job. He was going to study law, in the autumn, at the University of Chicago. He asked whether my companion and I were writers, and I asked him what made him think so. "I heard you using some words that you don't hear very much around here." When I afterwards asked the friend who was driving me what he thought these words could have been, he said he thought they must have been "T. S. Eliot." Yet in the Cook family, at any rate, such words were not of rare occurrence. The daughter who was studying to teach had talked to me intelligently about Latin poetry.

4. THE TUSCARORAS

The Tuscaroras, as has already been said, were the last of the Six Nations to be admitted to the Iroquois League. Driven out of what is now North Carolina by the whites in the second decade of the eighteenth century, they came north, and in about 1715, under the sponsorship of the Oneidas, were admitted to the Council of the League. They had already had a rudimentary league of their own and seem to have figured as the most important unit among the many unharmonious tribes that inhabited that part of the South. They belonged to the Iroquoian family, their language derived from the same linguistic stock, though it had now diverged so widely from those of the other five nations that they and the Tuscaroras could not understand one another. Though most of the Iroquois today are able to communicate in English, the Tuscaroras, if they do not speak English, have in the Longhouse to resort to an interpreter when the Iroquois languages are spoken.

There is an illuminating account of the troubles that preceded the migration of the Tuscaroras by the Indian scholar J. N. B. Hewitt, himself a Tuscarora, in the *Handbook of the Indians of North America* published by the Bureau of American Ethnology. Hewitt quotes John Lawson, the surveyor-general of North

Carolina, on the "many amiable qualities" of the Tuscaroras. Lawson says that they have been "really better to us than we have been to them, as they always freely gave us of their victuals at their quarters, while we let them walk by our doors hungry, and do not often relieve them. We look upon them with disdain and scorn, and think them little better than beasts in human form; while, with all our religion and education, we possess more moral deformities and vices than these people do." The whites made a practice of kidnapping the Indians and selling them into slavery. When it was found that this was rousing hostility and endangering the lives of the colonists, the Pennsylvania provincial council made enactments designed to prevent it; but these do not seem to have had much effect on the colonists. The prisoners taken in the war that followed were advertized for sale as slaves in the Boston *Newsletter* of 1713. And there were also on the part of the whites the usual provocations of broken treaties and encroachment on Indian lands. A Baron Christopher von Graffenreid, an adventurer from Berne, needed land for the immigrants he had brought to America, a band of Swiss and Palatine Germans whose governor he was to be, and he purchased from Lawson a tract, to be known as New Berne, which Lawson had assured him was not occupied but which was actually inhabited by the Tuscaroras. These massacred seventy of the settlers, and this set off a general war. Both Graffenried and Lawson were captured by the Indians, and Lawson was executed, but Graffenried bought his freedom by rum, ammunition and a promise of neutrality in the conflict that had been started by the massacre between Tuscaroras and non-Germanic whites. This conflict, however, went on, and Graffenried soon violated his truce. A Colonel Barnwell was now dispatched by the colonists of South Carolina to go to the rescue of the North Carolinians, and, supported by Indian allies who were hostile to the Tuscaroras, laid siege to their chief stronghold, a palisaded fort, and took it, in a savage battle, in January, 1712.

Barnwell now advanced on another Indian town, which the Indians successfully defended. In order to save the white prisoners, he made a truce with the Tuscaroras; then broke it by capturing a number of them and selling them into slavery. The war was continued on a larger scale. The small company of thirty-three whites, supported by nine hundred Indians, made an attack on another fort and slaughtered, burned, scalped, wounded or took prisoner—at the cost of small loss to themselves—a total of nine hundred and fifty Tuscaroras. The Indians who were working with the whites—some of them Tuscaroras at odds with the other group—also sold their Indian captives as slaves. The revolting Tuscaroras were crushed; but the Governor of New York for the Crown expressed concern because the Five Nations were "hardly to be diswaded from sheltering the Tuscarora Indians, which would embroil us all."

The first victory of Colonel Barnwell was the occasion for an incident worth noting, since it gives, at the risk of digression, an opportunity to touch on a matter of crucial importance in the Iroquois past. An enforced association on the part of the whites with the relative barbarism of their Indian allies is recorded by Graffenried. They "marched against a great Indian village . . . ," he says, "drove out the King and his forces, and carried the day with such fury, that, after they had killed a great many, in order to stimulate themselves still more, they cooked the flesh of an Indian 'in good condition' and ate it."

We find that the practice of cannibalism is a great theme in Iroquois folklore. Some of the Indians appear to have indulged in it; others to have held it in horror. The Canadian bugaboos called Windigo were supposed to be a tribe of cannibals. The Mohawks are reported to have eaten their enemies, and the word Mohawk itself is a corrupted form of the name for them of their enemies the Algonquins: "They Eat Men" (the Mohawks' name for themselves is "The People of the Flint"). That cannibalism was fairly common at the end of the seventeenth century is shown by the early white chronicles. There are a number of anthropophagous incidents in *The History of the Five Indian Nations* by the scientist Cadwallader Colden, who emigrated to America in 1710 and became first surveyor-general, then lieutenant-general of the colony of New York. In connection with events that took place in 1685—he is relying on French sources—Colden writes, for example, that "Two Old Men only were found in the Castle, who were cut into Pieces and boyled to make Soop for the French Allies.". . . "One of the Indian Prisoners was carried by them to Missilimackinack, to confirm this Victory, and was delivered to the Utawawas, who ate him.". . . "The Indians eat the Bodies of the French that they found. Coll. Schuyler (as he told me himself) going among the Indians at that Time, was invited to eat Broth with them, which some of them had already boiled, which he did, till they, putting the Ladle into the Kettle to take out more, brought out a French Man's Hand, which put an End to his Appetite." That the disdainful Europeans themselves could encourage these feasts on occasion if they did not actually care to take part in them would appear from such passages as the following: "He [the French Commandant] in the first Place assured them [the Indians], that the Christians abhorred all Manner of Cruelty, and then told them, that as the French shared with the Dionondadies in all the Dangers and Losses sustained by the War, they ought in like Manner to partake with them in any Advantage. The Dionandadies on this were persuaded to deliver up one of the [Iroquois] Prisoners. . . . That an End might be put to the Beginnings of a Reconciliation between these People and the Five Nations, the French gave a publick Invitation to feast on the Soup to be made on this Prisoner, and, in a more particular Manner, invited the Utawawas to the Entertainment. [The Utawawas had "stood neuter" as between the Five Nations and the French, and the French were attempting to embroil them with the Iroquois.] The Prisoner being first made fast to a Stake, so as to have Room to move round it, a Frenchman began the horrid Tragedy by broiling the Flesh of the Prisoner's Legs, from his Toes to his Knees with the red hot Barrel of a Gun; his Example was followed by a Uta-wawa, and they relieved one another as they grew tired. The Prisoner all this while continued his Death Song, till they clapt a red hot Frying-pan on his Buttocks, when he cried out, Fire is strong and too powerful; then all their Indians mocked him, as wanting Courage and Resolution. You, they said, a Soldier and a Captain, as you say, and afraid of Fire; you are not a Man. They continued their Torments for two Hours without ceasing. An Utawawa being desirous to outdo the French in their refined Cruelty, split a Furrow from the Prisoner's Shoulder to his Garter, and filling it with Gunpowder set Fire to it. This gave him exquisite Pain, and raised excessive Laughter in his Tormentors. When they found his Throat so much parched, that he was no longer able to gratify their Ears with his Howling, they gave him Water, to enable him to continue their Pleasure longer. But at last his Strength failing, an Utawawa flead off his Scalp, and threw burning hot Coals on his Scull. Then they untied him, and bid him run for his Life: he began to run, tumbling like a drunken Man; they shut up the Way to the East, and made him run Westward, the Country, as they think, of departed (miserable) Souls. He still had Force left to throw Stones, till they put an End to his Misery by knocking him on the Head with a Stone. After this every one cut a Slice from his Body, to conclude the Tragedy with a Feast." We learn later that "the French at Montreal being informed that a Party of the Five Nations were Discovered near Corlear's Lake, sent out a Captain with a Party of Soldiers and Indians, who being experienced in the Manner of making War with Indians, marched through the thickest Woods, and by the least frequented Places, so that he discovered the Enemy without being discovered. He surprised that Party, killed several, and took one Prisoner. The Utawawas being then trading at Montreal, the Count de Frontenac invited them to a Feast to be made of this Prisoner, and caused him to be burnt publickly alive at Montreal, in the Manner of which I have already given two Accounts from the French Authors."

It is perhaps significant that in Colden's history—in spite of the reputation of the Mohawks—the Iroquois are always the eaten not the eaters. The reformation of Hayówent'ha the cannibal is one of the most important episodes in the legend of Deganawídah. The reformer, Deganawídah, is a Mohawk; Hayówent'ha is an Onondaga, who has fled from the oppression of Tadodáho. (What follows is based on a version of the Daganawídah legend taken down in the Onondaga language by J. N. B. Hewitt and translated by Hewitt and William N. Fenton.) Deganawídah has set out to bring peace to his people, and his first step is to cure them of cannibalism. "I shall visit first," he announces, "the house of him of whom you say, 'He eats humans.'" He goes to the cannibal's lodge, finds him out and climbs to the roof and lies flat on his chest beside the hole that gives a vent for the smoke. The owner of the lodge soon returns, carrying a dead body. He throws it down inside the house, cuts it up and boils it in a kettle. When it is ready, he takes it off the fire, gets a bowl made of bark and prepares to eat, but he sees reflected in the water the face of Deganawídah, who is looking down through the smoke-vent, and he imagines it to be his own. He falls back and sits down. "Now indeed did he ponder many things." He takes another look and again sees the face. He thinks that someone may be playing a trick on him and looks up at the smoke-vent, but there is nobody there. He again becomes thoughtful, and presently he says, "So then it is really I myself who am looking up from the depths of the pot. My personal beauty is most amazing. But perhaps my behavior is not so beautiful when I kill people and eat their flesh. Perhaps I should cease from my habits. It may be that someone will come to my house and tell me what I ought to do to make up for the number of human beings to whom I have caused suffering." He goes out and empties the pot in a running stream, and now Deganawídah appears. Hayówent'ha tells Deganawídah that he is "seeking a congenial friend" and makes him sit down by the fire. He gives him a full account of what has taken place, at the end of which Deganawídah stands up and says, "Truly what has happened today is a very wonderful story. Now you have changed the very pattern of your life. Now a new frame of mind has come to you, [a longing for] Righteousness and Peace. At this moment, you are seeking for someone to tell you what you ought to do in order that peace may prevail in places in which you have done injury among mankind." Deganawídah, too, is seeking a friend, someone who is ready to work with him in the cause of Righteousness and Peace. Hayówent'ha agrees to join him. Deganawídah bids him fetch water while he himself goes hunting. He brings back a deer. It is on this, says Deganawídah, that the Creator intends men to live. They bury the remains of the human body, and cook and eat the deer. "What do you mean by Righteousness and Peace?" Hayówent'ha asks Deganawídah. "What will happen when these shall be realized?" "By these," says Deganawídah, "I mean that this very day you have changed the disposition of your mind, and it shall come about that all mankind shall change their present disposition. Thàt means that this reformation shall begin at once, and that Righteousness and Peace shall increase continually." "What will you call it when it has taken place, whatever you are talking about?" "It will be called the Completed House and also the Great Law." Hayówent'ha says he now understands and accepts. The next step is to prevent human beings from killing one another in war, and the organization of the League begins. As it proceeds, to Righteousness and Peace are added other ideal objectives: Reason, Justice and Health, and eventually, when it is further advanced, Power.

By the time the Tuscaroras, in the wars described above, had been defeated by the colonists and their Indian enemies, this "Power" of the League, as we have seen, was considerable. The Tuscaroras gave up their fight in the South and applied for admission to the

League, and by the end of 1722 they had been formally received as the Sixth Nation, but their gradual immigration north extended over a period of ninety years. Our Revolution split them again, and the descendants of the faction that sided with the English now live in the Six Nations Reserve in Canada, while the others, who sided with us, a group of about seven hundred, are living on a reservation of something over six thousand acres just northeast of Niagara Falls.

The Tuscaroras had, then, been admitted to the councils of the Iroquois Confederacy, but they had never been given quite equal status. It had been decreed by Deganawída, in the original constitution, that there should not be more than fifty hereditary chiefs, so this number could not be expanded to accommodate the Tuscaroras. They were organized internally like the other nations, and a Tuscarora representative was allowed to be present at the general council, but he had to ask permission to speak; and they have sometimes been treated with a certain hauteur which has made them perhaps rather sensitive. It was the Oneidas who sponsored their admission to the League, but they became the protegés of the Senecas, who turned over to them a part of their land. A Seneca called a Tuscarora "my son," and the Tuscaroras had to address the Senecas as "my father." They did not have the Handsome Lake religion, and the majority of them became Protestant Christians and burned down the Tuscarora Longhouse sometime in the eighteen-forties. They are even rather vague about their clans, seem no longer sure how many they have. A resourceful politician at the present time, if his chieftainship is called in question, may attempt to justify his title by claiming the support of some clan—the Sand Turtle clan, for example, as distinguished from the Turtle clan—which, absorbed by a stronger one, has been long ago allowed to lapse but the supposed descendants of which now split off and acknowledge his authority. There seems always to have been some regret on the part of the Tuscaroras over the triumph, in the early nineteenth century, of the influence of the Christian missions. It has alienated them, they feel, from their own tradition. Dr. David Landy, the author of a paper on *Tuscarora Tribalism and National Identity*,* asserts that he "has heard more than one Tuscarora say, sometimes with grudging admiration, sometimes with envy, sometimes with the pride of the distant relative of the more successful man, that adherents of the Handsome Lake religion on the other reserves are the 'real' Indians." They talk now of restoring the Longhouse. And this relatively inferior position vis-à-vis the other five Iroquois nations has operated, as sometimes happens, to stimulate them to special exertions in order to prove themselves. The more nationalistic ones like to emphasize the rôle that the Tuscaroras have played in Iroquois history. And lately, at this time of crisis, the Tuscaroras have added to their record the honor of a spectacular victory in the Iroquois fight against despoliation.

* *Ethnohistory*, Summer 1957, published by Indiana University.

In January, 1958, the Power Authority of the State of New York, of which Robert Moses is Chairman, got a license from the Federal Power Commission to start work on a hydroelectric project for utilizing the power of Niagara Falls. It was to cost $705,000,000 and to be financed by the sale of bonds to the people of the State of New York. It was supposed to benefit the public by generating thirteen billion kilowatt hours of electrical energy a year, thus supplying electricity at a cost of four and a half mills instead of the current rate of seven mills per hour. Construction was at once commenced, and Mr. Moses, with his usual dynamic drive and declaration of an iron schedule, announced that the load of power would be unleashed on February 10, 1961. A great upheaval at Niagara began. The installation of the powerhouse, the waterway and the intake to the power conduits was to involve relocation of the highways and the displacement of many people's homes. The town of Niagara Falls has long ceased to be an aviary of honeymooners. It is today almost indistinguishable from Gary, Indiana. The ashtrays, pennants and fans, all decorated with views of the Falls in garish metallic colors, the Indian dolls and jumbo postcards seem all to belong to an earlier day; the recumbent nude beauty in china, whose breasts are salt and pepper castors, removable from their sockets, could hardly have been offered for sale in the early nineteen-hundreds and yet she, too, essentially belongs to the era of Sherlock Holmes's Persian slipper. The Niagara Falls Museum—founded in 1830—was still housed in 1958 in a stiff old-fashioned building, with high ceilings, steep stairways and endless glass-cases, divided into rectangular panes. This museum displayed the old barrels and balls—one of the latter made of rubber tires—in which people have, sometimes to their deaths, made the descent of Niagara Falls, together with photographs of the fabulous Blondin balancing high on his tightrope above them; a collection of animals and human monsters: two-headed calves, Siamese twins, etc., stuffed or preserved in bottles; a moth-eaten panther sinking its teeth in the neck of a mangy stag; the skeletons of a mastodon and a humpbacked whale; a spooky room peopled with Egyptian mummies and desiccated corpses from Indian graves—the whole place and some of the exhibits hideously scrawled over with the names of visitors. The effect of this museum was grisly, yet I am sorry that the building has been taken down (its contents have been removed to the Canadian side). It was the last of the old Niagara. The all-crowding industrial life, which has ruined the landscape of the river, will soon have left little of the trippers' town, already full of chemical fumes and covered with dust and soot. And the inhabitants are beginning to feel that it is even more perilous to find oneself in the path of the Power Authority than to shoot the Falls in a barrel.

But the project has run into one obstacle which it has not found it easy to iron out. It was decided, in the interests of the project, to condemn, under the right of eminent domain, about a fifth of the Tuscarora reservation, 1,383 acres, in order to flood it as a storage reservoir for supplementing the power of the river in the seasons when the water runs low. This land of the Tuscaroras, as in other Indian reservations, is free from property tax, so no revenue would be forfeited by taking it; and it seemed to Mr. Moses much simpler to evict from their humble-looking homes a hundred and seventy-five Indians living in thirty-seven houses than to disrupt the neighboring town of Lewiston, in which, as Moses later explained, it would be necessary to dig up two cemeteries, to demolish a million-dollar schoolhouse and to destroy three or four hundred houses. Operations were therefore begun, without consultation with the Indians and in complete disregard of their rights. In March, 1957, the engineers of the Power Authority came to the house of Chief Clinton Rickard—without being aware, no doubt, that he had been one of the original organizers of the still active Indian Defense League— and asked for permission to make soil tests. There was no question yet, they said, of taking the land. Chief Rickard then called a council, and it was decided to refuse permission, and also to make it clear that the Indians were not prepared to "sell, lease or negotiate for any land transactions of any kind." Nothing further was heard by the Indians till they read in the paper the following September that a part of their land was to be taken for a reservoir. They sent a protest to the Power Authority, to which they received no reply; and it was not till the very last minute, November 8, that they succeeded in finding out that a hearing on the subject was to be held the next day in Washington before the Federal Power Commission.

Two chiefs and Chief Rickard's son William just managed to get there in time. They had had no chance to retain a lawyer, and on this account the lawyers for the Power Authority and the Power Commission itself tried to bar them from testifying, but these officials were at last prevailed upon to allow the Tuscaroras to talk. The Indians now told the Commission that their reservation was not for sale, that its inalienable use had been guaranteed by the eighteenth-century treaties, and they explained that it had been a part of Deganawída's teaching that the land "did not belong to us, we were only the custodians of it, and that we were to preserve it for the coming generations. As such, the land cannot be sold and is priceless, there can be no value placed upon it." This statement must have seemed to the power people either superstitious nonsense or a device for holding out for more money. The offered rate of compensation had at that stage been stated rather vaguely. "We estimate," said Robert Moses, "that the total payment we are prepared to pay for prompt settlement, considering the peculiar nature of Indian land, may be as much as $1000 an acre, not including houses of any value." The Tuscaroras were told at the hearings in Washington that they would be allowed to file a brief in protest, but that they would have to get a lawyer to represent them, and they retained Mr. Arthur Lazarus, Jr., of Washington.

On February 11 of the following year, 1958, Mr. Moses issued a printed *Open Letter to the Tuscarora Indians*, of which the peremptory tone was perfectly pitched to antagonize the persons to whom it was addressed: "The Federal Power Commission has now issued a workable license for construction of the entire project. We have borrowed from private investors the first $100,000,000 of the $625,000,000 needed to build. Contracts for turbines and generators and for construction of the main generating plant have been issued. This essential work already unduly delayed can and must proceed immediately. Constructions in the way of the project have already caused unconscionable economic loss to the whole Frontier Community and to the entire western part of the state. Absence of cheap power is aggravating the general business recession. Ten thousand construction jobs which will be provided when the project is fully under way are badly needed to offset rising unemployment. You yourselves have as much at stake as your neighbors, since the local industries where most of you are employed cannot invite much longer the economic difficulties resulting from increased power costs and uncertainties as to the completion of the project. . . . You claim that the inclusion of any part of your reservation in the reservoir will be a violation of existing treaties between the Tuscaroras and the United States. However, the treaties you talk about have nothing to do with your reservation in Niagara County, as you must know. . . . It will be necessary in the very near future for our engineers to enter your property . . . and also for the Authority's contractors to enter your property for construction purposes. . . . While we have understood your reluctance to part

with the land, we cannot delay longer. We are carrying out an urgent project of vital public importance
under double mandate of State and Federal law, and in
accordance with a Federal license. We have no more
time for stalling and debate. It is high time for expedi-
tious negotiation if you are in a mood to negotiate.
The advantages to your Nation of prompt friendly
agreement on the generous terms the authority offers
cannot be overstated. We hope you will decide to
proceed in this spirit, but we must go ahead in any
event."

A little later, in March, the Tuscaroras were informed through a non-official source that the surveyors were coming on the reservation. The Indians put up
notices at every entrance warning intruders off. Mr.
Moses, however, was ready for this. With his characteristic audacity in by-passing formal procedure, he
had had a bill put through the state legislature which
gave the Power Authority the right to appropriate,
without first condemning, any lands that were needed
for the project. All that was necessary in order to
take property was for the Power Authority to file a
map in the office of the New York Secretary of State,
and deposit with the State Comptroller a sum which
was supposed to correspond to the market value of the
land. The counsel for the Tuscaroras took the position
that this bill was invalid in its application to Indian
property, since it violated the original treaty; that the
taking of Indian land had not been authorized by the
license which had been granted the Power Authority
by the Federal Power Commission; and that a special

Act of Congress would be needed in order that these lands might be taken. The Power Authority contended that the area wanted for the reservoir was not covered by the old treaty, since it had not been included in the land which had been given the Tuscaroras by the Senecas, but had been deeded to them by the Holland Land Company, and so was not really tribal land and hence not protected by the treaty. The Tuscaroras' answer to this was that the land from the Holland Land Company had been bought for them by the federal government in 1804, and that its status as a reservation had been acknowledged by the government in a treaty made in 1838. The whole strategy in the reservoir case had been planned by Mr. Arthur Lazarus, who, as has been said, had been retained by the nation—that is, by the official chiefs; but individual Tuscaroras, who distrusted the official policy, took the step of retaining Mr. Stanley Grossman, a sympathetic and very able young lawyer practicing in Niagara Falls. Mr. Lazarus wants to have it made clear that neither he nor the chiefs who employed him had anything to do with the tactics adopted in the incidents that followed. Mr. Grossman was simply the counsel for the Indians involved in these incidents. Mr. Lazarus deserves all the credit for the handling of the litigation on behalf of the Tuscarora nation; yet the practical obstruction by one group of the Indians and the defense of them in their difficulties by Grossman gave pause to the Power Authority and influenced public opinion.

While the legal issue was thus undecided, it was

announced by the Power Authority, on the night of April 16, 1958, over radio and television, that the surveyors, under police protection, would come onto the reservation the following day. The Tuscaroras immediately notified the other nations of the Iroquois Confederacy to send members to be witnesses and uphold their hands. In consultation with Mr. Grossman, they were wise enough to fix on a policy of Gandhian passive resistance, and when the surveyors arrived in the morning, accompanied by no less than ten carloads of State Troopers, plainclothesmen and Niagara County sheriffs—estimated at more than a hundred— armed with tear-gas, submachine guns and revolvers, they were met by placards and signs saying, "Warning. No Trespassing. Indian Reserve," "Must You Take Everything the Indians Own?," "United States Help Us. We Helped You in 1776 and 1812, 1918 and 1941." About two hundred Tuscaroras stood in the way of the trucks. The leaders of this demonstration were William Rickard, the son of Clinton, the founder of the Indian Defense League who has already been mentioned above; John Hewitt, a great-nephew of J. N. B. Hewitt, the Smithsonian scholar, who has also been mentioned; and Wallace Anderson, known as Mad Bear, the man who had shaken hands with me at Onondaga. Mr. Grossman was also present, as well as the lawyers for the Power Authority, so what happened was amply witnessed by parties not directly involved.

"We urged them not to start anything," says William Rickard in a printed leaflet. "A James Williams of the New York State Indian Social Service was ordering the chiefs to send the people away so the surveyors could start work. I asked by what authority he was acting. He stated that he was going to carry out Governor Harriman's appropriation bill granting the State Power Authority permission to take 1,383 acres of our reserve. I promptly told him that bill was not worth the paper it was written on. He promptly cited the Criminal Jurisdiction bill passed in 1948 conferring jurisdiction in the State of New York over the Indians, also the Civil Jurisdiction bill passed in 1950. I told him I was well aware of how those bills violated the Constitution of the United States Government. They were passed over the objections of the Six Nations Iroquois Confederacy, who unanimously opposed those bills. I told him that I had been present at both hearings in Washington, D.C., and that the bills did not pass until the end of each session of Congress. He claimed ignorance of this and walked back to the police."

The women were much excited, and some of them lay down in front of the trucks. Those who lived in the threatened area had wept at the prospect of the loss of their homes. They had heard about what had happened at the Caughnawaga reservation, which had partly been destroyed by the St. Lawrence Seaway. The bulldozers had broken down the houses of the Mohawks who had refused to move, and one woman had her home crushed before her eyes while she was hanging out clothes on the line. I saw one of these bulldozed houses on the St. Regis reservation, and it remains in my mind as a symbol of the fate of the individual at the mercy of modern construction: the house had been scrunched like a cockroach, a flattened-out mass of muddied boards. The women of the Tuscaroras had this kind of thing in mind, and their methods of opposing the invaders were somewhat less well-disciplined than those of the men. According to Rickard's account, "the women punched and scratched the officers, and the children, some four and five years old, started to tackle the officers. Some bruises resulted but nothing serious. A surveyor kicked one of the women in the leg. After much argument with the sheriffs, we had him arrested for assault." In the scuffle, some well-drilling equipment was damaged, and the grass was set on fire. The police arrested Anderson, Hewitt and Rickard, the first two on charges of unlawful assembly, the third on that of disorderly conduct. Hewitt and Rickard were tackled and thrown to the ground by the deputies, who dragged them in the direction of the patrol wagon. Mr. Grossman told them not to resist but to allow themselves to be arrested. There were cries of, "This is Russia!," "Do you call this democracy?"

The three leaders of the demonstration were taken before a justice of the peace. Reporters were barred from the court. Mr. Grossman got the Indians set free in his custody, and a comedy now began on the part of the county authorities to keep the case from getting into court. The prosecuting parties would never appear, so the hearings were three times adjourned. Mr. Grossman moved dismissal, but this was denied, and finally, on May 21, the sheriff and the county district attorney pressed the charges against Anderson and Hewitt, again postponing the charge against Rickard. Anderson and Hewitt were sent to jail, with the bail, which they could not pay, set at $500; but Mr. Grossman got a writ of habeas corpus (which was upheld by the New York Supreme Court), and the next morning had them out. When Rickard's case came up for the fourth time, the sheriff failed again to appear. Mr. Grossman at this point succeeded in having the cases dismissed. In the meantime, a suit had been brought by the woman who had been kicked in the leg against the man who was said to have kicked her. For this charge on the other side, an opposite device was employed: the woman was not notified when the case came up, so she failed to appear in court.

It will be evident that in all this the Power Authority was guilty of a certain highhandedness. At the time of this showdown between it and the Indians, the Indians say the reservation telephones were tapped; that agents of the telephone company who were supposed to be line repairmen came and camped on the reservation in tents. The Tuscaroras, in talking to one another, were able to resort to their own tongue, but everything that was said in English they believe to have been reported. The telegraph offices, they believe, were watched, the news broadcasts rigorously censored. An entirely untrue statement was made over television to the effect that Chief Rickard

—who had devoted his life to championing Indian rights—had appealed to his people to call off
their resistance. This resistance, however, continued.
Though the Power Authority got a court order per-
mitting them to enter the reservation, the surveyors,
when they tried to take advantage of it, had fire-
crackers tossed at them by the children, and guns
fired over their heads, and then found that the air
had been let out of their tires and that the valves had
been removed. The Tuscaroras also, on their side,
succeeded in getting a court order which restrained the
Power Authority from actually taking the land. The
surveyors, however, went on with their work, and
one day when they were there, Wallace Anderson was
seen talking to some Indian children who had just
been brought in by a school bus. The children then
went into a field in which the surveyors were working,
and a United States marshal on duty there, anticipating
interference, arrested him and took him before a
United States commissioner. It had been hoped to
convict him of contempt of court, but since this action
had been taken without a warrant and no definite
charge could be brought, it was not difficult for Mr.
Grossman to have him again released.

I found in Niagara Falls—what rather at first surprised me—a certain amount of sympathy for the
Indians. The white people complain that they, too,
have had to suffer from the grandiose ambitions and
the domineering methods of Moses and from the
roughshod procedure of the Power Authority. The
Niagara Power Project is to be financed by the public,

and it is supposed to benefit the public; but the Power Authority, they say, behaves like an old-fashioned corporation, never consulting the public and assuming autocratic powers. The white citizens who lose their property under the right of eminent domain—if they think it has been condemned without sufficient justification—are unlikely to find redress in the courts, but the Indians do have a good case, and the whites have taken a certain satisfaction in seeing them score off the Power Authority. An extreme expression of this point of view on the part of a white resident of Lewiston, New York, Mr. Roger Alexander Millar, appeared in the Niagara Falls *Gazette* of July 16, 1958, in the form of an open letter to Governor Harriman. Says the writer: "What a shameful spectacle it is when the great State of New York, of many million people, of whom you are the Chief Executive, browbeats and intimidates a pathetic handful of Tuscarora Indians, whose mistake it is to spurn the almighty dollar and to stand up for what they and many, many white people hereabouts believe to be their historic rights. At the instigation of the State Power Authority, four separate arrests of Tuscaroras have been made. In each instance the case has been thrown out of court and the Indian freed. Once a writ of habeas corpus has been required to set the SPA back on its heels. . . . As for me, I say more power to the Indians. They have greater grievances than the American colonists had at the time of the Boston Tea Party. . . . Moses claims that the State Power Authority is perpetual in duration, and that a determination of necessity by the Authority is final and not reviewable by the courts. Whew! . . . Just how stupid can we get that we tolerate such dangerous, arrogant nonsense? Are we going Russian? Are we to permit Moses to brush aside the words of George Washington in 1790, when the Indians were living right where they are now: 'No state nor person can purchase your lands unless at a general treaty held under the general authority of the United States; and the general government will never consent to your being defrauded, and it will protect you in all your just rights.' More and more people are coming to detest Moses' methods. . . . He's one of the master politicians of our time, even as Hitler, but we can hope and believe that he is reaching the end of his rope on the reservation, thanks to the stubborn Tuscaroras."

When I spoke to one of the Indians of the sympathetic attitude of their white neighbors, he answered —I believe, truly—that the white people were watching what happened to the Indians in apprehension lest the federal and state authorities, having succeeded in bullying the red men, would be trying it on the white ones, too. An example of white resistance is afforded by the Wilson Hill case. This Wilson Hill formerly stood, between Massena and Waddington, on our side of the St. Lawrence River. In connection with the St. Lawrence Power Project, it was partially to be flooded by the power pool in such a way as to make it an island, and two thousand acres were taken. The people who owned property in this area declared

Gov. Harriman   Robert Moses   A. Thorne Hills

. . . a luncheon chat with Authority chairman and an SPA trustee

3 BRAVE +HANDSOME "LIBERATORS"

Page from a special number of *Indian Views*, published by the League of North American Indians. This issue is devoted to the struggle of the Tuscaroras with the New York State Power Authority. It is no doubt unfair to Mr. Harriman, Mr. Moses and Mr. Hills to show them appearing to such poor advantage side by side with pictures of Indians looking their best; but this picture represents with accuracy the aspect worn by these officials in the minds of many Tuscaroras.

that the Power Authority was condemning more land than it needed. It had been calculated, they said, by the engineers that the flooding would not extend beyond an elevation of 246 feet, but the property to be surrendered had been surveyed two miles back from the river. The landowners formed an association in the hope of saving part of this tract. They went to court and lost, and then also lost appeals to the two higher state courts. They were enraged by a statement of the solicitor general that, "It is no concern of the plaintiffs or former owners what use is made of their expropriated property." It is claimed by one of the landowners that she was told by the state's acquisition agent that if she refrained from going to law and would negotiate directly with the Power Authority, she would be permitted to keep part of her farm, and that, as a result of persisting with her suit, she had her whole estate taken away. The landowners, then, were defeated; and it was proposed by the Power Authority to "relocate" on what was left of Wilson Hill a certain number of persons whose camps along the river had been destroyed. They were to live in a model group of houses to be built by Robert Moses—who already had his blueprint ready—and were told to be prepared to move in on the dot of December 31, 1956. They were also told to sign an agreement to submit to certain conditions of residence drawn up by the Power Authority, from which they would be leasing these places: they were not allowed to sublease their houses without the Authority's permission, and they were not allowed to use them for offices or stores or for any

other purpose than residence. But the people assigned
to this blueprint, with only a few exceptions, refused to
accept such terms. They are reported to have written
Mr. Moses an extremely disrespectful letter declaring
that, though it might be possible in the neighborhood
of New York City, to subject people to such regi-
mentation, it would not go down in upstate New
York. They went for their camps to the Adirondacks
or elsewhere.

Let us return to the story of the Tuscaroras. As a
result of the Indians' resistance, Robert Moses now
raised his offer to $1100 an acre, and was dangling
before the Tuscaroras' eyes, in one of his handsome
brochures, a double-spread fancy drawing of a $250,000
community center in the approved non-ornamental
modern style, "to be located within the reservation, in
the event that an early agreement is consummated"—a
gift which, so far as I could see, left the Indians completely cold. At a meeting between the Indians and
the Power Authority, one of the Tuscaroras is said
to have infuriated the representatives of the latter by
remarking that, instead of all that money, they might
follow the policy of the early days and just give them
a few trinkets. The attorneys for the Indians and the
Power Authority continued to fight the case in the
courts. The latter scored a point when, on June 24,
a Federal district judge held that the Power Authority
could take the land and dissolved the restraining order.
Four days later, however, a judge in the Federal Court
of Appeals granted the Indians a few days' stay, and

on July 24 the three judges of this court reached a two-to-one decision that an incorrect procedure had been followed in taking the Indian land, since the special bill of April, 1958, put through by the Power Authority, would empower it to "move in, appropriate the land and remove the owner, before he has had a chance to have a judicial hearing." This prevented for the time being the clearing of timber or the razing of houses on the Tuscarora reservation. But the Court recommended that the Power Authority seek condemnation either through the New York State courts or through the Federal District Court of Buffalo. The two opponents now filed cross-petitions for rehearing in the Federal Court of Appeals. The petition of the Indians was denied, and they applied to the Supreme Court of the United States for a review of this decision, on the ground of the invalidity, in respect to the Indian lands, of the Power Authority's license. Mr. Moses put up a strong plea that the matter be quickly settled. They were losing, he said, $100,000 a day, and the lives of the construction workers were being endangered on account of a makeshift transmission line by which one man had already been electrocuted. Though other parts of the project could be postponed, the erection of the power lines on the reservation must be begun by September 15. (It was also true, it seems, that the banks—in view of the obstacles encountered—were becoming a little reluctant to lend money to the Power Authority.) In a statement of September 11 "On Tuscarora Reservoir Obstruction," Mr. Moses called the legal proceedings "a silly game." "We have been shunted about," he said, "and jackassed from court to court and judge to judge, and are faced with the prospect of more litigation and further delays, postponement of permanent financing and perhaps stoppage of work. . . . I have been involved in quite a few public enterprises with the usual conventional, outrageous and also comparatively innocent pressures, but nowhere in my experience has there been so much of this as on the Niagara Frontier." The final words of this statement are worth reflecting upon: "How our democratic system can survive such stultifying domestic weakness, incompetence and ineptitude in the ruthless, world-wide competition with other systems of government more incisive and less tolerant of obstruction, is more than I can figure out." The implication would seem to be that those "more incisive and less tolerant" systems have distinctly the advantage over us and that "our democratic system" can hardly survive without becoming less democratic.

The Supreme Court declined to review the case, but Justice Harlan deferred to a petition of the Indians by granting them a few days' stay, on condition that they file their appeal to the Supreme Court by September 19. The Power Authority now applied, as Judge Harlan had informed it it might, to the United States District Court for permission to proceed with the power lines—an operation, it was pointed out, which would affect only eighty-six acres. Bulldozers were now sent in and a good deal of timber was cleared away, but Wallace Anderson held up this work by calling out thirty Tuscaroras who were part of the clearance crew. The Federal Court of Appeals now jolted the Power Authority by ruling, in a unanimous decision of November 14, that the Indian land could not be taken unless it were definitely found by the Federal Power Commission that this "would not interfere with the purposes of the reservation." It justified the Tuscaroras in their contention that nothing could be done with their property without the approval of Congress, and pointed out that "it did not appear that the Indian land was necessary for the project but was desired solely for economy." "We fail to find anywhere," said the Court, "an inclination of the Congress to save costs for its sole licensee for this enormous project at the expense of Indians living on the reservation." The question was thus remanded to the Federal Power Commission.

Mr. Moses' response to this was to announce that the funds he could count on would be used up by January, 1959, and that as long as there was any uncertainty about the possibility of building the reservoir, he "could not undertake permanent financing"; that if the reservoir had to be shifted to "private property," the construction costs would be increased by from fifteen to twenty million dollars, with a thirty per cent increase in the cost of power; that if the project were to be abandoned, it would mean a loss of four hundred million, "with ensuing suits and utter confusion," and would throw three thousand men out of work. At the suggestion of the mayor of Niagara Falls, he offered to negotiate for an immediate cash settlement, but the

Tuscaroras would not meet him. In January, they turned down an offer of two and a half million dollars, holding out for half a million more, job preference on the construction work, free electric power and the extension of the privileges of their present status to whatever new lands they might buy. Mr. Moses agreed, six days later, to the sum of three million dollars, but would not accept most of the other conditions, declaring that he could not make the settlement contingent on subsequent action by Congress. The Indians rejected these terms, explaining to reporters that they were "fully aware that this was Moses's final offer. This proves that we valued our land and were not simply after the money."

On February 2, 1959, the Federal Power Commission more or less astonished everybody by ruling, in a three-to-two decision, that the Tuscaroras could not be compelled to give up any part of their reservation. "We regret," the majority commissioners wrote, "that we have not been able to reach any other solution," but "we cannot permit our judgment to be swayed by our personal views of what is desirable but must administer the laws as passed by Congress and as interpreted by the courts." Moses's retort to this was to characterize the decision as "gobbledygook," and, on account of the dissenting voices, as "indefinite, contradictory." "Our experience," he added, "before the commission indicated that time is no object in their prolonged, leisurely and expensive and incomprehensible consideration of urgent projects. . . . Then the five [commissioners] ask whether we want more time to argue some more. The answer is we do not." They could not, he went on to say, bring themselves to dig up the two cemeteries and disturb the "hundreds of private houses." Though he had written in huge capitals in one of his brochures, "IT WOULD BE COMPLETELY IMPRACTICAL TO BUILD THE RESERVOIR ANYWHERE ELSE," he now admitted that they would have to resign themselves to a reservoir on a smaller scale and not on reservation ground. On the same day Chief Black Cloud (Elton Green), who had initiated the litigation on behalf of the Tuscarora nation, declared to a reporter, "I'm delighted. I expected to get justice from the federal government, and we did."

Mr. Gunther, in the article already mentioned in the *Buffalo Law Review*, seems to regard the decision of July 24 in the Federal Court of Appeals as something of a turning-point in the conflict between the claims of New York State and the federal government to authority over Indian lands. "Federal supremacy," he says, had already been "emerging" in other cases that raised the same issue; and this had perhaps roused the state to its arrogant attitude. "Oft-repeated, tradition-laden contentions are perhaps the most difficult to dislodge. And the very weakness of a position may strengthen the reluctance to yield and may indeed blind its defenders to the crumbling foundation. So it may be with New York's assertion of a unique power over Indian lands; that may explain the state's broad claims in the *Tuscarora* case, despite all that has gone before. . . . The *Tuscarora* decision of the Court of

Appeals came, after all, in a case which the state deliberately chose to make the most elaborate presentation of its position and to argue on the broadest possible grounds. All the greater the significance, then —and all the more penetrating the likely impact— of the repudiation of New York's contentions. The court's insistence that federal guardianship over tribal land holdings persists thus furnishes an appropriate occasion to initiate, albeit belatedly, some needed changes in governmental attitudes, by the nation as well as the state." It should be added, however, that a new appeal on the part of the Power Authority is still pending before the Supreme Court.

It is said to have been found astonishing in Albany that the none too well off Tuscaroras should have rejected an offer of three million dollars for thirteen hundred and eighty acres; but this is not at all puzzling to anyone who has been among the Iroquois lately and seen something of their national spirit. Some of them, to be sure, would be glad to sell when they are offered large sums for their reservations; but a determined and effective group who are becoming more and more influential have put above everything else the recognition of their national identity and will repulse without hesitation any impingement on their ancient privileges. And, besides, the earth is their mother, and "you cannot sell your mother."

Robert Moses is a well-known figure. But who are this handful of Indians who have succeeded in stopping him short? (For only the second time. The first occurred when women with baby carriages blocked the bulldozers which were supposed to break ground for a huge parking lot in Central Park, and forced Moses to build a playground instead.)

I have spoken of the Rickard family. I called upon them in June, when the tension was still considerable. My son, who was driving me, and I had passed a sheriff's car patrolling the reservation, and when I presented myself at the Rickard door, they received me with some natural misgiving, and before they invited me in, asked me what my "transportation" was and looked around the side of the house to make sure I had not come in an official car. I found myself here in a household in which the tradition of Iroquois patriotism was at least two generations old. It reminded me of labor families in which the fight for unionization has been passed on from father to son and a knowledge of labor history is a part of one's home education. Clinton Rickard of the Indian Defense League, a veteran of the Spanish-American War, is now seventy-seven. This league, which was founded in 1925, has had for its principal object to provide a defense fund for Indians who have got into trouble with the white authorities and are too poor to be able to pay counsel. The first achievement of the Defense League, however, was to reëstablish the right of the Indians—included in the Jay Treaty of 1794 between England and the United States but eventually disregarded—to pass freely back and forth between Canada and the United States. The Indians were at one time classed as "orientals" and forbidden to cross the border. The removal of this bar by the League is now celebrated every July by a parade of Iroquois from both sides of the line across the Whirlpool Rapids Bridge. It was held, on an appeal to the Supreme Court of Canada, in 1956, that this provision of the Jay Treaty was no longer valid and that an Indian, like any white man, must pay duty, in coming to Canada, on goods that he has bought in the United States. This news has, however, either not yet reached the Indians or they are continuing their gesture in defiance as an assertion that they are neither British subjects nor citizens of the United States but the original North American inhabitants. The same principle was defended in cases of Indians who were facing deportation for entering the country illegally or for not passing the immigrant literacy test. The elder Rickard remarked to me that he had once told a Senate Committee that it used to be said to the Indians that there was a pot of money for them in Washington into which they could dip for expenses, but that this pot seemed to be now in Europe. His son, William Rickard, one of those arrested in the riot of April 17, spoke of the crisis with passionate excitement, but with none of the practical vagueness that one sometimes finds in the nationalists: he was exact about dates, facts and figures. When the Rickards were satisfied that I was not an agent, they became very friendly and helpful and invited my son and me to an abundant family dinner, at which children and grandchildren were present.

On a subsequent visit, in August, I had a talk

with Wallace Anderson, known among his people as Mad Bear; he later came to see me at my summer home, when returning from a meeting about taxes at St. Regis; and I saw him again at Brantford, Ontario, where he had gone in connection with events that are presently to be described; so I have had some opportunity to make his acquaintance. Though his mother is a member of the Bear Clan, Mad Bear is not, he tells me, a proper Indian name. Since the Tuscaroras now have no Longhouse, they have no ceremonies for biennial namegiving; but Anderson has adopted the name by which, on account of his hotheadedness, he was called by his grandmother in his childhood (*mad* in the sense of *angry*). He told me that he thought he had seen me before and reminded me of the Onondaga council. Without prejudice to the other Tuscarora chiefs, I may say that, at thirty-one, he struck me as already a leader. Mad Bear is not himself a chief, and this makes his position the more impressive, and, also, perhaps, his policies and his movements freer, since he is not involved in the traditional web of the relationships and rankings of the Iroquois League. His growing importance to his people was shown by his having been called in by the Mohawks of St. Regis at the time when they were making their stand against paying the state income tax. On this occasion he led four hundred Indians into court and tore up the summonses that had been served on them. With something of Standing Arrow's power of appealing to the imagination, he has combined the effective qual-

ities of a self-controlled audacity and—as I later
found in playing checkers with him—a certain tac-
tical shrewdness. He has also a robust enthusiasm,
a sly humor and an easy affability which contribute
to a personal magnetism of the kind that commands
allegiance. I found that people strongly took sides
either against him or for him. When I first saw him,
he had not long before been rather unaccountably
attacked and slashed across the face with a knife by a
cousin of his who, he said, had spent some time in a
mental institution. Mad Bear is somewhat rotund but,
I should say, very powerfully built. He has the round,
not the aquiline Iroquois face, and the scar of the
huge gash only serves to add to his aspect of pug-
nacious durability. When I called on him at Tuscarora,
I was on my way to a pageant at the Six Nations
Reserve in Canada, and he told me that he would be
at a certain time at one of the Longhouses of that
reservation. I waited for him there two hours. Sunday
games and contests were going on, and I felt among
the people assembled the atmosphere of quiet expectation that precedes the arrival of a leader. When he
did not appear at the time he had said, I made
inquiries and got replies that indicated that, since the
assault on him, he had had to be circumspect in his
movements.

A passionate fervor for the Indian cause seems early
to have possessed Wallace Anderson. He tells me that
in their school on the reservation, the white teacher
would rap them over the knuckles or keep them after
school if they were heard talking Tuscarora. Clinton

Above: Mad Bear, taken in July, 1959.

Preceding plate: Mad Bear (Wallace Anderson), taken at Inchon, Korea, in January, 1957, while he was serving on U.S.S. *Seagarden.*

Rickard became his hero, and he wanted to carry on Rickard's work. He has informed himself about Iroquois history, and, unlike some of the other nationalists, he has seen a good deal of the world. He went into the Navy when he was sixteen and remained there till he was twenty-one. He drove a landing craft in the Pacific war in the Seventh Amphibious Fleet; was at Saipan and Okinawa; and he later served in Korea. He applied, he says, after the war, for a loan under the GI Bill of Rights, but discovered that this was impossible because he lived on reservation property. Up to the time of the war with the Power Authority, he spent every winter in the Merchant Marine.

"Sometimes I feel," he told me—when the fight was still undecided, "that the struggle is completely hopeless. Then again I don't know. I think that maybe some day the Iroquois will come into their own again." And he recited a remarkable prophecy supposed to have been made by Deganawída. I took it down as he told it and give it here in his own words:

"When Deganawída was leaving the Indians in the Bay of Quinté in Ontario, he told the Indian people that they would face a time of great suffering. They would distrust their leaders and the principles of peace of the League, and a great white serpent was to come upon the Iroquois, and that for a time it would intermingle with the Indian people and would be accepted by the Indians, who would treat the serpent as a friend. This serpent would in time become so powerful that it would attempt to destroy the Indian, and the serpent is described as choking the life's blood out of the Indian people. Deganawída told the Indians that they would be in such a terrible state at this point that all hope would seem to be lost, and he told them that when things looked their darkest a red serpent would come from the north and approach the white serpent, which would be terrified, and upon seeing the red serpent he would release the Indian, who would fall to the ground almost like a helpless child, and the white serpent would turn all its attention to the red serpent. The bewilderment would cause the white serpent to accept the red serpent momentarily. The white serpent would be stunned and take part of the red serpent and accept him. Then there is a heated argument and a fight. And then the Indian revives and crawls toward the land of the hilly country, and then he would assemble his people together, and they would renew their faith and the principles of peace that Deganawída had established. There would at the same time exist among the Indians a great love and forgiveness for his brother, and in this gathering would come streams from all over—not only the Iroquois but from all over—and they would gather in this hilly country, and they would renew their friendship. And Deganawída said they would remain neutral in this fight between the white serpent and the red serpent.

"At the time they were watching the two serpents locked in this battle, a great message would come to them, which would make them ever so humble, and when they become that humble, they will be waiting for a young leader, an Indian boy, possibly in his teens, who would be a choice seer. Nobody knows who he is or where he comes from, but he will be given great power, and would be heard by thousands, and he would give them the guidance and the hope to refrain them from going back to their land and he would be the accepted leader. And Deganawída said that they will gather in the land of the hilly country, beneath the branches of an elm tree, and they should burn tobacco and call upon Deganawída by name when we are facing our darkest hours, and he will return. Deganawída said that as the choice seer speaks to the Indians that number as the blades of grass and he would be heard by all at the same time, and as the Indians are gathered watching the fight, they notice from the south a black serpent coming from the sea, and he is described as dripping with salt water, and as he stands there, he rests for a spell to get his breath, all the time watching to the north to the land where the white serpent and the red serpent are fighting. Deganawída said that the battle between the white and the red serpents opened real slow but would then become so violent that the mountains would crack and the rivers would boil and the fish would turn up on their bellies. He said that there would be no leaves on the trees in that area. There would be no grass, and that strange bugs and beetles would crawl from the ground and attack both serpents, and he said that a great heat would cause the stench of death to sicken both serpents. And then, as the boy seer is watching this fight, the red serpent reaches around the back of the white serpent and pulls from him a hair which is carried toward the south by a great wind into the waiting hands of the black serpent, and as the black serpent studies this hair, it suddenly turns into a woman, a white woman who tells him things that he knows to be true but he wants to hear them again. When this white woman finishes telling these things, he takes her and gently places her on a rock with great love and respect, and then he becomes infuriated at what he has heard, so he makes a beeline for the north, and he enters the battle between the red and white serpents with such speed and anger that he defeats the two serpents, who have already been battle-weary.

"When he finishes, he stands on the chest of the white serpent, and he boasts and puts his chest out like he's the conqueror, and he looks for another serpent to conquer. He looks to the land of the hilly country and then he sees the Indian standing with his arms folded and looking ever so nobly so that he knows that this Indian is not the one that we should fight. The next direction that he will face will be eastward and at that time he will be momentarily blinded by a light that is many times brighter than the sun. The light will be coming from the east to the west over the water, and when the black serpent regains his sight, he becomes terrified and makes a beeline for the sea. He dips into the sea and swims away in a southerly direction, and shall never again be seen by the Indians. The white serpent revives, and he, too, sees this light, and he makes a feeble attempt to gather himself and go toward that light. A portion of the white serpent refuses to remain but instead makes its way toward the land of the hilly country, and there he will join the Indian People with a great love like that of a lost brother. The rest of the white serpent would go to the sea and dip into the sea and would be lost out of sight for a spell. Then suddenly the white serpent would appear again on the top of the water and he would be slowly swimming toward the light. Deganawída said that the white serpent would never again be a troublesome spot for the Indian people. The red serpent would revive and he would shiver with great fear when he sees that light. He would crawl to the north and leave a bloody shaky trail northward, and he would never be seen again by the Indians. Deganawída said as this light approaches that he would be that light, and he would return to his Indian people, and when he returns, the Indian people would be a greater nation than they ever were before."

"Some people believe," said Mad Bear, "that the white serpent stands for the white race; the red serpent for Soviet Russia; and the black serpent for the Negro race." The white hair that flies through the air and speaks to the black serpent is Eleanor Roosevelt. "When the news of the Mau Mau rebellion reached the shores of this country, the black serpent was infuriated into making a stand for himself, and Eleanor Roosevelt was exalted like a god by the colored people." According to one interpretation, the prophecy covers five years. The red serpent appeared among us when the immigrants came from Hungary. (Mad Bear, so well-posted about his own people, seemed to imagine that these refugees from Communism were Communists.) The battle between the red and the white serpents was then (1958) in its third year. (Mad

Bear has written me more recently that the Eisen-
hower-Khrushchyóv exchange of visits is now believed
to be the moment when the white serpent "takes part
of the red serpent and accepts him.") The colored
people would fight the whites that autumn. It would
be four years before the Indians could assemble in the
hilly country (they were, he said, not yet sure where
this was). The Russians would bomb America, and
the Tuscaroras themselves would be bombed; but
after a big war—in 1960—the United States would
come to an end, and at the same time a great light
would come to the Indian people. Some Indians
thought that this was the white man's God.

Mad Bear explained to me, as had Philip Cook, that
the expectation of a Savior was common among the
Indians. He had heard this prophecy, he said, from
the head clan mother of the Senecas, who lives on the
Tuscarora reservation, and from a number of other
sources. It had "remained in the Longhouse for years,"
but had not been understood, though it had always
been expected that the people of the Longhouse would
someday be strong again.

To many this prophecy may seem fantastic, but is
it so much so as that of Jehovah's Witnesses, who
believe that "millions now living will never die," since
the end of the world will come first, and who were
able in the summer of '57 to assemble, in the Yankee
Stadium, recruited from forty-eight states and a hundred and twenty-two foreign countries, 194,000
adherents who held that faith? And does not every
nation—especially when at war—sustain itself with a
more or less similar myth?

5. THE SENECA REPUBLIC

We now come to a special phenomenon which complicates even further the situation of the Iroquois Six Nations. Of these nations, the Seneca people are usually considered the most highly developed. Estimates made by the colonists in the middle of the seventeenth century seem to show that at that time the Senecas composed about half the Iroquois population. They occupied the whole western half of what is today the state of New York, and there is a theory that their exceptional qualities were stimulated by their peculiar position between the western non-Iroquois Indians, against whom they had to stand as a bulwark and who kept them alert and resourceful, and the rest of their people to the east of them, who protected them from the pressures of the English and Dutch, to which the Oneidas and the Mohawks were obliged more or less to succumb.

The Senecas have produced more remarkable men than any of the other nations. The Indian General Ely S. Parker, who collaborated with Morgan on *The League of the Iroquois*, who acted as military secretary for Grant and made the draft of the terms at Appomattox, and who was afterwards appointed by Grant Commissioner of Indian Affairs, was a Seneca chief of the Wolf clan. It was said of him by his great-nephew Arthur C. Parker that he was "the only American Indian who rose to national distinction and who could trace his lineage back for generations to the Stone Age and to the days of Hiawatha." Arthur C. Parker himself, who has been mentioned above as a scholar, was the first state archaeologist of New York and afterwards director of the Rochester Museum. He wrote a biography of his great-uncle Ely and *An Analytical History of the Seneca Indians;* he edited texts (in translation) of the Iroquois Constitution and the Handsome Lake Code; and he assembled a fascinating collection called *Seneca Myths and Folk-Tales* (which was supplemented later by the *Legends of the Longhouse* of his tribesman Jesse Cornplanter). The Parkers were descendants of Handsome Lake (and so related to his half-brother Cornplanter) and also of Jee-gón-sah-seh the "Peace Queen," who is supposed to have been associated with Deganawídah and Hayówent'ha in the founding of the Iroquois League. This family—intermarried to some extent with the whites and the Tuscaroras— makes today a whole complicated web that provides one of the strongest fibres uniting the Seneca people. The legislature of Pennsylvania, in 1791, as a recognition of Cornplanter's services in mediating between Iroquois and whites, presented him with three tracts of land, one of which, just over the line from New York, is still owned by Cornplanter's descendants, who now number over five hundred. About forty of them live permanently on the Cornplanter tract, and there are family reunions there that run to hundreds. Cornplanter himself was half white and felt that he had been badly treated by his father, a white trader in Albany, who, when the son had just got married and gone to him for some rudimentary equipment—"a kettle and a gun"—had sent him away empty-handed and without, as he afterwards complained, his father's even having warned him that the colonies were about to rebel. He thereafter with a certain stubborn bitterness accounted himself an Indian and—in spite of the conciliatory office which he performed with so much success (he had a son who interpreted for him)—he would not learn, or admit he knew, English. In his last years, he came to believe that the Creator had ordered him to repudiate the whites, and he destroyed a belt and a sword that had been given him in reward for his services. It has, however, been characteristic of the notable individuals of this Cornplanter-Handsome Lake stock that they were at home in both the white and the Indian worlds. I was therefore not surprised to learn, in the course of a visit to the Senecas, that a family by whose obviously superior qualities and ease in their relations with outsiders I had particularly been impressed belonged to the Cornplanter connection. (The name of this family is Nephew, so called from a nephew of Cornplanter who, having no non-Indian name, had so signed below his uncle on a treaty. Though all Indian names mean something and are the property of particular clans, the names that they use in their intercourse with the whites are arbitrary or accidental. The Parkers were named after an English officer who had been captured and adopted by the Senecas. Ely took the Christian name of a much-respected Baptist missionary, and Arthur Parker's middle name, Caswell, was that of a woman missionary. Ely's original Indian name meant Coming to the Front, and from the moment of his being invested with the hereditary title of his family, this title—It Holds the Door Open —became his name and designated him the Keeper of the "Western Door" of the geographical Iroquois Longhouse. The names of his great-grandfather, his grandfather and his father had been Vanishing Smoke, Little Smoke and Dragonfly. The family among themselves used only these Indian names.)

One finds thus at the core of the Seneca people an intelligence and a practical ability, a kind of irreducible morale, which, in the course of their difficult relations with the whites, has always in the long run retrieved them from the disasters inflicted upon them and the results of their own vices. The first great disaster was Sullivan's raid in 1779, when, to prevent them from helping the British, Washington sent one of his generals to invade the Seneca country. Sullivan burned almost all their villages, destroying their stock of corn, and cutting down their crops and their orchards. Our soldiers are said to have skinned a young Seneca in order to make leather for leggings, and when the Senecas caught two of our men—with the connivance, it is said, of a British officer—they cut off the head of one and subjected the other to their most terrible tortures. The Senecas took refuge with the British in their stronghold of Fort Niagara, and some drifted

away to the West. They were amnestied after the
Revolution, but had been shaken by their wholesale
defeat, and this led them to take to drink to an extent
that demoralized them further. The creation of the
Handsome Lake code was an assertion of moral principle and of social common sense in a degrading situation. But, later, in the forties and fifties, when, following our treaties with the Iroquois, the wilderness of
western New York had become available for settlers
and the greedy land speculators were ranging the state,
the Senecas barely escaped being totally dispossessed.
At that time the state of New York, in the interests
of this land speculation, had adopted a deliberate
policy of inducing the Iroquois to emigrate. The
Senecas, in 1837, were in possession of about 125,000
acres—comprising four reservations: Buffalo Creek,
Tonawanda, Cattaraugus and Allegany, in the western
part of the state—the title to which had been guaranteed by the Pickering Treaty of 1794. But these
lands were all on rivers and particularly rich, and an
attempt was made in 1838 by the agents of the Ogden
Land Company to get this area away from the Senecas. The disintegrative effect on the Confederacy of
the contact of the Indians with the whites has been explained by the Reverend Asher Wright, the remarkable
Congregational missionary who lived among the Senecas from 1831 to 1875. Asher Wright had graduated
from Dartmouth, which had been founded to educate
the Indians, and was a scholar who read Sanskrit and
Hebrew, so was not afraid to tackle Seneca. He
preached to them in their own language and translated

the New Testament into it. Wright's memoir of his ministry to the Senecas survives as one of the few inside documents that throw light on what was happening among them. The land of the Six Nations, says Wright, had originally been held by the Confederacy in common, but the immediate splitting-up by the whites of the great tract that had been granted the Indians was designed to break up the Confederacy— which had already been partly wrecked in the throes of our Revolution—by confining its six constituents to separate reservations. The principle of unanimity in arriving at important decisions had also by now been destroyed. It had been part of the machinery of the League that any measure proposed by an individual "must first," in the words of Wright, "gain the assent of his family, then [of] his clan, next of the four related clans in his end of the council house, then of his nation, and then in due course of order the business would be brought up before the representatives of the Confederacy. In the reverse order, the measures of the general council were sent down to the people for their approval. It was a standing rule that all action should be unanimous. Hence, the discussions were always, without any known exception, continued till all opposition was reasoned down, or the proposed measure abandoned. Hence, the great and constantly increasing power of the Confederacy until their councils were divided by the bribery and whiskey of the whites." Taking advantage of the weakening of the structure of the League, the Land Company almost succeeded in bringing off an immense fraud.

Discovering that about fifteen sixteenths of the Senecas did not want to sell their property, they induced a United States Commission to "insist that a majority must rule, according to white custom, and the unanimity principle . . . be set aside. At that time, the Indians were too feeble (or too wise) to risk a war on that account." It was possible for the agents of the land company—resorting, if necessary, to liquor (since Handsome Lake's campaign against drinking had, of course, not completely discouraged it)—to get the signatures of some of the chiefs by bribery; others, who were ill, were induced to sign without knowing what they were signing; in other more difficult cases, the victim was made drunk in a tavern and engaged in conversation while, without his being aware of it, his hand was guided to make its mark. They also set up bogus chiefs. "The Company," according to Arthur Parker, "was reduced to the necessity of taking debauched Indians to Buffalo and penning them in an inn, where they were 'elected and declared chiefs' by company agents, and then for pay forced to sign the treaty." As a last resort, the agents forged signatures. In this way, they produced a "treaty" by which the Senecas, for a consideration of $202,000, were supposed to have sold all four of their reservations. The Indians not involved in the fraud now protested to the federal government, and the evidence of corruption they brought was examined by a Senate committee and by the President, Martin van Buren. The treaty was then amended, but, even in its modified form, it was returned to the Senate by the President, who asserted that "the assent of the Seneca tribe had not been given, nor could it be obtained to it" and that "there was every reason to believe that improper means had been employed." But, as Asher Wright says, "the policy then in vogue in Washington favored the concentration of all the Indian tribes in what was then the Western Territory"; and eventually, against his conviction, the President ratified the treaty.

The news of this ratification, says Wright, "caused a general outburst of anguish, and was followed by . . . determined and desperate efforts to break it up." At this point the missionaries intervened. They collected more evidence of bribery and fraud, and, through the influence of the Quakers, this was brought to the attention of Daniel Webster and of the Secretary of War, the latter of whom appealed to the Land Company and suggested that, in order to avoid litigation, it arrange to settle the matter out of court. The result was a "compromise Treaty" of 1842, which provided that two of the Seneca reservations, Cattaraugus and Allegany, comprising 53,000 acres, should be given back to the Indians, and the two others, Tonawanda and Buffalo Creek, be surrendered to the Ogden Land Company. What was formerly the Buffalo Creek reservation is now part of the city of Buffalo; but the Senecas of Tonawanda refused to relinquish their land, and were supported by the people of Genesee County, who, in 1846, held a convention and appointed Lewis H. Morgan, the author of *The League of the Iroquois*, to carry a memorial to Washington. Through his efforts and those of others, they finally, in 1868, obtained a special act of Congress which authorized them to buy back the land—6,500 acres, a tenth of their original grant—from which they had never allowed themselves to be dislodged.

The Senecas of Buffalo Creek had, in the meantime, either emigrated to Canada or moved in on the other reservations. The Land Company had promised to establish such Senecas as were willing to move to the West on new lands beyond the Missouri. The government agreed to provide an agent for a party of not less than two hundred and fifty, but this number could not be recruited, and the exodus was postponed till the May of 1846, when it started with only two hundred and nineteen. These Indians were simply dumped in the wilderness, with no food and no shelter, and more than half of them died of typhoid or ran off and disappeared. The Quakers sent them $500 to relieve them and bring them back. Some of them died on the way, and those who arrived home spread typhoid in the Cattaraugus Reservation. Wright says that this "produced an impression of horror on the subject of Western Emigration not readily to be effaced; and served to render the people more determined than ever to resist every future effort to remove them from their paternal heritage." All this—despite the aid of the missionaries in their struggle against dispossession —did not make it at all easy to convert them to the white man's religion. The early French Jesuit fathers, whose mission among the Senecas had been established in 1657 and lasted thirty years, at the end of which the Indians expelled them, had "left behind them," says Wright—it is the sentiment, I suppose, that I met in my Mohawk friend Philip Cook—"an intense hatred of the Christian name, resulting from the traitorous acts which occasioned their expulsion; which has been perpetuated to this day, though its cause and origin [are] almost wholly forgotten." "The influence of Christianity," says Wright, "had been almost paralyzed by the intense excitement of the popular mind during the treaty struggle." "In prosecuting our work, it soon became apparent that fresh difficulties must be encountered. The pagan portion of the two reservations availed themselves of the opportunity of union to build up and strengthen their cause against Christianity. Dances were multiplied, old ceremonies revived, and great effort was put forth to add interest and éclat to all their proceedings." The religion of Handsome Lake was, from Wright's point of view, a device of the Devil for sidetracking the Indians from the path toward conversion. A summary added in a different hand to Wright's memoir of 1859 estimates that "about three hundred and fifty persons have made a Christian profession, on the different reservations belonging to the Senecas under the care of the American Board [of Missionaries]. Of these, as might be expected, some have apostatized, but the majority have given as satisfactory evidence of the genuineness of their piety as could under the circumstances be reasonably anticipated." In 1859, there must have been in these reservations about three thousand Senecas. Arthur Parker corroborates Wright in his *Analytical History of the Seneca Indians*: "Many Indians were embittered so deeply that they said, 'If this be an act of a Christian nation, we will cling to the faith of our fathers and reject Christianity forever.' The strength of the non-Christian party of the Six Nations dates from the fraudulent treaty, and to this day [1926] they recite the frauds of Buffalo Creek as a reason why Christians should not be trusted."

I do not, however, want to let Asher Wright—good and honest man though he was and champion of the Indians in their struggle over the treaty—put the whole burden of blame on the Catholics for prejudicing them against Christianity. It was the Protestant part-Indian preacher, Eleazar Williams, who, as agent of the Ogden Land Company, had lured the Oneidas to Wisconsin; and one can see from the interesting memoir called *Our Life Among the Iroquois*, by the Bostonian Mrs. Harriet S. Caswell, who had worked as a young woman with the Asher Wrights, that the methods of these Protestant missionaries could also be somewhat unscrupulous. An Indian girl of an anti-Christian family was dying of tuberculosis, and her mother came to Mrs. Caswell. "It was a great comfort to the Indians in their last hours to be permitted to see the clothes in which they were to be buried. 'But there is one thing,' she [the mother] continued, 'which we cannot make. She wants a pair of lace sleeves like those she has seen you wear.' Some flowing lace sleeves, after the fashion of the day, had been embroidered for me by my mother, and I had occasionally worn them, to the great delight of the Indians, who are very fond of embroidery. The mother said,

'We cannot make these sleeves for her. Can you do it?'
I said, 'Yes, I can do it; and I will do it upon one
condition.'" The condition was that Mrs. Caswell
should make the sleeves at the daughter's bedside and
preach to her the Christian religion. This the mother
could not accept. "This was hard for me, but I
believed that through the pleading of the daughter I
should in the end be allowed to have my own way.
The daughter was in consumption, and would probably linger for some time. I must wait." The mother
came again to plead, but the missionary was adamant
about her condition. The mother at last gave in, and
Mrs. Caswell spent an hour each day—with a group
of Indian women present—at the bedside of the dying
girl. "The result was that the dear child died a triumphant death through faith in Christ, and the women
commenced from that time to attend the mission
church and to hear the regular preaching of the
Word."

The scandal of '38, with its sell-out or surrender
on the part of the chiefs, was, in two of the Seneca
reservations, Allegany and Cattaraugus, to set off a
revolution. A group of young Senecas of warrior
rank denounced these hereditary chiefs for their in-
competence, bad faith and venality, and also charged
them with graft in collecting and distributing the
monies from the rental of the sawmills on these reserva-
vations. The three leaders of this revolution were pupils
of Asher Wright, who had been sent by him to college
in the East. A recorded speech by one of them, made

in 1848, shows that they were informed about and evidently influenced by the events of that year in Europe: "Is there one here"—he is speaking to the Baltimore Quakers—"whose philanthropic and patriotic spirit is not aroused with the thrilling tidings come over the great salt waters that millions of human beings are becoming free; that the spirit of freedom has crossed from America over the great ocean into the old world and there planted the standard of liberty?" In December, 1848, a majority of the non-ranking Senecas of Allegany and Cattaraugus declared a Seneca Republic. They proceeded to depose their chiefs, to separate Church and State, and to draw up a constitution which established legal monogamy; which vested the legislative power in a council of eighteen (now sixteen) members, with a president and other officers to be annually elected (now every two years) by universal manhood suffrage (a sharp departure from the matriarchal system, which, however, continued to prevail in the clan); and which set up a judiciary consisting of three "Peacemakers," who were to deal with all offenses except major crimes and all suits involving sums under fifty dollars, the more serious kinds of cases to be handled by the courts of the state. No laws were to be passed by the Council in contravention of those of the state of New York or of the United States.

The framers of this constitution applied to the federal government and got from it a charter which established them, now detached from the councils of the League, as a self-contained Seneca community, with 3792 enrolled members; and this Seneca Republic still flourishes with its semi-independent government —very much, on a smaller scale, like Andorra or San Marino—in the southwestern corner of New York. (Though the name of this Seneca common-wealth is officially the Seneca Nation, I shall continue to refer to it as the Seneca Republic in order to avoid confusion—since it does not include the Senecas of the Tonawanda reservation and Canada—with the original Seneca nation which was one of the Six Nations of the Iroquois League.) The political ma-chinery of the Seneca Republic is simple and seems to be practical. I could not help contrasting it with the anarchy of the supposedly constitutional Republic of Haiti, in which the President is always attempting to alter the constitution in such a way as to prolong his term of office and is usually thrown out by a coup d'état, which results, if he survives, in an escape to Jamaica. A President of the Seneca Republic is elected for his two-year term first from one, then from the other of the two reservations. Thus, although he can serve more than once, he cannot succeed himself. His second in command, the Clerk, must be chosen from the other reservation, to which the President does not belong. Since the Church and the State function sepa-rately, the Longhouses on the two reservations are no longer used for councils but only for religious cere-monies. The business of the government is carried on in two little town halls, one at Jimerstown on Allegany and the other at Four Corners on Cattaraugus, as well as in a general office which seems to have been purposely located outside both the reservations in the town of Gowanda. There are two parties, the People's Party and the New Deal, formerly the Veterans' Party, which make mutual charges of corruption. "Would you know it if somebody was telling the truth?" I was asked by a Seneca ex-president (who was married to a woman of the Cornplanter connection). "Would you know if I was telling the truth if I told you how the Indians vote. Would you know if somebody told you something else that he wasn't telling the truth?" I said that I thought I would. "Well, when an Indian goes to vote, there are two ballots on separate papers. First, one party hands him its ballot, and gives him ten dollars with it—then the other party gives him twelve dollars and hands him the other paper. How is that different from the way you vote?" My companion replied that we were only paid once, which brought a laugh from the Indians.

My impression was, nevertheless, that the affairs of the Seneca Republic were handled, on the whole, pretty well. These Indians are well-enough off to have employed a first-rate attorney (a lawyer to look after their interests was a feature of their original program): Mr. Edward E. O'Neill of Washington, a former New Dealer in the Department of Justice, who was retained by the Senecas in 1954 and who has spent many months at Gowanda. He has prepared for them an annual printed report which covers the business of the Council, balances the Republic's books and records its commercial transactions; and he has persuaded them—in order to ameliorate the situation described above—to·

reform their electoral system: the two ballots are now printed on the same sheet, so that the briber has to trust the bribee and can no longer be sure of his vote. When the Thruway was put through the Cattaraugus reservation, he got the Indians $100,000 for individual claims and $75,000 for compensation to the nation, which, however, when divided, amounted to little more than $22 apiece. The President of the Seneca Republic, when I visited it in 1958, was the influential Cornelius Seneca, who has been elected four times and who struck me as one of the ablest men I had met in the Iroquois world. In physique and in personality, he is the opposite of Wallace Anderson (Mad Bear), the Tuscarora leader. He belongs to the classical aquiline type and, when photographed in his feathered headdress, might figure as the ideal American Indian. He is said to be an eloquent speaker in a somewhat traditional style, but is quite free from the mythology of the nationalist movement. When I talked to him, he was perfectly matter-of-fact—with the Indian nuance of ironic humor—and exhibited a detailed and practical grasp of everything connected with the affairs of the Republic. Mr. Seneca was educated in the district school and then spent two years at the advanced school for Indians at Carlisle, Pennsylvania. When he left there, in 1914, he became a structural steel worker and was for thirty years superintendent of the Bethlehem steel-erection department. His wife is a teacher in the Cattaraugus school, and their small house—set back on its well-kept lawn—with its bookcase and upholstered chairs, its

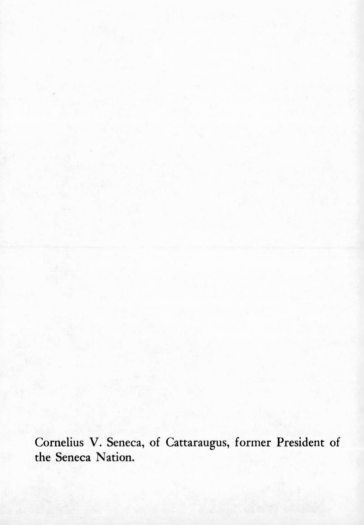

Cornelius V. Seneca, of Cattaraugus, former President of the Seneca Nation.

piano and phonograph, its bright spotless dining room-kitchen, is a model of neatness and comfort.

The position of the Seneca Republic is peculiar in several ways. It functions independently of the League, as well as of the other Senecas. The Senecas of Tonawanda did not feel themselves responsible for the débâcle of 1838, for the reason that, though the signatures of the Tonawanda chiefs were forged by the Land Company on its treaty, they had actually had nothing to do with it. Arthur C. Parker, himself of Tonawanda descent, asserts that "not a single wary Tonawanda chief could be kidnapped, bribed, or induced to touch the rum of the unscrupulous agents." They had, therefore, no need of a revolution, and when the republicans of the other two reservations deposed their hereditary chiefs, the Tonawandas took over their chieftainships. The Tonawandas seem more sure of themselves than the Iroquois of other reservations. It was to Tonawanda that Handsome Lake, the prophet, came when he and his followers were driven out of Allegany; it was there that his grandson and disciple Soshéoa established the Handsome Lake Code; and it has remained the headquarters of the Handsome Lake religion. These Senecas have fewer problems than the Iroquois on most of the other reservations. They are in touch with the nationalist movement, but they have not yet been threatened by public works, and seem not much excited about it.

I shall return to Tonawanda later, but I want at this point to devote some space to the first Tonawanda

Seneca with whom I had any extensive conversation and who seems to me in some ways typical of the spirit of this reservation. Mr. Nicodemus Bailey is an extremely clever man, who spent five and a half years at Carlisle and who speaks and writes English with something like the literary quality of, say, a Russian of the old regime who has achieved a real elegance in a Western language without ceasing to speak like a foreigner. He told me that there were hardly two men now left on the Tonawanda reservation whose Seneca was really excellent—the "criterion," as he said, being the speeches made at the councils. He is a musician—who has played the flute in the Buffalo Philharmonic Orchestra—and something of an Iroquois scholar. He is a man of strong opinions, and his point of view sharply contrasts with that of the nationalists. His own political activities have all been directed toward obtaining for the Senecas of Tonawanda the privileges of United States citizenship. He worked for the transference of jurisdiction, in both civil and criminal cases, to the courts of the state of New York; and he expressed to me his satisfaction at seeing on the reservation a school bus taking the children to a non-segregated school. He is, I think, the only Iroquois I have talked with who votes and wants others to vote. His face and his tone light up when he speaks of his years at Carlisle, which he says were the best of his life. He distinguished himself on the Track Team and was a champion hammer-thrower. It had been possible only at this all-Indian school to get to know one's fellow-Indians from all over the United

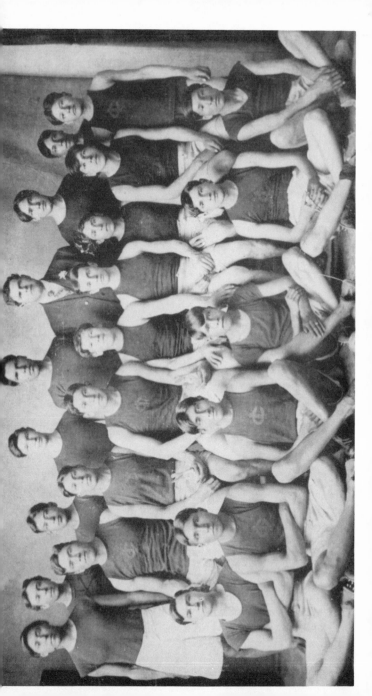

The track team of Carlisle Indian School, photographed about 1908. Nicodemus Bailey is the fourth from the left in the second row. By his side, on the right, sits Jim Thorpe, who was Olympic Champion in Stockholm in 1912 and, according to a memorial in the city of Carlisle, voted in 1950 "the greatest athlete and football player of the first half of the twentieth century." He was an Oklahoma Indian, Sac and Fox, with an admixture of French and Irish blood.

States. When I said that I could not believe that
the obstinate and self-sufficient Indians of the Zuñi
pueblo in New Mexico would let their young people
go to Carlisle, he told me that, on the contrary,
at the time he was there, the art teacher had been a
Zuñi woman (the Zuñis once excelled at pottery and
now make jewelry and silverware). This school at
Carlisle, which was formerly run by the Indian Bureau
and the War Department, was converted into a barracks in the First World War, and has not been opened
again. The reason for this was official dissatisfaction
with the results of educating young Indians in a college exclusively Indian. It turned out that though the
Indians who went to Carlisle did become proficient in
English and got a grasp of the world of the whites
that would otherwise have hardly been possible,
they also learned about one another and were for-
tified in their Indian self-consciousness. Like the
Russian who has sojourned in Western Europe and
found out what it has to teach him, a good many of
the graduates of the Carlisle school, instead of trying
to share the life of the white man, would return to
their own people, better qualified to work for their
interests. Carlisle, Mr. Bailey writes me, "turned out
educated Indians who developed the 'intestinal forti-
tude,' plainly guts, to stand up and talk against corruption in the federal Indian Service; plead their own
cause for justice for their people and demand to be
recognized and treated as humans; all of which so
nettled many Western politicians and office-holding
beneficiaries that it prompted the several attempts at

closing the institution long before it happened. The war furnished the pretext to justify the act." I remembered the jokes that I used to hear about men from Carlisle who had been famous at football and then "gone back to the blanket" and taken part in their tribal ceremonies with an equal enthusiasm, and I realized now the stupidity of the assumptions that made this seem grotesque. Was college football less barbarous than these ceremonies? Why should the educated young Indian be expected to turn his back on festivals and sacred rites which perhaps antedated Christianity? Mr. Bailey—although a Christian and a thirty-second-degree Mason—took, I found, a great deal of interest in the Handsome Lake religion, and was worried because the grave of Soshéowa had had a communal cookhouse built over it. He played me some excellent recordings of the songs that accompany the War Dance, performed by a singer, now old, of whose voice he had wanted to preserve an impress, and he so aroused my interest in the Little Water Ceremony, a song cycle based, he said, on a "fanciful tale" of death and resurrection, which was sung in the dark with rattles and ended, just at dawn, "with a flourish of the flute," that I decided I must try to hear it. Though the views of Mr. Bailey are by no means those of the nationalists, though he has long ceased to act as a chief, and though the ancient oak cabin in which he was born has been set up in the Buffalo Museum, he still has his base in the Indian world. "The Indians," he observed to Dr. William N. Fenton, who had taken me to his house, "are like a boiling pot. From time to time somebody comes along and takes off the lid and looks in. Then he puts it on again and goes away." He added, after a moment, to Fenton: "You've looked into it longer than most people."

The Seneca Republic, then, is somewhat at odds with the Confederacy, at least on the latter's more nationalist side, and its relations with the neighboring whites who now occupy a part of the Senecas' land are also a little awkward. For 95 per cent of the town of Salamanca, with its population of over 9,000, is situated on the territory of these Indians, as are also the white villages of Vandalia, Killbuck, Carollton and Great Valley. Salamanca grew up with the railroads at the time—the eighteen-forties and fifties—when they were being extended West. A little sawmill town called Hemlock which stood on the line of a pass through the hills grew into a railroad junction, and its name was changed to Salamanca in honor of the fact that the Duke of Salamanca had invested in a large quantity of Erie stock—an event which has been also commemorated by a poster of a Salamanca bullfight in one of the principal bars. The adjoining land belonged to the Senecas, and—without the authorization of the federal government—the railroad workers leased it from them. These leases were, however, later validated by special acts of Congress, the last one of which, of 1890, approved renewal of the leases for terms not exceeding ninety-nine years. But the white settlers, as the years went on, were to become more and more reluctant to recognize the Indians as their landlords, let alone acknowledge that the value of the land had increased since they first leased it. One block in the business district was up to the nineteen-thirties still renting for a dollar a year; and many rents were not paid at all. But eventually the Senecas brought suit against one of the local leaseholders, who was eighteen years behind in payment, and in 1942 the Court of Appeals affirmed the Indians' right to cancel this lease—as a result of which they also cancelled some two thousand of their five thousand other leases, and new leases were issued with an increase of rent and new provisions for protecting the Indians. Through a bill passed in 1950, it was arranged to have the whole annual sum of the rentals collected by the town itself as an addition to the local taxes. This sum in 1958 amounted to little more than $13,500 for land which has a far greater value, but even this moderate rent makes the white Salamancans uncomfortable. Outsiders who have lived in the town say the whole place is rather neurotic, that it suffers from a sense of frustration, on account of having the Indians as landlords —just as those who know the Indian world well say the Indians are made uncomfortable by the constant pressure of the whites, and that their feudings and jealousies among themselves, of which the Senecas have had their share, are a backfiring of bitterness against their neighbors.

These Senecas have, in fact, now been threatened with a disaster that is almost comparable to the 1838 dispossession.

In August, 1941, an act was passed by Congress which authorized an "Allegheny Reservoir Project" as part of a flood-control program for the Ohio River Basin. This project, of which the cost was first estimated at something over $37,000,000, had been obstructed by Harold Ickes, the then Secretary of the Interior, on the ground that so considerable an operation ought not to be undertaken entirely at government expense but should be partly financed by the state. His opposition had no effect, and the cost of the dam to be built was raised to $112,000,000. But the war intervened, and the project was dropped and not taken up again till the summer of 1956. The Senecas, by this time, were much alarmed. The great dam was to be constructed at a narrows called Kinzua in Pennsylvania on the Allegheny River, only twelve miles downstream from the Allegany reservation (these two names, though derived from the same Indian word, are spelt in different ways, and there is a third spelling for the Alleghany Mountains), and to accumulate water in a reservoir which would produce a thirty-three-mile lake extending to Salamanca. This lake would cover 9000 acres of the habitable land on the reservation and—since some 12,000 acres of the Seneca preserve are rocky and precipitous hills—leave only 2300 habitable acres. The United States Corps of Engineers, who were taking the operation in hand, particularly angered the Senecas by telling them that the whole of this area would be flooded only perhaps once in a hundred years, and that, for the rest, they would be free to return and make use of their former property during the months when it was not under water. The

Cornplanter tract described above—particularly sacred to the Senecas as the place where Handsome Lake the prophet had lived arid had his revelations—would also be flooded by the dam. Cornplanter's grave and its monument would have to be moved somewhere else, and his descendants would lose their sanctuary.

The agents of the Corps of Engineers had at first approached the Senecas in the usual ignorance of Indian affairs that has characterized these sweeping projects. These agents, who seem not to have known of the existence of the Seneca Republic, had supposed it would be simply a matter of paying off individual householders, and their ranking district head, Colonel H. E. Sprague, was proceeding, like Robert Moses, on a schedule that demanded quick action and did not allow for uncertain factors. They were somewhat taken aback when they found that they would have to struggle for the acquisition of land held in common, under the protection of the United States, by a semi-independent republic, and that its government could challenge their right to appropriate Indian territory by producing the Pickering Treaty of 1794, signed by an envoy of Washington, according to which "the United States acknowledge all the land within the aforesaid mentioned boundaries, to be the property of the Seneka Nation; and the United States will never claim the same, nor disturb the Seneka in the free use and enjoyment thereof: but it shall remain theirs, until they choose to sell the same to the people of the United States, who have the right to purchase." The President of the Seneca Republic announced that his government would acquiesce in any project of which it was possible to prove the public necessity; but he sought a non-official opinion on the expediency of the Engineers' project. Mr. Edward O'Neill, the Senecas' lawyer, now had a special study made of the problem of flood control in connection with the Allegheny River by two well-known engineers who had worked for the government, Mr. Arthur E. Morgan, the former chairman of the Tennessee Valley Authority, and Mr. Barton M. Jones, the construction engineer for the TVA, who had, respectively, planned and built the Norris Dam. Mr. Morgan and Mr. Jones reported that the Kinzua dam was a needlessly expensive device for dealing with the dangers of flooding, and that its purpose could be achieved, and even more effectively achieved, without inundating the Seneca Reservation. It was proposed to "divert the flow of the Allegheny River through a six mile channel into a large glacial depression which has about three times the capacity of Kinzua, where it would be stored for flood control and for increasing the low water flow." It was estimated by Morgan and Jones that the project they recommended would not cost much more than eighty million dollars, whereas that of the Engineers would be likely to cost about half as much again as their estimated hundred million. The Senecas, accordingly, on August 30, 1957, brought an action against the Secretary of the Army and the Chief of Engineers (the Corps of Engineers is under the War Department) for an injunction directing them to "refrain from the construction of the Allegheny

River Project," which had already been "authorized by Congress." (A million dollars for this purpose was appropriated in 1958 by the Public Works Appropriation Act.) The Seneca Republic insisted, as the Tuscaroras were later to do, that a special act of Congress was necessary to deprive them of any part of their territory. This intention was to be supported by a precedent created in 1958 when a Federal District Court in South Dakota ruled that the lands of the Sioux could not be taken for a similar project without "the requisite authority" of Congress. This resistance to the Kinzua dam has had the result, I am told, of uniting, within the Seneca Republic, the various parties and factions to a degree that has not been known within the memory of the oldest generation. On a visit to the Allegany Reservation in June of 1958, I found that an "Indian Village," set up in the summer for tourists, with booths that sold souvenirs and a platform for "social" dances, had been rendered a little forbidding by a stuffed effigy of Colonel Sprague hanging from the branch of a tree, with an arrow sticking out of its back.

This resistance to the dam by the Senecas has now come to be backed to a considerable extent by disapproval on the part of the whites. Since the lake would reach to Salamanca, the people there, too, are becoming alarmed. A long article on the front page of the Salamanca *Inquirer* (the local Democratic weekly) of June 20, 1958, began with a statement by Mr. Morgan that the dam "would increase flood hazards" for the town of Salamanca. He is quoted as

saying that "the Kinzua dam will only protect Warren
and Pittsburgh from floods resulting from only half
the greatest probable rainfall computed by the U. S.
Weather Bureau for the region, and that a flood only
50 per cent greater than the Kinzua Dam can control
would be worse than the disastrous flood at Warren
two years ago." Such a flood would "hit Salamanca
harder than if there were no dam at Kinzua." The
project has been opposed, in both New York and
Pennsylvania, by the various organizations of sports-
men, who believe that their hunting and fishing
will be spoiled by the wrecking of the Allegheny
Valley. Even the huge artificial lake—since its shore-
line would be constantly fluctuating—would become so difficult of access for boating that special
highways at the public expense would have to be
built to reach it. And, finally, public confidence has
received a *coup de grâce* since it was learned that
genuine flood control has never been the object of the
Kinzua Dam, but has merely served as a pretext for
putting through at the public expense a particularly
costly contrivance intended to serve the interests of
a group of industrialists in Pittsburgh, who now appear
as its principal advocates. Though Pittsburgh itself
is not seriously in danger from the flooding of the
upper Allegheny, certain Pittsburgh manufacturers
have their reasons for wanting the river diluted at the
seasons when it is running low. The sulphurous drain-
age from the coal mines is from their point of view
deleterious because it ruins their boilers by rusting
them. Hence pollution of the water must be reduced

and the Allegheny kept at a uniform level. Mr. O'Neill, on behalf of the Indians, contends in one of his statements that industrial pollution could be reduced by the action of the industrialists themselves at a cost of three or four hundred thousand dollars. "Is this government," he asks, "to expend one hundred and fifty millions of dollars to afford relief to private industry at a cost to the taxpayer of three hundred and seventy-five times as much?"

The history of the Senecas' attempts to avert the construction of the dam shows the usual fluctuations of policy where Indian affairs are concerned. Their petition for an injunction on the grounds given above was rejected by the Federal District Court for the District of Columbia, by the United States Court of Appeals for the District of Columbia circuit, and finally—on June 15, 1959—by the Supreme Court of the United States, which left standing the opinion of the Court of Appeals: "We think Congress has authorized the taking of these lands." In the meantime, however, on June 2, the House Appropriations Committee, in reporting the Public Works Appropriation Bill for 1960, which included the $1,400,000 for the Kinzua dam, had ordered "an independent investigation of the merits of the alternative proposals advocated by the Corps of Engineers and the engineering consultants for the Seneca Indians." But the Senate supported the project and the investigation was dismissed. A compromise bill reported to and passed by both the House and the Senate, which carried in it the Senate's version, was vetoed by Eisenhower, and his veto was sustained in the House by one vote. A new bill had now to be written, but its only departure from the former one was to reduce the amount of the appropriation by 2.5 per cent. The President vetoed this bill, too, but on September 10, 1959, his veto was overridden in both the House and the Senate. The only hope now for the Indians is that Eisenhower may use his prerogative to withhold the expenditure of appropriated funds for a further consideration of federal projects. There has been submitted to the White House, in response to the President's request, a list of the projects included in the bill in which the ratio of benefit to cost is less than 1 to 1. In the case of the Kinzua Dam, this ration has been reckoned as 1.5 to .8.

6. SENECA NEW YEAR'S CEREMONIES

I was able to see something of this Seneca com·munity which our government desires to flood, when, in the last week of January, 1958, I went with Dr. William N. Fenton to attend the New Year's ceremonies on the Allegany Reservation. Dr. Fenton is an anthropologist of an altogether exceptional sort. His family came from Cattaraugus County, in which lie the two reservations that make up the Seneca Republic, and he has from childhood spent a good deal of time there. Some of these Senecas he has known all his life. Both his grandfather and his father were interested in the Indians, and they accumulated a valuable collection of masks, weapons and other objects, which is now in New York City in the Museum of the American Indian. William Fenton was graduated from Dartmouth, which, founded in the eighteenth century with money raised by an Indian preacher, was originally intended for the education of Indians and still offers scholarships to Indian students. Here Fenton first realized that the Iroquois—who, though more has been written about them than about any other group of North American Indians, are still rather imperfectly known—could provide for him a field of research. This research has turned into a lifework. He studied anthropology at Yale under Clark Wissler and Edward Sapir and served under John Collier in the Indian Bureau, spending two years and a half as a community worker in the Tonawanda and Tuscarora reservations, then thirteen years in the Bureau of Ethnology of the Smithsonian Institution. He is today the leading Iroquois scholar and probably knows more about this remarkable people than any other white man has known. He has brought to the subject an intelligence at once scrupulously scientific and humanly intuitive of a kind which, on any large scale, has probably not been applied to it since the work of Lewis Morgan. The writer has thus been peculiarly fortunate in having been given an opportunity of visiting the Seneca reservations in the company of Dr. Fenton. Not only is Dr. Fenton an Iroquois scholar, understanding spoken Seneca and having some grasp of the other languages, but he is on quite non-anthropological terms with the Indians in this part of the world. He was thus able both to take me into their homes, as a friend and former neighbor, and, as an expert, to explain to me, at the ceremonies, the meaning of what was being said and done.

My visit in winter to the Seneca country was a novel and impressive experience. This was the region that, a century and a quarter before, in the days of Asher Wright, had been still a primitive wilderness, with forested hills and rough rivers, in which Wright's young New England wife and three or four white woman teachers had had to find the courage, in their little log houses, to withstand the snows and winds of winter; to live with the disquieting queerness of the customs and beliefs of the Indians, of their "weird, plaintive" unintelligible songs; to hold meetings in the mission schoolhouse, at which Christian hymns were sung, accompanied by a lonely melodeon, and to return late at night—which they "dreaded"—by rude trails that were "long, dark and dangerous... through the woods, through mud holes, over broken bridges, through streams which we had to ford. . . . Two lone women, the old mission horses and wagon, the dense forest on either side, the young Indians in a variety of indescribable costumes, with their long hair streaming in the wind, running before, behind, and on either side, holding high the torches and singing the Christian songs taught them by us." They had to stiffen themselves not to shrink from the hostility that was always lurking and that broke out in truculent threats and in practical jokes meant to test their nerve. Mrs. Wright was always unhappy when her husband was away from home. The letters she sent him by messenger show a strange world of cold and danger and inflexible Protestant faith:

Seneca Mission, December, 1835

Tuesday evening. Deacon Blue Eyes came this evening, and is to spend the night with us. We expect to kill hogs to-morrow. Thermometer eight degrees below zero to-day. I took cold yesterday, and have a dreadful face, I assure you. Can scarcely see out of my left eye. My jaw is somewhat painful and I have been obliged to keep still all day. Your letter was truly welcome, and the more so as it was entirely unexpected. You were in the woods at the very time I feared. I should not have slept that night had I known that. You must not do so again! No, no! You must be willing to stop where darkness overtakes you, and not risk your life and health by traveling in the night. I am glad you have bought a cow, and I shall do my best to make a great deal of butter, but you must not form too high expectations.

Monday evening. . . I send you your compass, that you may have a guide through the woods. But oh, keep near to the great Guide of feeble, wandering sinners! There is safety only there, and peace only there. Tell Indian Robert he will need a true compass to guide him through the wilderness of this world, where are a thousand snares into which he may fall at any moment.". . .

"This evening," she writes him a little later, "I received your precious letter and could scarcely keep from crying when I found you had not heard from me. You must have met my messenger before this time, however, and received at his hand the letter and other things which I sent to you. . . .

"I am now writing in our own little room again. It is the pleasantest place in the house for me, although it seems so lonely since my other half has deserted it. But you know there is a secret joy sometimes in indulging loneliness when it reminds us so strongly of the cause of our past happiness and present sadness.

"I hope, my dear, that you are making rapid progress in the Indian tongue. Do not faint or be discouraged. Go forward, keep looking at the crowd of precious souls going down to death, and at the example and command of our divine Master."

It was interesting to contrast this world with the world we were now entering and to try to note what elements remained the same. The weather—from which our motel protected us—was of course what it had always been. There was snow on the ground when we got there, and it snowed a little harder and grew colder every day. The young men were playing a game called "snow-snake" as they had been for no one knows how many hundred years. They had made in the snow along the edge of a road a groove half a mile or more long by dragging a log that was fastened to a pole and guided by two men who held the ends of the pole and walked on either side of the track. Then the groove was iced by pouring on water. The snow-snakes are javelins made of hard wood—maple, hickory, birch or ash, with slightly lifted serpentine heads. These are owned by the "snow-snake doctors," older men who polish and grease them; they use a wax which is made by a secret method and is supposed to owe its special virtue to magic. The snakes are carefully cherished and transported in cases of cloth with compartments like those in which table silver or the disjointed parts of fishing rods are carried. These owners, however, get younger men to throw them. The javelin is held with the forefinger against the base, and the

thumb and other fingers grasping the shaft, and is
launched, with a running start, from a mark at which
the thrower must halt. One of the contenders we
watched, who tried to put all his force behind the
throw, always ended by turning a somersault. It requires a good deal of skill even to make the snake slide
in the groove, and, if not started straight enough, it will
often, before travelling far, jump out. A great deal of
betting goes on—the Iroquois are passionate gamblers.
One reads tales from the early days of men betting
everything they had: their weapons, their homes, their
wives. Today rolls of bills are flourished.

Not far from the snow-snake course stood a dark
unpainted frame house of an old-fashioned gabled
kind. On the evening of our first day, we attended
in this house a ceremony which is called in English the
"Dark Dance." This belongs to a class of rituals that
are not performed in the Longhouse but are "put up,"
as the phrase is, in private homes, in which the family
makes the arrangements and pays for the "feast" that
accompanies them. There were two or three of these
taking place that night, and Fenton thought that this
was the most interesting. The Dark Dance is a kind of
oratorio, a set of song-sequences which are sung in
the dark. One was admitted by way of the back of
the house, and we stumbled with a torch through the
snow. Unfortunately we arrived after the singing had
begun and could not enter before the first of the sequences was finished. We waited between the outside
privy and the back porch of the house—on which latter
lay a pile of cans that had provided the corn for the fes-

tive soup. The darkened house in the snow seemed quite spooky. From within came the sound of singing, which, given its beat by the rattles and drums, pounded on, through episodic pauses, with a steady compelling rhythm.

At the first intermission, the lights were turned on, and we went in by the back door. We found ourselves in a very large kitchen, in which the singers and musicians and the audience were sitting along the walls, leaving the rest of the floor clear for the dancers. An immense boiler of soup was keeping hot on an old-fashioned wood stove. In the next room—what rather surprised me—a group of young people and old people both, including the master of ceremonies and the very old lady who was putting up the feast, were listening to television. The double door to this room had been opened, and we could hear from it the flat mechanical crackle of the jokes of some TV comedian. The old people no doubt knew the Dark Dance so well that they did not care to hear it again, and for the young it was too archaic. At the end of the intermission, the folding doors were closed and the singing began again.

This ceremony, very ancient and somewhat mysterious, has to do with the Great Little People. Years and years ago an Iroquois boy was out hunting with bow and arrow. He came to a deep ravine, with a tall tree growing out of it, whose top was on a level with where he stood. On the top of the tree was a black squirrel, which he was just about to shoot when he heard strange voices at the bottom of the cliff. He crawled to the edge and looked down, and there he saw two little men, who were shooting at the squirrel with tiny bows but could not manage to make their arrows reach more than halfway up the tree. The boy shot the squirrel and it fell, and the little men were much excited to see the enormous arrow. They tried to pull it out but they could not. Then they looked up and saw the boy and begged him to come down and extract the arrow. He did so, and they asked him if they could have the squirrel, telling him that black squirrel for them was what buffalo meat was for the Indians. The boy not only let them have it but gave them also two gray squirrels he had shot. They made with him a pact of friendship and invited him to come to their home. He accepted and, since it was all they could do to carry the black squirrel between them, he carried the two gray ones himself.

They went to a cave in the rocks, and inside were a little old man and a little old woman, the mother and father of the two little men. The woman was pounding corn with a tiny pounder, and they gave him corn soup in a tiny wooden bowl. He thought that this would hardly be enough, but no matter how much he ate, the amount of it never grew less. They explained to him who they were. There are three tribes of the Great Little People. One lives along the streams and under the falls of the Genesee River, and these are called the Stone Throwers. They are terribly strong and can hurl rocks and uproot trees. Another takes care of the plants: they wake them up in the springtime, they see that the flowers bloom and they turn the fruit so that it gets the sun. The third live in caverns, and their special task is to guard all the entrances to the underworld and prevent the white buffalo that live there from breaking out and wreaking havoc on earth. When these buffalo do escape, the Pygmies have to herd them back. So they are working for the Indians as well as themselves and have long wanted to make their acquaintance. The mother now prepared a feast: corn soup, with the meat of the squirrel, and a beverage of berry-juice. She gave three raps on a tiny drum, and the rest of the Pygmies came trooping. They burned the sacred tobacco and then covered up the fire. In the dark, they sang songs to the beat of the drum, and they told the boy to learn them. He stayed for several days, and the same thing took place every night, till the boy could go through the whole ceremony. Then they told him to perform this ritual three days after he should have returned to his people, and the Pygmies at ten days' distance would hear the first beat of the drum and come to feast with the Indians. If the Indians heard the Pygmies drum or sing, they would please to go to the gulches from which the sound was coming and throw some tobacco down to them; and they would also be grateful if the young people would make bundles of their fingernail parings and throw these down to them, too, for when the animals that the Little People fear caught the smell of the fingernail parings, they would think that there were humans about and let the Pygmies alone. They gave the boy a round white stone which would act as a hunting charm, and he assured them he would perform the ceremony and return their hospitality.

They took him to the cliff where he found them, and he made his way back to his settlement, but he found it completely changed: it was now overgrown with the forest, and there was nobody living there. He searched for his people and found them. But they did not recognize him now; he saw that they had grown strangely older. Every day he was gone was a human year. He told them about his adventures, and from that time the Indians have never failed to give feasts for the Little People.

The Dark Dance begins with an invocation, which implies that neglect of the Pygmies has resulted in somebody's illness. (The "members" referred to in the passage that follows are the members of the medicine society which has charge of the Great Little People ceremony. It was attempted by Handsome Lake, when he instituted his other reforms, to abolish these ancient societies, so incompatible with his modernized teaching; but, as is likely to turn out in such reformations, the religion to be expelled went on flourishing by the side of the new one.) After the usual thanks to the Creator and to his deputies, the Sun and Moon, the Pygmies are addressed as follows:

"So now you get tobacco—you, the Great Little People.
Now is the time when you have come;
You and the members have assembled here tonight.
Now again you receive tobacco—you, the Great Little People.
You are the wanderers of the mountains;

You have promised to hear us whenever the drum
   sounds,
Even as far away as a ten days' journey.
You well know the members of this society,
So let this [the illness] cease.
You are the cause of a person, a member, becoming
   ill.
Henceforth give good fortune, for she [or he] has
   fulfilled her duty and given you tobacco.
You love tobacco and we remember it;
So also you should remember us.
How the drum receives tobacco,
And the rattle also.
It is our belief that we have said all,
So now we hope that you will help us.
Now these are the words spoken before you all,
You who are gathered here tonight.
So now it is done."

When the Little People enter the room, its occupants are heard to shift their feet. The visitors, in the
darkness, are stumbling over their legs. The Little
People sing in their own language, which nobody
understands. The purpose of performing such ceremonies in the dark is evidently to produce the illusion
that the characters who are being sung about or are
themselves supposed to be singing are actually in the
room. In any case, the effect is extraordinary—exciting
and at first even frightening. The singing fills up the
room, as if something had opened out that was larger
than those who released it, and that had some kind

of independent existence, embodying some projection of the human spirit which has survived through uncounted centuries, some collaboration of man with Nature—we have only this unsatisfactory word—which was now still alive in this shabby old house, rising up and renewing itself, taking over and animating the darkness. One was aware of the texture of the music in a way that one would not have been if one had seen the room and the singers. One wondered whether all oratorios ought not to be sung in the dark. Single voices are answered by choruses, which sometimes seem to sing against them. In a moment of accumulating crisis—liberating, menacing, exulting—I became aware of great bulks of darkness blocking the light under the crack of the door from the room in which that other audience was looking at television. It was the large-looming women of the chorus —the main singers of the drama are male—who at this point get up and dance, intensifying the rhythm by their stamping. This sequence of songs has more variety than any Southwestern Indian music I have heard—most of which has been rather monotonous. There are constant changes of tempo, and the great climaxes are followed by quieter passages. This ceremony, when performed in its entirety, is a cycle of a hundred and sixty-eight songs. The unit that is called a song is something like the stanza of a ballad: two lines that are once repeated, with the change of a single word; and like ballads they have nonsense refrains of the "Hey, nonny nonny!" type.

Of the four parts that constitute the Dark Dance,

one was omitted on the evening we heard it. This was the section devoted to the charm-holders, usually sung second, which is apparently an interruption to the development of the drama of the cycle. Its relevance to the Little People is by way of the round white stone which was given the boy by the Pygmies. Other charms have been bestowed by the Little People and also by various animals, and these have been passed on from person to person, each one, before he dies, appointing the next possessor. The complete set of charms is supposed to consist of—besides the white stone of the Pygmies—the scales of the Great Horned Serpent; the claws of the Blue Panther, which heralds the approach of death; the feathers of the Giant Exploding Wren, which was described to me as bursting from a hollow tree and soaring away "like a jet plane"; the castor of the White Beaver; the sharp bone (an evil charm); the dried corn bug; the small mummified hand; the hair from the flying head of the Wind; the bones or the powder made from the bones of the Great Naked Bear; the small whistle or flute made from the wingbone of an eagle; the bag of sacred tobacco; the powder to be used against witches; the claws or teeth of several wild animals of the non-supernatural kind; a small war club; a small bow and arrow; a small pestle and mortar; miniature wooden bowls and spoons; a wooden doll; and the clairvoyant eye-oil. All of these charms—even those that are beneficent, such as the feathers of the Exploding Wren—must be sung to, because, like the Pygmies, if neglected, they may become angry. People do not talk about

these charms, but the members of the society know
the owners. If—as happened on the evening we attended this ceremony—the host does not possess such
a charm, the section that is devoted to them is not
performed.

In the second intermission of the cycle—as had happened when the boy was entertained by the Pygmies
—a saucepan of strawberry syrup, which at that season
had to be made of frozen strawberries, was passed
around in a ritual manner, and everybody took a taste
of it from a paddle-like wooden spoon. At the end
of the final section, the Little People "go back to their
rocks, over the hills, beyond the horizon," which is
imagined as an enormous inverted bowl, under the rim
of which one may crawl. "Ten campfires"—that is,
nights—"they take." I was later shown the kind of
terrain in which the Pygmies are supposed to live:
the rocky heights on the reservation which for human
beings are uninhabitable but among which the Pygmies
could perhaps keep dry after the flooding of these
lands by the Engineers.

When the lights were turned on at the end of the
performance, the hostess and the master of ceremonies
emerged from the neighboring room in which they
had been occupied with television. The sound track
was now turned off, but the rest of the TV audience
remained and watched the silent shadows. The old
lady took her seat in a chair as if on a kind of throne,
and the twelve women who had sung the chorus paid
her homage by dancing before her—that is, they
paraded past her, circling a chair in the middle of the

room, and when they came to where she was seated, turned toward her and did special steps. They were likely to laugh in their effort to sustain the crescendo spurts that are the pattern of most Iroquois dancing, and to encourage one another with gentle little pushes not to let down the dance. Then the master of cere- monies, in a formal speech, expressed thanks to the hostess, the musicians and the singers; and finally the corn soup was served and a platter of chunks of meat, which they ate, old style, with their fingers. Every- one, as the custom is, had brought a pail and took it home filled with soup.

On a subsequent evening we were asked to dinner by a lady of the Cornplanter connection. Her hus- band—a railroad man and a veteran of Anzio who had been wounded twice—was a descendant of one of those "white captives" who had been adopted by the Indians. The captive had been Pennsylvania Dutch, and the family had kept the German name. Its present bearer, our host, came downstairs freshly shaved and in a fresh gray nylon shirt. With his well-brushed iron-gray hair and a face more expressive than most Iroquois faces, he seemed rather European than Indian. The Seneca pronunciation has something of a singsong drawl that might be mistaken for that of some Scan- dinavian language. Our hostess was a clever and attrac- tive woman who often received white visiting scholars. The house, which had been built in the eighties and had belonged to her husband's father, was low-ceil- inged, light and pleasant. There was a piano on one side of the living room, and we sat on two couches that faced one another across one of those low long tables such as white people but not Indians use for cocktails and on which were lying copies of *McCall's Magazine* and some clippings about the Kinzua Dam. The family felt strongly about the dam, and we talked about this before dinner. Our hostess was an excellent cook and gave us potroast, mashed potatoes and frozen peas, with celery and pickles on the side, fruit salad in a jellied form and a homemade lemon pie. (When I returned for the Strawberry Festival in June, she regaled my son and me with a magnificent strawberry shortcake.) Just after we had finished dinner, the daughter, only child of the family, came in with a young admirer. She was a very pretty girl, more oriental in type than either of her parents seemed, who wore a black dress in good taste and red leather high-heeled shoes. She was a teacher and wanted to try for a scholarship at Teachers' College, Columbia, in order to train herself to deal with "exceptional children." Fenton said he would recommend her and tell them how strong she was, how, the afternoon before, when we had called there first, she had handed him up from the cellar, as if it had been nothing at all, a sixty-pound sack of potatoes that had almost had him reeling. Later on, when her application was being discussed with more seriousness, she remembered this and cautioned Fenton, "Don't you dare say anything about those potatoes!" This surprised me, for the strength of these Seneca women is usually a source of pride; but in the case of this fine-featured girl, I imagine that

Indian muscle had somehow come to seem to her incongruous with the academic career she had trained
for. Her companion was a quiet boy, with spectacles,
a crew cut and a yellow sweater, but dark-skinned,
unmistakably Indian.

In the living room, after dinner, Fenton introduced
the subject of the Dark Dance, which had been something of an institution in the family of our hostess's
father. It was strange—but a phenomenon I had noticed before—to see this intelligent woman, who was
easy and gay in her dealings with whites, become,
when these matters were touched on, so silent, sober
and thoughtful. The instinct to preserve Indian secrets
seems to be felt by almost every Indian; but in this
case I thought that our hostess had been carried back
to something very ancient which had been also a part
of her childhood world and which was difficult to
explain to outsiders. She had not thought of it, I felt,
at all in terms of her white contacts in which English
was spoken. Her father, she however explained, had
regularly put up the Dark Dance because he had felt
that his family owed the Great Little People a special
debt. An uncle of his, when a boy of ten, had disappeared one day in the woods and had not reappeared for a month. They thought he had been lost
or killed. He came back, but he could not remember
what had happened to him during his absence. They
guessed that he had been taken by the Pygmies, in
order—as their habit was—to save him from some
threatening misfortune. Our hostess thought a moment and then added—as if to bridge over the gap

between the world of the Little People and that of *McCall's* and the Kinzua Dam: "It was wild here then."

We inquired about the handed-down animal charms. This matter has remained obscure. Are there really, among Indians today, individuals who believe themselves the guardians of such amulets as the scales of the Great Horned Serpent? But she could not tell us much about this, and Fenton went on to ask about passages in the songs that he did not understand. One expression she at first translated as, "You are about to go,"—then, after a moment's pondering, said that the English of it was really, "Get out!" But what was the crow, Fenton asked, which was mentioned at the end of the cycle? He had told me of this as a charming touch. When the Little People return to their rocks—"over the hills, beyond the horizon"—they were evidently followed by a crow, the last thing to disappear. Was this bird a messenger? If so, it seemed strange that it had not been introduced before. "You've got that a little wrong," she answered. "That's not about a crow—it says, 'Let's eat.'" In Seneca words, apparently, the presence or absence of a glottal stop may make all the difference in meaning: *ga-ga*, crow (with glottal stops after each of the vowels); *ewonde-gáhga*, "They will soon eat with us." (Dr. Fenton tells me, however, that the second of these words has the first for its root: to eat in this sense is to pick like crows.)

Our hostess had said that it was wild out there in the days of the Little People. I was to learn that it was still fairly wild. They also discussed, after dinner, the encounter of a nephew of hers with a bear. This boy, who had been then sixteen but who, as I afterward found when I met him, belonged to the Seneca giant breed, enormously tall and strong—his nickname was "Horse"—had been out hunting with his dog in the snow and, through stumbling on a snow-covered stone, had started sliding on a frozen slope. He had heard his dog barking, and at the bottom he saw a black bear, which had been feeding on a dead skunk. The dog—a big "Indian collie," a shaggy mongrel with police-dog blood—tried to attack the bear, which knocked him away with a blow of its paw. The dog ran to his master and the bear came after him. The boy shot twice at the bear, wounding it in the neck and head; but the bear continued its charge and knocked the rifle out of the boy's hand. It now tried to get its arms around him in order to hug him to death. The dog began to bite its hind legs, and while its attention was thus distracted, the boy slugged the bear in the head. The animal clawed the boy and slugged back, and the boy was attempting to strangle it when, weakened by its wounds, it fell backwards, holding the boy in its arms. He fainted, and when he came to, the dog was standing over him, and the bear lay beside him dead. The boy and the dog got home, and the boy spent some time in the hospital, where his lacerated torso and legs were dressed. The dog, too, had been badly clawed. I later met "Horse's" father, who told me that the bear had weighed six hundred pounds and that he had had to drag it in with a truck. They had skinned it, and it was eaten by the family.

This actual adventure reminded me of certain of the Seneca folk tales. Niágwaihégowa, the Great Naked Bear, is the most terrible of the mythical animals. He is sometimes overcome by a boy, and there is a story in which a dog also figures. Here the dog makes a rush at the bear but the bear opens its jaws and takes a breath, and the dog disappears down its throat. The boy picks up a stump and dashes at the bear, crying, "I'm after you, you cannot escape me!" Now, these are the very words which Niágwaihégowa is in the habit of using himself, and which put a spell on his prey so that they helplessly fall into his claws. The monster has to flee from the boy and is eventually worn out by the chase and compelled to ransom his life by surrendering the magic teeth which, along with the powder from his bones, were to figure among the charm-holders' amulets.

The closeness of the Indians to the animal world is thus even today much in evidence. The problem of relations with the animals among which the Indians lived and which were their only fellow-creatures is at the center of the Iroquois culture. Says the last of the Stone Giants (the only survivor of those who were crushed to death at Onondaga by the Holder-up of the Heavens) to a hunter who, lost in the woods, has discovered his hiding place: "Be wise and learn my secrets, how disease is healed, how man and beast and plant may talk together and learn one another's missions. Go and live with the trees and birds and beasts and fish, and learn to honor them as your own brothers." And the Iroquois still, through their clans,

bear the names of these animal brothers; they invoke
them in their medicine societies and they imitate them
in their dances. It seemed to me natural enough, in one
of my visits to Onondaga, to find Louis Papineau,
the tree surgeon, feeding with milk from a bottle a
baby raccoon which, abandoned by its mother, he had
picked up on a walk through the woods and which
accompanied our conversation with an almost spar-
rowlike chirping. But it did surprise me a little that
President Cornelius Seneca, who had spent the best
part of his life as superintendent of construction for
Bethlehem Steel, should say to me, "I sometimes
wonder whether I mightn't have been better off in
our original state of life in the woods. We didn't fight
each other much—our life was peaceful then. I
wouldn't have known about modern civilization, so
I wouldn't have known any better. I could have lived
with the animals then."

But here as in other connections—like the television next door to the Dark Dance—one runs into incongruities. There is a state park near the Allegany
Reservation, which, since located on higher ground,
would not, like the Seneca country, be subjected to
annual flooding by the proposed flood-control dam
and in which the raccoons and the bears are being
cherished with so much kindness that they fearlessly
come out to meet visitors in the hope of getting something to eat. This park was stocked at one time with
bison, which—in spite of the respect for that animal
expressed by the Buffalo Dance—were to become a
great nuisance to the Senecas. The bison liked to

visit the reservation and they would sometimes look in at the windows. A woman once opened her door and found one standing before her, as if he were about to come in. The Indians were afraid of these bison. They could not hunt them: these animals belonged to the white man. Neither could they treat them as brothers. They could establish no relation with them. They could only shoo them away without permanently getting rid of them, as they have done with the white police, the surveyors and the engineers who have recently been invading their reservations.

The first event of the New Year's ceremonies proper is the giving of names to children who have been born during the previous six months (the ceremony occurs twice a year). This is called "They Boil the Babies"— which means merely that the kettle has been hung for the feast. The English names chosen by the Indians— either because they have become Christians or for convenience in dealing with the whites—seem often the results of caprice or accident. One finds among the Senecas such names as Cecil and Basil (pronounced Ceecil and Baysil) and Beverly Joyce, which sound as if they had been chosen out of fiction magazines. But the Indian names are traditional and have always some appropriate meaning. There are in our sense no family names—there are only the clan designations—but each clan has its own set of personal names, and it is said to be possible for an Indian to be able to tell from the name alone to which clan another Indian belongs. Thus one clan will specialize in names that have to do with hunting, another with gambling, etc. Two members of the same clan may not have the same name simultaneously: the child has to be given a name that is not at the time in use. At puberty, the boy or girl is given another name, which has been that of a maternal relative who has in childhood had the same name as hers. In the case of an hereditary chief, his title becomes his name. The heads of the religion, the Keepers of the Faith, have also their special titles.

It had snowed the night we arrived, and when we went to the Longhouse the following morning, they were only just digging it out, and the services did not start till the afternoon. The Longhouse at Allegany is larger than the others I saw, but not so well kept up as some. The two doors for the men and the women are on the lengthwise front facing the road. There are high windows both front and back. The inside of the building must once have been white and the benches for the audience red; but it is a long time now since they were painted and these colors now are hardly to be recognized. The benches stretch along the wall, in tiers like shallow bleachers; and in the middle of the room is a backless bench—probably at one time white —on which the singers and drummers, while performing, sit astride or sideways. There is a wood-burning stove at each end of the room, and these heat it so effectively that even on a very cold morning one would be roasted if one sat too close to them. The only things that seemed new and clean were a couple of brooms hung up high on the wall. There is an attic above the ceiling, in which equipment is kept and which is only accessible through a trap-door with no ladder or steps to reach it. When they want to get anything out, they simply upend a bench so that it makes an inclined plane, and one of the boys—with the Iroquois sureness of foot—runs up it like a squirrel, only steadying himself with one hand on the back.

When we returned in the afternoon, the ritual had already begun. The master of ceremonies was murmuring the prayers and putting pinches of tobacco in the open stove. He sounded much like a priest or a Protestant minister in the more routine parts of a service. He was gray-haired and spectacled, with features that did not seem strikingly Indian, very sober and in his delivery a little monotonous: his only inflection of tone came at the end of a sentence. With a handful of others to hear him and assent to his admonitions with a "*Nyoh*" ("It shall be done"), which sounded very much like "Amen," he was thanking the Creator and His appointed helpers—the Sun, the Moon and the Stars, the Thunders and the Winds—for the blessings they brought to the Indians, under the roof of the shabby old Longhouse, in the midst of the smothering snow that was keeping the congregation away. A few more people did arrive, but this made only twelve in all, and the man who was to take us to the Dark Dance that night "put up" a modest feast in the women's half of the room—the sexes sit at opposite ends—which was accompanied by a modest dance that circled the bench in the middle, to the beat of the water-drums and the cowhorn rattles. I asked this man on a later occasion whether they ever did the War Dance nowadays, and he answered, "Not very often—only once in a while when people ask for it." The young people did not care for it. The War Dance is likely to be long on account of the interruptions which are one of its special features: at any hiatus in the dancing, a speech, facetious or serious, may be made by anyone taking part. I asked how the warwhoop sounded, and he gave it with the mildness of reluctance. "I ought to have a tomahawk," he said. It occurred to me that it might be embarrassing, out of key with their present situation, for them nowadays to perform the War Dance. I learned later, from an account in Parker, that "the attitudes are those of the violent passions and hence are not very graceful. In this dance may be seen at the same time or instant one in the attitude of attack, another of the defense; one drawing the bow, another striking with the war club; others listening and others striking the foe."*

The dances and the preachings of the following days—the ceremonies as a whole are always known in English as "the doin's"—presented a variety of entertainment and brought out a better attendance. The male dancers in the Buffalo Dance do not wear buffalo skins, as they do in the Southwest (though they used to wear black buffalo masks, with bristling hair and leather ears, human noses, huge glaring eyes and huge grinning teeth), but simply move heavily with a

* From a lecture by Nicholson H. Parker on "Indian Dances and Their Influence," included as an appendix by Arthur C. Parker in his *Life of General Ely S. Parker.*

stamping step. When a little boy came too near and
threatened to get in the way of the herd, the leader
tossed his head at him, buffalo-fashion. In the Bear
Dance the dancers gave grunts and growls. A plate
of honey or a saucepan of strawberry syrup was taken
first to the door and a spoonful or so spilled outside as an offering to the powerful beast to whom
homage is being paid; then it was set on the bench in
the center so that the dancers could help themselves.
They are supposed to plunge into it greedily, pawing
it with their hands. This is the dance of a medicine
society, and one of its features is that the dancer may
become possessed by the bear. The women may be
members as well as the men, and are supposed to be
especially liable to this. Fenton says that Jesse Cornplanter, an intelligent man, who had studied the customs of his people, once told him that, watching these
performances for years, he had always assumed that
the frenzy of the women was something deliberately acted till he had noticed that the persons affected
were likely to be high-keyed or excitable types, and
came to the conclusion that—as in Voodoo possession
—they were really carried away. Though the Bear
Dance was many times repeated in the course of the
ceremonies I watched, I saw nothing that suggested
this phenomenon. The only thing approaching it I
noted was the behavior of a young man, at the end
of the dance, who sat down and—somewhat ostenta-
tiously—gobbled up all that was left of the syrup.

There were also two dances devoted to the corn.
The women carried ears of corn, and they sang what

the ears were supposed to be saying, "We are happy to be home,"—that is, to be hung up for the winter. It is a part of this ceremony that baskets are taken around to the houses, where they receive contributions of corn. There were other dances, also, which made these rounds. The dancers had originally, it seems, called at every house in the village; but in latterday Allegany, they had visited only seven on the reservation—omitting, I suppose, the Christians; today they visit only two. When they were leaving, a gun was fired outside, and, to herald their return, it was fired again. I was crippled at the time with gout, and I could not accompany them on these expeditions, which, in the deep snow, were heavy going, but stayed behind and talked with an anxious old man, who was one of the pillars of the Longhouse. I asked about the Sacrifice of the White Dog, which was still in Lewis Morgan's time the central event of these mid-winter rites. A special breed of dogs was kept for this purpose—the whiteness represented purity, any dark hairs had to be pulled out—and one of them was ritually strangled on the day that the ceremonies began. The body was then hung on a pole, with many colored ribbons tied to it, the offerings of individuals, who were supposed to be rewarded with blessings, and on the last day it was burned at a wooden altar. He answered that so far as his memory went this had never been performed in Allegany; but I was to find that in at least one of the other reservations the custom had lasted longer, and a description of it was later given me by a man who had got it firsthand from an

older person who had actually seen it. The killing of
the dog had taken place a little way off from the
Longhouse. They had wrapped the dog in bright ribbons and put wampum around his neck. The man who
was officiating had cleaned him up carefully. He
caressed the dog, then slowly choked him to death,
and he died "without even a kick or a flinch." (I
heard from another source that the strangling was
done with a rope, the ends of which were held by
two men who stood on either side of the dog.) "He
knew that he was going to die and wanted to die.
They burned him, and there came up a high wind
blowing thirty or forty miles an hour, but the smoke
was not affected. They dropped the tobacco into the
fire, and the smoke went straight up like a ray of
light, and it never even shook when it hit the high
wind above the trees. The Indians watched the smoke
until they couldn't see it no more." The man who had
told the story had "tried to leave the fire, and something was pushing him, and he couldn't see exactly
what it was. The Indians prayed with tobacco, and
they asked the Creator for something and it was
granted to them afterwards. The smoke took the message direct to the Creator." There is a movement
now—though not yet, I believe, of any very considerable proportions—to return to the White Dog Sacrifice. Some of the more extreme nationalists seem to
feel that the recital of the Handsome Lake Code and
the mere words of the invocations are, without this,
not sufficiently effective. The people who want the
White Dog are, as it were, the Fundamentalists—or,

better perhaps, the High Church party, in the Iroquois religious world. But since the ceremonies I saw were performed in the Allegany Reservation, a part of the Seneca Republic which has dissociated itself from the League and separated Church and State, they had no political significance, as they did sometimes in the other reservations, where they contributed to the nationalist movement, and nobody was worrying about the White Dog. The Longhouse here was free from fanaticism and had, in fact, only a moderate following. "Come around here in two years' time," said the apprehensive old man with whom I was talking, "and you'll find the Longhouse empty." Yet this may have been partly the illusion that we all of us tend to have when our energies begin to slacken: the notion that the world which we knew and of which we ourselves were part is dying out along with *us;* for others, I found, took a different view. There were obviously younger men who were training themselves to carry on. One of them was a husky broad-shouldered ex-soldier, who was sometimes allowed to preside. Outside the Longhouse one day he talked about the Kinzua Dam. He had served, he said, in Europe under Eisenhower, and he had always been loyal to his general: "I did whatever he said." And now he thought he "might expect that the thirty-third President of the United States would redeem the promises of the first President." This was said not with indignation but with the solemn-faced dry Indian humor.

The fourth day of our attendance at the ceremonies was rather an off-session at the Longhouse. A blizzard seemed commencing; it was colder than ever. But in the morning they played on the floor the traditional peachpit game. The clans of a tribe are divided into what the anthropologists call two "moieties," and in this game a man or woman from one of these halves plays against a man or woman from the other. The play is started off with a warwhoop, quite startling in the quiet room: it was the only time I heard it in the Longhouse. The pits are black on one side and white on the other. They are dropped into a wooden bowl, and the object is, by bumping the bowl on the floor—on which a folded blanket is laid—to bring all of one color up. The supporters of each of the moieties stand over the kneeling players and, by their sharp cries of encouragement in rhythm with the brisk rap and rattle of the bowl, keep up a high pitch of excitement. One wonders whether there can possibly be any technique for obtaining the desired result. Perhaps not: the game, it seems, may go on for days. But on the morning we saw it played—since this perfect score was never attained—they must have decided the winner on the basis of the highest proportion. This game, too, was taken around to the houses.

The other main feature of this day at the Longhouse is the annual guessing of dreams. To the Iroquois, these are of enormous importance. Their conception of dreams, as has been explained by Mr. Anthony F. C. Wallace in a paper to which I am much indebted,* has a good deal in common with Freud's, and

---

* *Dreams and the Wishes of the Soul: A Type of Psychoanalytic Theory among the Seventeenth Century Iroquois,* in the *American Anthropologist* of April 1958, published by the American Anthropological Society.

the dreams of the Iroquois, like the Freudian ones, had sometimes to be interpreted by someone else. There is a strange account of their influence on the Iroquois's cousins, the Hurons, in one of the early Jesuit "Relations," by Father Paul Ragueneau, who is writing in 1648: "In addition," he says, "to the desires which we generally have that are free, or at least voluntary in us, [and] which arise from a previous knowledge of some goodness that we imagine to exist in the thing desired, the Hurons believe that our souls have other desires, which are, as it were, inborn and concealed. These, they say, come from the depths of the soul, not through any knowledge, but by means of a certain blind transporting of the soul to certain objects; these transports might in the language of philosophy be called *Desideria Innata*, to distinguish them from the former, which are called *Desideria Elicita*. Now, they believe that our soul makes these natural desires known by means of dreams, which are its language. Accordingly, when these desires are accomplished, it is satisfied; but, on the contrary, if it be not granted what it desires, it becomes angry, and not only does not give its body the good and the happiness that it wished to procure for it, but often it also revolts against the body, causing various diseases, and even death. . . . In consequence of these erroneous [as thought Father Ragueneau] ideas, most of the Hurons are very careful to note their dreams, and to provide the soul with what it has pictured to them during their sleep. If, for instance, they have seen a javelin in a dream, they try to get it; if they have dreamed that they gave a feast, they will give one on awakening, if they have the wherewithal; and so on with other things. And they call this *Ondinnonk*—a secret desire of the soul manifested by a dream."

Of the Iroquois themselves, says another of the Jesuits, Father Jacques Fremin, "[they] have, properly speaking, only a single Divinity—the dream. To it they render their submission, and follow all its orders with the utmost exactness. The Tsonnontouens [Seneca] are more attached to this superstition than any of the others; their Religion in this respect becomes even a matter of scruple; whatever it be that they think they have done in their dreams, they believe themselves absolutely obliged to execute at the earliest moment. The other nations content themselves with observing those of their dreams which are the most important; but this people, which has the reputation of living more religiously than its neighbors, would think itself guilty of a great crime if it failed in its observance of a single dream. The people think only of that, they talk about nothing else, and all their cabins are filled with their dreams. They spare no pains, no industry, to show their attachment thereto, and their folly in this particular goes to such an excess as would be hard to imagine. He who has dreamed during the night that he was bathing, runs immediately, as soon as he rises, all naked, to several cabins, in each of which he has a kettleful of water thrown over his body, however cold the weather may be. Another who has dreamed that he was taken prisoner and burned alive, has found himself bound and burned like a captive on the next day, being persuaded that, by thus satisfying his dream, this fidelity will avert from him the pain and infamy of captivity and death—which, according to what he has learned from his Divinity, he is otherwise bound to suffer among his enemies. Some have been known to go as far as Quebec, travelling a hundred and fifty leagues, for the sake of getting a dog that they had dreamed of buying there." Another Jesuit, Father de Quens, writes of a Cayuga that, "having dreamed that he gave a feast of human flesh, invited all the chief men of the Country to his cabin to hear a matter of importance. When they had assembled, he told them that he was ruined, as he had had a dream impossible of fulfillment; that his ruin would entail that of the whole Nation; and that a universal overthrow and destruction of the earth was to be expected. He enlarged at great length on the subject, and then asked them to guess his dream. All struck wide of the mark, until one man, suspecting the truth, said to him: 'Thou wishest to give a feast of human flesh. Here, take my brother; I place him in thy hands to be cut up on the spot, and put into the kettle.' All present were seized with fright, except the dreamer, who said that his dream required a woman. Superstition went so far that they adorned a girl with all the riches of the Country—with bracelets, collars, crowns, and all the ornaments used by women—just as victims of old were decked for immolation; and that poor innocent, not knowing why she was made to look so pretty, was actually led to the place appointed for the sacrifice. All the people attended to witness so strange a spectacle. The guests took their places, and the public victim was led into the middle of the circle. She was delivered to the Sacrificer, who was the very one for whom the sacrifice was to be made. He took her; they watched his actions, and pitied that innocent girl; but, when they thought him about to deal the death-blow, he cried out: 'I am satisfied; my dream requires nothing further.'"

The New Year's ceremonies of the Indians involved, when the Jesuits first witnessed them, what these Frenchmen called "the Festival of Fools." On February 22, 1656, "immediately upon the announcement of the festival . . . nothing was seen but men, women and children running like maniacs through the streets—this, however, in a far different manner from that of masquerades in Europe, the greater number being nearly naked and apparently insensible to the cold, which is well-nigh unbearable to those who are most warmly clothed." They demanded that people should guess their dreams, which were only "expressed in riddles, phrases of covert meaning, songs and occasionally in gestures alone. Consequently, a good Oedipus is not always to be found. Yet they will not leave a place till their thought is divined; and if they meet with delay, or a disinclination or inability to guess it, they threaten to burn up everything—a menace which is only too often executed, as we very nearly learned to our own cost. One of these maniacs stole into our cabin, determined that we should guess his dream and satisfy it." It turned out that his dream had been that he had killed a French priest, and the man with whom the Jesuits were staying presented him with a coat which was supposed to have been taken from the body of a Frenchman.

This custom in a milder form has continued to the present day. The dreams are sometimes satisfied, as in the case above, by purely symbolic means. A Seneca of the Cornplanter tract, sometime in the nineteenth century, once dreamed, Mr. Wallace tells us, "that a certain young woman was alone in a canoe, in the middle of a stream, without a paddle. The dreamer invited the young lady to a dream-guessing ceremony at his home. Various people gathered, and each one tried to guess what the dream was. Finally the dream was guessed. A miniature canoe with a paddle was thereupon presented to the girl." It seemed logical to the Senecas that by this means a real accident could be averted. It may be mentioned that Cornplanter himself, when he knew that his services to the whites had aroused the disapproval of his people, made the rounds of his neighbors at New Year's, explaining that he had just had a dream and inviting them to guess what it was. He was "nearly naked," says Morgan, and "shivering with cold." On the third day, a clairvoyant friend told him that his nakedness certainly meant that he had dreamed he would be stripped of his title of chief; "that he had had a sufficient term of service for the good of the nation."

The propounding and satisfying of dream desires is no longer, as it was in the seventeenth century, allowed to create dangerous situations. This custom has dwindled today to a point where it is said to resemble

that parlor game in which the company, by a series
of questions, has to guess what historical character
somebody has in mind. But on January 27, 1958, we
did not see even this in the Longhouse. The officials
were there to receive the dreamers, and we waited for
over an hour, but in that time not one applicant
arrived.

The following night, however, was the ceremonies'
highest point. We went at six and stayed till twelve.
There were more than a hundred people, and the
evening was supposed to have been unusually successful. There was, if anything, an even wider variation of
types than I had seen in the other reservations—owing, says Parker, to the Senecas' having taken in, when
they themselves had been crushed by Sullivan's Raid,
the remnants of twenty "broken tribes": notably,
the Delawares, the Mohicans, the Foxes, the Cherokees, the Nanticokes, the Shawnees, the Wyandots,
the Neutrals, the Eries, the Mingoes and the Chippewas. And yet there seems to be a dominant Seneca
character and, I should say, even a dominant physical strain. (I understand that from the records of the
Civil War it would appear that the Senecas who
took part in it were of unusual strength and stature.)
There are some scrubby ones, but there are also
the stalwarts, who are very imposing figures. The
wife of the master of ceremonies, who was herself
a Keeper of the Faith, was enormously broad and
enormously tall, a strong character and a good
kindly woman, who had had two sons in the war

—one killed, one imprisoned by the Germans; a third is at present serving with the American forces in Germany. She had herself served as a boilermaker during the war, and her prodigies of strength were legendary. Bespectacled, she sat on the highest bench, only dancing—her legs were great columns—in special important ceremonies; but she descended on one occasion to remove the hats of the drummer and the singer, and when a child was running about the floor, she captured him and, since, having no lap, she was unable to put him on it, she simply held him out before her while he loudly and steadily howled. The children were much underfoot. The one whom the giantess had sought to restrain was a lively and bright little boy, with whom I played in the intermissions, amusing him with a jumping mouse made out of a pocket handkerchief. He danced with his elders in certain of the dances. At three, he had perfectly learned the steps, and, holding on to the hand of his mother or father, he participated with earnestness and energy. When I winked as he was dancing past me, he would not give me a smile. His mother was also an enormous woman—though not so tall and monumental as the other—whose feet, as is characteristic of Seneca women, were astonishingly small and mobile and whom a nose red and swollen with acne did not prevent from being attractive.

The dances were many and varied. The highly valued Bear Society, at the instance of those it was supposed to have cured and who desired to insure themselves against a recurrence of their ailments, had to perform its dance some fifteen times, once for each of its patients, till the singer's voice had pretty well given out. The Fish Dance is a young people's ceremony performed by men and women both. They take first a few steps to the right, and then a few steps to the left—which is supposed to represent the technique of salmon in making their way upstream. For this, the girl chooses her partner. They dance not side by side but face to face, so that every other person is dancing backwards, and they reverse at the end of each song, so that each is now facing a different partner. We also saw the Naked Dance done, but in a very much modified form from that which once horrified the Jesuits. The men and girls had then danced stark naked, and on this night alone in the year did a couple who belonged to the same clan have license to go to bed with one another. This dance is now called Shaking the Bush— the explanation of which name that was given me was that each of the dancers is imagined to be holding a small branch. They dance in pairs, two boys, two girls, and reverse as they do in the Fish Dance. There are speeches between the dances. At one point, the master of ceremonies admonished those present that the people must make a better showing at the Longhouse —"or how will the Great Spirit know you are Indians?" It was curious to hear them switch from the solemnity of their ancient language to colloquial American speech. "Well," said one elderly man, after a particularly strenuous performance, "it's a great life if you don't weaken!"

Drinking is supposed to be barred, but at one point

two drunken young men came in and sat behind us. "How would you like to be scalped, white man?" asked one, leaning over my shoulder. He was a rather good-looking fellow, who evidently fancied himself as Ronald Colman, since he had grown a narrow Colman mustache. I pointed to the bald patch on the top of my head and said I had been scalped already. They then demanded what clan I belonged to, implying that I had no right to be there. Fenton astonished them by turning around and telling them in their own language that he belonged to the Hawk Clan, of which in that reservation he had been made an honorary member. "Who am I?" said the first young man. "Who's he?" Fenton gave them both their names. They were more civil after this, though still aggressive. The young man told me not to "get mad." His companion was garrulous, boastful and boring in a very un-Indian way, offering to explain the ceremonies: "What do you want to know? I can tell you anything!" The other began to rib him, telling me that his father was Polish and that he himself was a Falseface—a kind of grotesque demon—who didn't need to wear a mask. I now resorted to the rather mean device of trying him with a little Russian, to which he mumblingly replied and shut up. It was evident that the other young man had an itch to take part in the dances but did not quite dare to trust himself. He finally got to the point of going on the floor for a round or two, then gave up and went out to drink more beer.

The evening was not, however, a mere string of de-tached events. It had a certain dramatic structure. The

A Huskface mask, made on the Cattaraugus Seneca Reservation and now in the Museum of the State of New York at Albany. *Photograph Courtesy of New York State Museum and Science Service.*

Falsefaces were present and the Huskfaces were coming to celebrate the New Year. Three times in the
course of the evening do the Huskfaces invade the
Longhouse. The first and the second times it is merely
their heralds who appear. A prodigious rattling and
scraping of sticks is heard on the clapboarding outside. "Watch that door! Watch that door!" said the
young man behind me. The two doors at either end
of the Longhouse partly open, then close again. The
audience waits in suspense; the same thing is once
more repeated. Then the doors are thrown violently
open, and two supernatural figures appear. They are
of towering height and wear overalls; their faces are
round masks, quite expressionless, which have been
braided out of straw-colored cornhusks—the eyes
two round holes, the mouth small, the nose a tiny
ear wrapped in husk—and are fringed, like the sun
in an old-fashioned drawing, with an irradiation of
fine little corn-leaves. These heralds charge through
the room, holding before them, horizontally, long
staves. They pass by one another without touching,
and each goes out the opposite door, which is immediately closed behind him.

An hour of dancing now passes, toward the end of
which the masked clowns appear. Some of these are
conventional Falsefaces—a term to be more fully explained: red masks with distorted features. Others are
original comic creations: a Chinaman; a hooligan with
a grinning mouth, a brown derby and an old tailcoat
worn with pyjama bottoms; a creature who is evidently a caricature of the white man's conception of

an Indian, a mask painted bright red, with a deeply furrowed forehead and a profile which looks like a parody of the Pontiac signs that punctuate the New York State roads; and another who is evidently a parody of the paleface's ideal of feminine beauty— bulging with enormous bosoms and enamelled with a cold-cream complexion—of the type of Jayne Mansfield and Marilyn Monroe. (These costumes are often improvised from the donations of incongruous old clothing that are sent them by the white charities.) It is a feature of this masquerade that young and old disguise their ages, and that the sexes exchange their clothes. The men and women, it seems, even sometimes swap costumes between the acts in order to fool the audience and one another. I tried to spot the women by their smaller feet, then discovered that the Seneca men, in spite of their sometimes gigantic build, had very small feet, too. All this must give a certain sense of liberation. As somebody said of a mimed flirtation taking place between the hooligan and the Hollywood beauty, it might be that an aged woman—without either of them being aware of it—was making passes at her little grandson. The clowns first approach the spectators with a curious nasal grunting—"Hon-hon-hon-hon" (the *on* pronounced as in French)—which is their only form of speech, and holding out a gloved right hand with the fingers wide apart. They are asking for cigarettes. When you give the clown one, he or she takes it with his left hand, jerks it up in a formalized gesture and sticks it between two of the fingers of the other hand. A second or third cigarette goes between two other fingers, so that the clown is clipping them stiffly very much as a magician does his billiard balls in the multiplying billiard ball trick. The clown, in return for this gift, after putting the cigarettes in his pocket, hands the donor the turtle-shell rattle which he has been holding under his arm. While the spectator beats time with the rattle, he performs, to the delight of the audience, a kind of frenetic breakdown. The actors, too, obviously love all this. There is something rather sexy about it. The man who is playing the beauty abounds in seductive appeal; the girls who are male goblins abandon all feminine decorum. There is a game of stealing cigarettes out of one another's pockets. But suddenly the frolic stops: the banging on the door is heard again. Consternation seizes the clowns. The bogus Indian and the Hollywood beauty huddle together in panic. The heralds of the Huskfaces again flash through with their wonderful suddenness and swiftness that makes them seem truly from another world. When they are gone, the stage Indian stands forth and shakes his fist at the door.

This is followed, when the clowns have left, after an interval of more commonplace dancing, by the ritual of the real Falsefaces, one of the most important medicine societies, which requires some explanation. I have told how the Stone Giants were destroyed at Onondaga and how one of their number escaped, and I have also mentioned that a hunter later came upon him by accident in the forest, and that the Giant admonished this man to "be wise and learn how disease is healed." The hunter, after this, fell asleep, and in

his dreams he beheld strange faces, and when he
wakened, he found himself lying at the foot of a great
basswood tree, which, as he looked at it, took on a
face like the ones he had seen in his dreams. For the
giant had proliferated a new race of beings. When
the Creator had made mankind and the rest of the
natural life of the earth—for He had not himself made
the earth—He met, on a tour of inspection, this last of
the Stone Giants, who claimed to be master of the
world. He carried an enormous rattle, a snapping
turtle's shell with a handle, and he shook it so hard that
he scared all the beasts, and he also made a frightening
sound with his mouth. "Very well," the Creator said.
"Let us have a trial of power. Let us see which of us
can move that mountain." The Stone Giant commanded the mountain to move, and when he and the
Creator looked again, they saw that it had come just
a little nearer. Then it was the Creator's turn, and the
giant felt a rush behind him, and, quickly turning his
head, he was hit by the mountain, which was right
at his back. The Creator said, "I am the master of
this place. I can create life. What has happened to
your face that makes it so twisted?" Hence the bent
nose of the mask which Standing Arrow had shown
me at Schoharie Creek; hence the writhen mouth,
which is uttering a cry of pain. But the giant had still
his power, he had already infected the world, and
he would always be able to send illness on men. He
told the hunter who had found him in the forest
that mankind, if it wanted to get rid of disease,
would have to make faces like his out of the wood

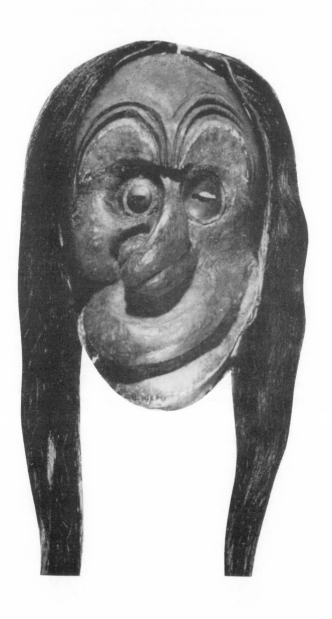

A Falseface mask made on the Six Nations Reserve on Grand River, Ontario. *Photograph courtesy of New York State Museum and Science Service.*

of the basswood tree and wear them and perform certain rites. Such a mask is called Ga-gón-sah (*on* nasal), Its Face. They are not, I understand, any longer produced by the method prescribed by the Giant, though there still survives a special ceremony performed in the presence of the tree itself. The mask was supposed to be made while the tree was still alive, so that its life might be retained by the mask. The face was first drawn on the trunk, then carved to a depth of six inches, then, finally, gouged out of the tree. But the makers of Falsefaces today simply carve out their masks at home. The head of the Gagónsah Society is a woman, the only woman official, who is called the Keeper of the Masks. The Falsefaces were mobilized at Tonawanda as late as 1849 to ward off a cholera epidemic, and they are still sometimes called in today.

The Falsefaces played a conspicuous rôle, very weird and yet genuinely impressive, in the ceremonies as I saw them at Allegany. They crawled in—I think, three of them—on their hands and knees through the door at the women's end, wearing their frightful masks with long manes of black or white horsehair and uttering that "awful sound" of which I had first heard from Standing Arrow and by means of which the Stone Giant had attempted to dismay the Creator. Of this sound the mock-Falseface clowns had been able to give only amateurish imitations. But these were the real thing, not clowns but true celebrants and accomplished performers. I thought that their loud nasal grunting, like a bubbling of liquid metal, must be produced by some instrument like the "swazzle" that is used for the voice of Punch in the Punch and Judy shows, but I was told that this was not the case. The Falsefaces gather around the stove, and persons who have been cured by the society may apply to have their cure renewed. On this occasion only one man came forward. The Falsefaces, with their ritual of glug-glug speech that seems to be saying something, smear the patient unmercifully with ashes, rubbing them in his hair, on his bare arms and down his trousers: the joints—shoulders, elbows, wrists, hips and knees—are supposed to get special attention. So far as the Gagónsah actors are playing their medicine rôles, they are assumed to be completely invulnerable to the red hot coals and ashes they handle. They ignore the blisters and bandages that appear on their hands the next day, and these are also ignored by others. The irrepressible little boy and his father were now sitting on the bench behind me, and the little boy was frightened by these demons and burst into tears again. He continued to bawl through the ceremony, and the father could do nothing about it: the Indians are gentle with their children; but when the False-faces had left the Longhouse, the darling big mother came over and removed him to the women's side.

Now occurred the third eruption of the Huskfaces, which constitutes the climax of the evening and brings it to a triumphant end. At this point a terrific bang-ing was heard all about the Longhouse, as if it were being bombarded. The heralds again appeared, both this time at the door at the women's end. Since these

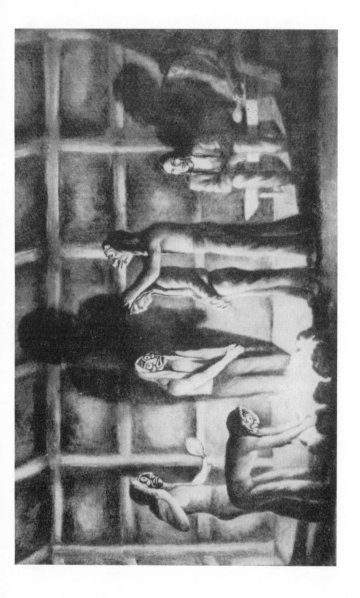

The healing rite of the Falsefaces, from a painting by Ernest Smith, a Seneca artist of Tonawanda. This painting is the property of Dr. William N. Fenton, who, in a paper called "Masked Medicine Societies of the Iroquois" in the 1940 *Annual Report of the Smithsonian Institution,* has supplied the following explanation of it: "The setting is the interior of a bark house, common among the Iroquois before 1800, and the time is presumably an evening of the Midwinter Festival. In response to a dream, the host has prepared a kettle of mush, of Falseface pudding, and summoned the Falsefaces. The announcer, who is painted sitting on the bench, has returned thanks to all the Spirit-forces, explained the purpose of the feast, and invoked the Faces-of-the-forests with burning tobacco. They have entered. The singer straddles the bench to beat out the tempo for their dance, which they energetically commence, scattering ashes everywhere. They hasten to finish curing the patient, their host who stands before the fire, since they crave tobacco and hunger for the kettle of mush which he has set down for them. A tall, red-faced fellow vigorously rubs the patient's scalp before blowing the hot ashes into the seat of the pain. A dark one moans anxiously while rubbing hot ashes between his palms prior to pouncing on his victim's shoulder and pumping his arm. Across the fire, a red face stoops to scoop live coals, while another impatiently shakes a turtle rattle. They are naked above the waist, but wearing the masks is said to protect their bodies from cold and their hands from the burning embers." *Photograph courtesy of New York State Museum and Science Service.*

beings cannot speak at all—they can only make a queer blowing sound (the rustling of the cornhusks, perhaps), less articulate even than the voices of the Falsefaces—they are obliged to commandeer an orator in order to deliver their message, which in some mysterious way they manage to communicate to him. This orator is said to be "kidnapped." He is taken outside and briefed. I was told by Nicodemus Bailey that this had several times happened to him. The oration of the Huskfaces' spokesman is supposed to be satiric and witty, and I imagine that he was excellent at this. The Huskfaces inhabit a country where everybody is happy and prosperous, the opposite of Iroquoia. It is known as the Country of the Burnt Stumps, which suggested to me desolation till I learned that—so much less advanced technically than the early white inhabitants of New York State, who were able to destroy their stumps—the Iroquois, in order to get sun for their crops, had simply burnt out patches of their forests, so that a country of burnt stumps was a country of special fertility. But the Huskfaces of Allegany had evidently no eligible satirist, and they conscripted the master of ceremonies, whom they summoned outside the door. When he returned, unaccompanied by the Huskfaces, he delivered a long homily, which was apparently less witty than moralistic. In the Country of the Huskfaces, he told them, the corn grows so high that it is over their heads, and they all have vegetable gardens—which few people in Allegany do. The children there obey their parents instead of romping all over the place when ceremonies are being held. I noticed that a self-conscious silence descended at these words on the children. I was told about this last point by Ronald Colman, who was back for the Huskfaces now and with whom I now found myself on friendly terms. But beyond this, we were up against the language barrier, with the two different worlds it divided. "I know what it means," he would say, "but I don't know how to explain it."

At the close of the spokesman's speech, the Huskfaces arrived *en masse*. All the men were dressed in women's clothes and all the women in men's. Mr. Frank Gouldsmith Speck, in a study of the Iroquois,* says that he was told in Canada by the leaders of a Cayuga Longhouse that they distinguished "five variant types" of Huskface masks: "eyedropper, cornflower, bisexual face, 'disappearing image,' which denotes a huskface of normal size with a miniature mask attached to the right or left, and 'old man,' a chief of the mask company, whose hoary age is symbolized by puffy cheeks, nose and lips and wrinkles." But I did not note very much difference among those I saw at Allegany. The expressions of all of them were vacuous: yet the heralds, when they charged through, seemed quite terrible, and when the whole tribe thronged in to dance—with their long gowns or overalls and sunflower faces—they gave an impression of benevolent power that corresponded to that pro-

---

* *The Iroquois: A Study in Cultural Evolution*, Bulletin 23 of The Cranbrook Institute of Science, Bloomfield Hills, Michigan.

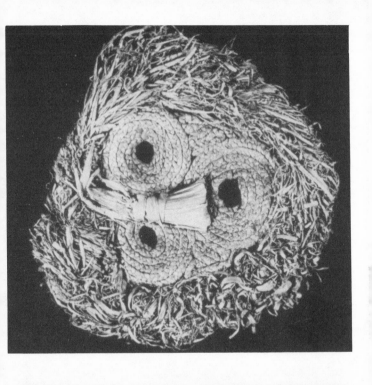

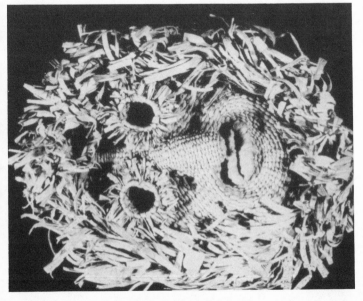

Huskfaces. These illustrate the two methods of making the masks: by twining a cornhusk cord, beginning with the mouth or nose (*left*), and by coiling a braided strip (*right*). *Photographs courtesy of New York State Museum and Science Service.*

duced by the New Year's Shálako birds at the Zuñi
pueblo in New Mexico, or for that matter by our Father
Christmas: they are the bringers of joy and abundance.
One of the shorter seemed playing the rôle of an
apple-cheeked and blank-faced Englishman, a country curate perhaps, dressed in a mackintosh, out of
rhythm with the other dancers and somewhat at a
loss as to what to do in that purposeful ebullient company. A little girl? An old woman? One could not
tell. When the Huskfaces are dancing at first by
themselves, the men do the women's steps and the
women the men's (quite distinct)—to the great amusement of the audience. Then the dancers seize partners
from the audience, grasping them by the arm and
propelling them on to the dance floor, and the great
dance of the evening begins. All these dances of the
Iroquois are done in spasms, each of which mounts to
a climax then abruptly comes to a stop, and the test
is to assert one's energy by keeping them up as long
as possible. Again and again the Huskfaces seemed to
lapse after their stamping at the end of a song (they
dance mostly on their heels, not on their toes, as we
do); again and again they revived, as if they had been
recharged, and put on a better dance than before. One
expected them to tire, to peter out; on the contrary,
they seemed to grow more dynamic, constantly gathering strength. The Huskfaces are leading the others,
challenging them not to give up; and at the end, when
they stopped at midnight, everybody seemed deeply
satisfied. "Hurray for the Huskfaces!" one felt that
they glowed, "who live in that marvellous country and

encourage us to live in ours." And the Huskfaces were proud and glad to know they had imparted some power to their friends the Seneca Indians.

The next morning the great dance of the Husk-faces was capped by the Great Feather Dance. This, too, is a costume performance, and it, too, brought out a large attendance, though not so large as the night before. The Great Feather Dance—which I saw again at the Strawberry Festival the following June—makes one feel in a more intense way than the big jolly jamboree of the Huskfaces the need of the human being, among spaces and wildernesses, between the so often indifferent earth which he still regards as his mother and the mysterious bowl of the heavens beyond which he cannot see, to declare, to create, himself, to occupy the vacuum of the universe. Like the other important dances, this dance is again and again renewed. The dancers all wear their best Iroquois costumes. The women have bright blouses over darker skirts, and under the skirts leggins, which, at the bottom, are split a few inches in front. All their garments are handsomely embroidered in traditional floral designs, usually with beads at the lower edges. The men wear magnificent war-bonnets. These are not a tradition with the Iroquois, who, as they say of themselves, were "bush Indians" and could never in their dense woods have carried such elaborate crests. In the old days, they wore simply round caps, which tightly fitted the head, with a couple of feathers that hung down in the

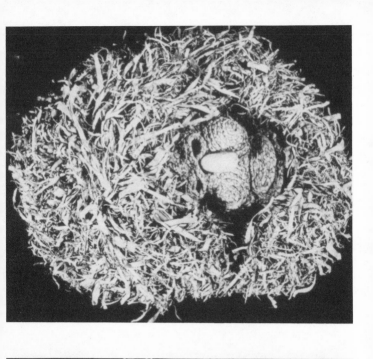

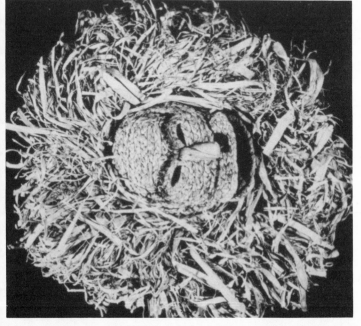

Grandfather and Grandmother Bushyhead, ranking senior Huskfaces—probably Seneca work. *Photographs Courtesy of New York State Museum and Science Service.*

back and an eagle feather that stood straight up and spun round when the wearer moved. The big bonnets were invented by the Indians of the plains, and I was told by Nicodemus Bailey that this fashion was adopted by the Iroquois after they first saw, at Fort Niagara, the Ottawa chieftain Pontiac in the pomp and splendor of one; but the white scholars seem to believe that they saw them first worn by the Sioux at Wild West shows toward the end of the nineteenth century and realized that without such ornaments they could never compete with these more colorful Indians. Now, in any case, they love to wear them. The more authentic-looking bonnets are constructed of eagle feathers, brownish with white tips, at the base of which have been stuck in, along the band, a row of smaller feathers of rusty red. And there are also gaudier ones, with dyed feathers of pink or orange. They order these, it seems, from plume companies. Yet this evidence of modern methods hardly weakened for me the force of the Feather Dance. It had some connection, I felt, with the old life of Talcottville—the village where I spent my summers—at the time when the early white settlers, too, had had to occupy the vacuum, by making roads and pulling up stumps, by building houses and managing the cattle, by cooking and spinning and quilting, by two trips a year to Utica with long lists made out by the ladies, by sleighing and dancing in winter, by picnics on the gray rocks of cataracts, by singing around the piano, by playing backgammon and reading Byron.

We left Salamanca the following morning, but we

went first to say goodby at the Longhouse. It was the final day of the ceremonies, and they had reverted to the solemnity of the first. We found the elders alone, with their benches pulled around the stove. They were preparing for the homage of tobacco, after which they would sit and smoke.

On the way back to Albany, we turned off from the Thruway to find out what had happened to Standing Arrow. There were only a few of the Indians now left on Schoharie Creek, living miserably, in the midst of the snow, in the old grounded bus and a multi-family shack that reminded me a little of a primitive longhouse. There were some children playing around in the snow. The farmers on whose property these Mohawks had camped, finding that the winter floods were failing to drive them away, had at last had an eviction notice served on them, and they were due to be turned out in ten days. Standing Arrow himself, they told me, had withdrawn to more comfortable quarters in a farmhouse a good distance off. To get there we waded through a field of snow. There were an old gray barn and two or three shacks, with smoke coming out of one of them. The pretty Mrs. Standing Arrow appeared from this shack and told us that her husband was in Onondaga. She sent a child to bring the swarthy Mohawk steelworker whom I had met when I was there before. He came down from a hill pushing a small cart on runners by which he had been hauling wood—a traditional Iroquois vehicle that dated from the untold centuries before the white man had brought them wheels. He said that he had just come back from the New Year's ceremonies at Onondaga and that they were going to have a council there as to what was to be done about the scheduled eviction. Standing Arrow was planning to apply to Albany for an interview with Governor Harriman.

This squatting of Standing Arrow's was to end in a curious way. A man who was described in the newspaper accounts as "an unemployed Schenectady mechanic" of "German-English stock" had read about the homeless Mohawks and had felt, he was quoted as saying, that they were "up against a wall." He had been moved to make over to Standing Arrow the title to a tract of land of a hundred and twenty acres—apparently useless to him—which he owned in Schoharie County. But now the dehorned chief's few followers swiftly melted away. The stories that reached me—like so many Indian rumors—were contradictory and vague. It had been part of the legal formalities that Standing Arrow had to pay a dollar to the man who was giving him the land, and some said that the dollar had made all the difference. Since the land had been legally purchased, the Indians would have to pay taxes: their leader had surrendered on the fundamental issue. Others said that Standing Arrow only wanted the land for himself, that he would not share it with anyone and would probably eventually sell it; others that he did not want to work but only wanted to talk and that the prospect of having to make habitable and profitable this unimproved patch of country would be enough to cause him to drop it. And there was even a story that Standing Arrow had now made himself an outlaw, so far as their religion was concerned, by claiming to be Deganawídah. I learned that the step he had taken in thus moving in on land that had once belonged to the Indians and which they felt that they still had a right to claim was one which had been contemplated by the Iroquois patriots but which had never been entrusted to Standing Arrow. If any exploit of the kind were attempted, it was to be put in the hands of responsible persons who would be able to make out a good case. Yet the fact that, despite his dehorning, he had still had some status at Onondaga and had invited me to the Council there seemed to show that there were some, at least, who had been giving him the benefit of the doubt. Could one be sure that his eloquence did not come from the Creator? Now, however, he was definitely discredited.

I believe that the truth was that Standing Arrow had been trying—not without some talents—to fill a traditional rôle which had been looming anew in the Iroquois world: the rôle of Messiah and captain. What I had learned since my talk with Philip Cook confirmed the assertion he had made that, among the North American Indians, the expectation of a Savior was recurrent. The most conspicuous example, perhaps, of an attempt to assume this leadership was the aborted attempt of the Shawnee Tecúmseh to organize a powerful confederacy of the Western and Southern Indians in order to maintain the Ohio River as a boundary to white expansion. He was supported by his twin brother Tenskwátawa, who, a few years later than Handsome Lake, had had a vision and had announced a revelation. Like Handsome Lake, he denounced the medicine societies and wanted to abolish drinking, and he prophesied that within four years there would take place a universal catastrophe, from which only his followers would be spared. He was militant against the whites and was able to rally an army of over a thousand converts. But both his movement and Tecumseh's confederacy were crushed at the battle of Tippecanoe, in November, 1811, when William Henry Harrison defeated their forces. Today all the pressures I have mentioned have been threatening the Iroquois people, and the need for a Savior has again been felt. Standing Arrow has failed as deliverer; but Mad Bear, who inspires confidence as well as commanding eloquence, has been coming more and more to seem one.

7. THE SIX NATIONS RESERVE

Since I paid my first visit to Standing Arrow in October, 1957, and discovered the existence of a nationalist movement among the Iroquois Indians, this movement has been growing in strength with a rapidity I did not anticipate. The kind of thing that I should have said if I had written this book even in the summer of 1958 would now be quite out of date. I should then have said that the Iroquois needed a leader, and Mad Bear has emerged as a leader. Even after the emergence of Mad Bear, I should have said that the political machinery of the League was too archaic and cumbersome to deal with the current crises. It was striking that the two most effective campaigns that had been brought to bear on these crises had been organized outside the League: the action of the Seneca Republic to avert the Kinzua Dam and that of the Tuscaroras in opposing the Power Authority. As for Mad Bear, he is not even an hereditary chief, so was free to pursue his own policy, as would otherwise have been hardly possible. I had found them complaining at Onondaga, before the Tuscaroras had won their decision, that these youngest brothers of the League, who had to ask permission to speak in the Council, had gone ahead without the Council's approval. But when I mentioned later on at St. Regis that I thought some more modern organization was needed to look after the Iroquois's interests, I was told that a revision of the League constitution was then being prepared by two Mohawks and that it was soon to be submitted to the Council.

This last news especially surprised me. The two Mohawks were Philip Cook and a man named Ernest Benedict, whom I had also met. I had observed among the middle-aged nationalists—believers in the old Confederacy and in the old religion of the Longhouse—that they were likely to be men who were still so much a part of the ancient Iroquois world that they had not wholly mastered English or really got to know the ropes of the white one. The problem, as Louis Papineau had said to me, was for them to find someone well enough educated to be able to present their claims and to deal with the whites about them. The Indians, on the other hand, who did know the white world, had been educated in white colleges, and were likely to have been made to feel that the odds against their people were overwhelming; to be cynical or ironical about the Iroquois's situation. Ernest Benedict, a graduate of St. Lawrence College, I had taken, when I met him the summer before, for an example of this latter type. He had made himself a test case of Iroquois non-citizenship, at the time of the last war, by going to jail for resisting the draft, but had got bored with it and ended by serving. Today he is an active collaborator in the effort to restore the

Confederacy. Nor is this the only evidence I have
noted, in the course of something less than two years,
of a rapidly increasing coöperation, not only among
the Six Nations, but between men of different tem-
peraments and of different degrees of adaptation.

What I least expected to see, however, was any real
coördination between the Iroquois living in Canada
and those in the United States. The Six Nations
Reserve near Brantford in Ontario is the largest of the
Iroquois reservations: over 43,000 acres, with a population of perhaps 7,000; and the only one that includes
groups from all the Six Nations (as well as a remnant
of the Delawares, once so harshly humiliated by the
Iroquois but eventually taken in by them, and a certain
number of Chippewas). There are no less than four
Longhouses here, two of which belong to the Cayugas,
who have no separate reservation in the United States
but are strongly represented at Brantford. These Iroquois are descendants of those who, as a result of their
siding with the British at the time of our Revolution,
afterwards took refuge in Canada and were given, in
1784, this large tract of land on Grand River by an arrangement which the Canadians call the Haldimand
Deed but which the Indians insist is a treaty since they
are described in it as "His Majesty's faithful allies."
This created for the Iroquois a peculiar situation in regard to the government of the League. At the present
time the 20,000 Iroquois are probably about equally
divided between Canada and the United States, and
the hierarchy established by Deganawídah exists on
both sides, but in duplicate. On each side, there are

fifty hereditary chiefs, each group with its own Tado-dáho. The capital, Onondaga, is of course on our side of the line, and the Indians in the United States insist that their Tadodáho is the only authentic one. I found on one occasion in Canada that when I spoke of the Canadian Tadodáha as if he were the opposite number of the one in the United States, I was corrected by an Indian from the other side, who said that the Canadian chief was merely an "acting" Tadodáho. Not only have the Iroquois, therefore, been scattered in separate reservations: the League is now a two-headed organism, and, as a result of this, official procedure seems sometimes to become rather complicated. The headquarters for the Iroquois in Canada is at the Six Nations Reserve, where the Onondagas have a Longhouse, as the headquarters of those in the United States is at the Longhouse in Onondaga. But the two branches, on certain occasions, send delegates to one another's councils, and the two Tadodáhos in council occasionally sit side by side. And since the problems of the two groups of Iroquois had separately to be settled with their respective governments, which had different machinery and different laws, I did not see how it was possible for them to work together.

Nor did I notice any signs of recalcitrance, such as were evident in our own reservations, when I visited the Six Nations Reserve in the August of 1958—though it is true that I did not at that time have anything but the most casual conversation with anyone except Miss Emily General, the organizer of an annual Six Nations Pageant, which I had gone up

to Brantford to see. This pageant takes place in the
depths of a forest inside the Six Nations Reserve, on
a charming natural stage, a loop in a little stream that
encloses what is almost an island. The audience sits
on long benches on a slope that overlooks this scene.
Strong spotlights in the northern darkness isolate the
tableaux of the action; warwhoops rip from the woods;
the characters appear from behind the trees or arrive
and depart in canoes that glide away out of sight.
But there is nothing of the Wild West show. The
performance is a quiet shadowing forth of events from
the Iroquois past, and as one listens to the solemn
speeches, given first in Iroquois and then in English,
one becomes aware that its purpose—as Miss General
afterwards told me—was didactic. The pageant is
aimed primarily at the national consciousness of the
Iroquois, with some thought of entertaining the white
visitor but also a firm design of making plain to him
the predicament of the Indian.

The next morning I went to call on Miss General,
who was for many years a schoolteacher on the Six
Nations Reserve and who now, with her brother, runs
a farm on a somewhat larger scale—ducks, pigs and
corn—than is usual for Indians on a reservation. She is
a woman of the serious and noble kind who can work
all her life for a cause. It is probably significant that
she gave her first pageant in 1924, a black year for
these Canada Iroquois. The government had become
dissatisfied with the slowness of the Indians to "inte-
grate"—they had been notably apathetic in the First
World War—and, making use of an earlier amend-

ment to the Canadian Indian Act, which gave the Governor General in council the power to take this step, "if deemed necessary," the authorities announced, in September of that year, that the hereditary chiefs were deposed and that a "Council of Twelve" were to take their place. The regional superintendent, a Lieutenant-Colonel C. E. Morgan, flanked by two Mounted Policemen, appeared at a meeting of the chiefs and read them an order in council proclaiming that they were banished from the Council House (at Brantford not identical with the Longhouse) and that this would now be the meeting place of an "elective" council, one "chief" and twelve councillors, actually appointed by the government.

Since that time, on the Six Nations Reserve, the supporters of the Iroquois Confederacy have been struggling to get rid of the "puppet government," as they call the Council of Twelve, and to recover their original autonomy. They had already been stiffening in resistance before the imposition of the puppet council. They had resented the presence of the Mounted Police, who had been installed among them in barracks early in the nineteen-twenties, and they were becoming aware that the authority of the chiefs was no longer respected by the government. They knew that the amendment to the Indian Act would make a sudden deposition possible. They began by protesting to the Canadian government; then in 1922 they wrote to Winston Churchill, at that time Colonial Secretary, who referred the matter back to the Governor General of Canada. At the same time, one of

Emily General's brothers issued his own passport and, accompanied by an attorney from Rochester—to the scandal of the Canadian authorities—applied at Geneva to the League of Nations, which said it had no jurisdiction. In 1930, Miss General and her brother were members of a delegation to England. They failed to see the King but were received by Members of Parliament, with whom, on the Terrace at Westminster, they took tea and smoked a peace-pipe. They wanted to establish their status as allies, not subjects, of the British Crown, but they were not encouraged in this. A parliamentary subcommittee was appointed to hear their grievances and decided that these were the business not of the Westminster but of the Dominion Parliament. The Iroquois were, however, persistent and appealed in 1945, with the usual lack of success, to the United Nations in San Francisco. In 1947, a Canadian Civil Service Act was passed which demanded that civil servants should swear an oath of allegiance to the Crown. Miss General, who for twenty years had taught school on the reservation, refused to take this oath and resigned her job. I did not get the impression, in talking with her on this first visit to the Six Nations Reserve, that she thought that the nationalist movement was far enough advanced to be very effective.

It was Sunday, and I went, as I have already mentioned, to the Onondaga Longhouse in the hope of finding Mad Bear there. They were having their Sunday games, and the cookhouse was serving refreshments. My companion and I had some Indian corn soup, which I had not tasted before, though I had seen the Seneca women boiling it in two great cauldrons, one with pork and one with beef, at the Allegany Longhouse. My companion asked what was in it, and the woman who was serving said, "You'd be surprised!" In the old days, it was made with the head of a bear—occasionally with the head of an enemy. Today they are reduced to a pig's head. The corn is a kind of white corn which has been stripped of its hulls by boiling it with ashes and then swollen by boiling it again till it has almost the dimensions of popcorn. It was cheap and extremely good. Our heads were not requisitioned, but we ran into a virulent expression of atavistic Iroquois hostility. A very old man, with slits for eyes, sitting alone and facing us at a nearby table, suddenly began to talk. He told us that his father had died in 1920 at the age of a hundred and two, and seemed to think that he remembered the way things were at the time of the Revolution—though, if the son's calculation were true, he would have had to be born in 1818. The Indians had been all right in those days, and he railed against the whites who had ruined them. It was our schools that had destroyed the Indians (Handsome Lake the prophet, it will be remembered, had coupled white schools with liquor as a cause of his people's deterioration). My companion, who was not used to the Iroquois, said later that this bitter old man made him feel that he would not care to be out alone on the Six Nations Reserve at night.

The next news I had from Grand River was that a
nationalist *coup d'état* had occurred. On March 5,
1959, the supporters of the hereditary chiefs—about
thirteen hundred strong and including both Christians
and Longhouse people—marched to the Council
House, where the elective chief and his council were
holding a locked session, and, while these latter got
away by the back door, they removed the front door
from its hinges. Mad Bear, who is said to have had a
good deal to do with deciding them to strike at this
time, presided at the meeting that followed, which
was attended by about five thousand. A proclamation
was read and nailed to the Council House door, which
abolished the elective council, restored the hereditary
chiefs and appointed an Iroquois police force of a
hundred and thirty-three, including a number of
women, who were to take the place of the "Mounties." A program was announced for the future which
was designed to make the reservation more or less
self-sustaining. They were to build an abattoir and a
canning factory; to manufacture their clothing as well
as souvenirs and cigarettes; to engage in coöperative
farming and provide a storehouse for grain and vegetables; to get loans for able students who could benefit by higher education; and to build an historical
museum. They prayed to the Great Spirit, and Chief
Logan, the son of the Tadodáho, expressed his belief
that the success of their action was due to His intervention.

The young men of the new police—who wore arm-
bands with IP on them for "Iroquois Police"—began

by arresting six drivers, four Indians, two for drunken driving, and two whites (reporters from local papers) for failing to obey a stop sign, and fined them five dollars each. At the instigation of Mad Bear, who said that the hereditary chiefs ought not to be criticized, a schoolteacher who had written to the Brantford paper that the movement to restore these chiefs did not have as much popular support as the nationalists were claiming for it was arrested and tried for treason. He was made to swear on wampum that he would henceforth support the chiefs and was warned that if the offense were repeated, he would be exiled from the reservation. Such procedure would seem to give point to a statement made by "Tonto," the Indian companion of the hero in the "Lone Ranger" television series, a Mohawk whose mother and seven brothers reside on the Six Nations Reserve. "My brothers on the Reserve must be careful," Tonto is reported to have said, when interviewed by the press in Hollywood. "They must set up a democracy, not a dictatorship."

Between the Tuscarora decision and the Canadian *coup d'état*, Mad Bear who had previously, in accomplishing his ends, exhibited both astuteness and restraint, seems to have come under the influence of a certain Herbert Holdridge, a retired U.S. brigadier general, who—I depend here on newspaper stories—announced himself in 1948 as a candidate for the presidency, running on a dissident platform of which vegetarianism was one of the planks, and declared, in the course of the campaign, that, if elected, he would do his best to see that certain prominent people were hanged. These included Harry Truman, General Bradley, Cardinal Spellman and John Foster Dulles. "I'm going to have them tried," he is reported to have said. "The Nuremberg Trials condemned war criminals after the fact. The way to prevent war is to condemn them before the fact." He has been vocal in the defense of civil liberties, and he has recently taken up the cause of the Indian. On March 19, 1959, accompanied by Mad Bear and about a hundred other Indians, he led a kind of raid on Washington. They attempted without success to present a petition to the President, demanding, among other reforms, the recognition of the Iroquois League as an independent nation and the dismissal of the Indian Commissioner, Mr. Glenn L. Emmons, who is said at the time of his taking office to have had no previous knowledge of Indian affairs and with whom—on account of an attempt to authorize the purchase by whites of Indian community lands—the Indians had long been dissatisfied. General Holdridge, after visiting the White House, led the group to Mr. Emmons's office, with the object of making a citizen's arrest, but was not allowed to see him. At a meeting of the Indian Defense League, he is reported to have advised the Indians "to resist with all their power, even to gunfire, if necessary, in defense of their territory."

The trial of George Beaver, the schoolteacher, had, a week before this expedition, brought a telegram from Mrs. Ellen Fairclough, the Canadian Minister of Citizenship and Immigration, warning the Indians that the Iroquois Police must cease to make arrests: "I must further inform you that steps will be taken without delay to restore and maintain peace and order on the Six Nations Reserve." This telegram, received on March 11 by the older Chief Logan, the Tadodáho, was read at a meeting by Mad Bear, who is reported to have commented on it: "My reaction is this—she can go and jump in the lake. She has previously announced she will have nothing to do with us. Are we going to have anything to do with this woman who knows nothing about the situation?" Shouts of "No! No!" The next day, no doubt as a retort to this, the Mounted Police attacked. The Council House was now always kept occupied by members of the new police, and the night when the attack was expected—the Indians had been tipped off—about a hundred and thirty people, who included young Chief Logan and Emily General, had been summoned to hold the fort. There were also reporters present. About three in the morning, police cars drove up and a group of sixty Mounties invaded the house. They ordered the Indians to leave, and the latter put up some resistance. The men, I am told, "just stood," and the women started fighting first, trying to push out the Mounties. A general mêlée followed. The men were dragged along and clubbed; the women got black eyes and bruises, and the wife of young Chief Logan had one arm so badly hurt that she was for some time unable to use it. There were several cameramen present—one of whom had got permission to cover the affair for the CBC; but when the riot got

under weigh and one of the Mounted Police noticed
that another photographer—according to the Brantford *Expositor*—was "filming a woman's injuries," he
smashed the camera with his riot-stick. The stick de-
scending on the camera was the last thing recorded in
the film. This film, in an edited version, was shown in
Toronto on television, and, I gathered—since Canadians pride themselves on their orderly British procedure
—made rather a bad impression. Young Chief Logan
called a halt to resistance. "We might as well go out,"
he said. "We can't do much anyway. Look what they
have here! We'll have to get help from outside." The
Indians then left the building. The Mounted Police issued thirty-three warrants on charges of kidnapping
(the schoolteacher), impersonating policemen and
obstructing the police; but, on the assurance presented by the Indians' lawyer, Mr. Malcolm Montgomery of Toronto, that the pro-Confederacy people
would no longer use militant methods but depend on
"peaceful negotiation and litigation in the civil courts,"
these charges were later dropped.

The first step in this litigation was a writ, submitted
by the nationalists, for an injunction to restrain the
elective council from selling three and a half acres
of land which had been leased, during the last war,
to a farm equipment company and on which the
company had built a factory. Out of the whole population of seven thousand, only fifty-four people had
voted on this sale, and only thirty-seven of these in
favor of it, and for two years the hereditary chiefs
had been trying to take the matter to court, but the

hearings had been always deferred. Mr. Montgomery
had succeeded, however, in obtaining an interim injunction, so that the land was frozen and could not
be sold. Now—beginning on April 15—the hearings
were finally held. In the atmosphere created by the
revolt and the raid, this occasion attracted a good
deal of attention all over the Iroquois world. The
larger question at issue was, of course, whether the
elective council or the hereditary chiefs of the
League had the authority on the Six Nations Reserve.
Many Indians from the States came to Brantford in
order to attend the hearings. Mad Bear was in court,
though, according to rumor, the Mounties had threatened to run him out. He wore feathers and a regalia of
yellow and blue which left one arm and shoulder bare
and suggested a masquerade. This was not well received in Canada, where such Indians as appeared in
costume wore the sober conventional buckskin. The
Tadodáho from Onondaga was there in a dark suit. A
good many of the chiefs from the Reserve were old.
It had been the younger men, the "warriors," as all those
males not chiefs are called, who pushed them to their
insurrection. One of them could only speak Onondaga
and had to testify through an interpreter. Another
attempted English, but mumbled and had a great deal
of difficulty in explaining what the Iroquois League
was. A Tuscarora from the States who sat next to me
said—truly, no doubt—that the trouble was that the
old chief was "thinking in Indian" and did not have
any English vocabulary to deal with Indian institu-
tions.

This Canadian court made a very good impression on a visitor from the States. It was in some ways rather different from one of ours and yet was not quite like England. The judge and the barristers did not wear wigs but had black gowns with white yokes. Mr. Justice J. M. King of the Ontario Supreme Court was obviously intelligent and conscientious. When speaking to the lawyers and the witnesses, he combined informality and dignity in a way that I imagined could be called Canadian. The proceedings were conducted with a quietness and a courtesy not always in evidence in American courts. (In Canada they complain that our lawyers "rant.") The Iroquois and their defenders did not, however, seem very hopeful. I called on Miss Emily General the afternoon before the hearings—at which she was to testify—and found her in bed with a temperature. I could see that she had taken the crisis hard. The Brantford Museum had put up on its door a gigantic reproduction of a False-face mask. Said Miss General, "We'll need every inch of that!"

There is of course a good deal of inconsistency in the position of the Iroquois nationalists. Even such a desegregationist as Nicodemus Bailey at Tonawanda wants exemption from property tax and buses to public schools both. At St. Regis they want exemption from every kind of tax, yet are dependent on the Hogansburg Fire Department. The April declaration of independence on the part of the Grand River Iroquois had focused attention on these contradictions.

The object of the nationalist program is to make the reservation self-sustaining, and it is probable that at the present time a majority of its population are in favor of restoring the hereditary chiefs; but the fact is—though the purest patriots have refused to accept anything from the government—that most of the Indians on this reservation have been collecting government old age pensions, disability pensions, mothers' allowances and other benefits. (The expenses of Indian schools in Canada are met out of a special fund accumulated from the sale of Indian lands.) The difficulties of the situation were brought out in a whole series of letters from Indians that—following George Beaver's protest—appeared in the Brantford *Expositor*. It was pointed out by one correspondent that, not long after the *coup d'état*, the hereditary chiefs in a television broadcast were appealing for aid from the government whose interference they had just repulsed. The same writer, who signed himself "Thankful Indian" —asserting that the Brantford rebellion had been mainly the work of Mad Bear, who had come in from the United States—expresses doubt as to whether a leader could be found among the Brantford Indians who would be capable of running the reservation as a self-dependent unit; and another correspondent writes that the hereditary system is out of date: "A chief might be an imbecile but he was still chief for life. That sort of government does not belong in this age. It is still practised only by a few tribes in Africa. . . . If the chiefs ever got in again on the hereditary principle, they could do what they liked, and we would be helpless. The thought of some of them as life members makes me reach for an aspirin." This writer seems to forget that an hereditary chief may be deposed on the motion of his clan mother. But one recognizes here, nevertheless, the ever-recurrent illusion, characteristic of revolutions and not unknown in our two-party system, that a brand-new set of rulers, though selected from one's own community, will be able to make a clean slate of the past and to behave like a new order of human beings.

Justice King, in a decision of September 3, concluded that since the Six Nations Indians, in accepting the lands assigned them, had put themselves under the protection of the Crown, they "owed allegiance to the Crown and thus became subjects of the Crown"; and that though "it might be unjust or unfair under the circumstances for the Parliament to interfere with their system of internal government by hereditary chiefs, I am of the opinion that Parliament has the authority to provide for the surrender of Reserve land." The injunction was therefore denied. But, in addition to the reservation included above, he pointed out that the provisions of the Indian Act make it clear "that the Governor-in-Council may accept or refuse a surrender of land so that it is still quite possible" for him "to take the position that the surrender of the land in question . . . should be refused. From the evidence given at the trial, it is difficult to see what advantage would accrue to the Six Nations Indians by surrendering the land in question."

The problem at this point for the Iroquois's counsel is to find some way of taking a poll that will show that a majority of the Indians are in favor of the hereditary chiefs. This is likely to prove rather difficult, since the Longhouse people on principle refuse to vote on anything whatever. It is hoped that the Ottawa government may appoint a committee to study the matter, and compromises of a typically British kind are at present under discussion. They may not, however, be acceptable to the uncompromising nationalists, who, in the meantime, are appealing to the Queen.

8. GROWTH AND CAUSES
OF IROQUOIS
RESURGENCE

The nationalist movement of the Iroquois is only one of many recent evidences of a new self-assertion on the part of the Indians. The subject is much too large and complicated even to be outlined here, but one should note that the successes of Mad Bear have led to his being sought out by certain non-Iroquois tribes who are struggling with similar problems. I am told that his correspondence has now become enormous. He has given up his old occupations and, financed by his own people, is devoting himself entirely to Indian affairs.

The Miccosúkee Indians, for example, are a small and obscure group who inhabit, in southern Florida, the Everglades and cypress swamps. They have in the past been associated with the Seminoles, but, by one of the innumerable anomalies of the Indian situation, their status in relation to our government is different. The Seminoles have a charter from the government and, approved by them, an elective council; their three reservations are incorporated as the Seminole Tribe of Florida. They have recently been modernizing their land and leasing it to tomato-growers and cattle-grazers, and they have embarked on a "Disney-land Project," which will involve sending tourists in dugout canoes down a stream infested with alligators. But the more primitive Miccosúkees do not live on a reservation, and their interests are now at odds with those of the Seminoles. They have never been con-quered by the white man and have never surrendered their lands, and they now want the federal govern-ment to acquire for them and hold in trust some 300,000 acres of swampland which only they have cared to inhabit, living on little islands and content to subsist on their hunting and fishing, but of which they may now be deprived by an Everglades Reclamation Proj-ect, which would flood about half their domain and eventually, by leading to improvements, expel them from the other half. These Florida Miccosúkees, who have never been rounded up and have never submitted to white domination, are said to be among the most stubborn of all the Indian bands, and when they heard of the success of the Tuscaroras in standing up to the Power Authority, they appealed to Mad Bear to advise them. He made the trip South to see them and also met there with representatives of other Southern Indian groups. They discussed, he reports, a project of uniting all the Indians of North, South and Central America, and they sent a buckskin of recognition to Fidel Castro's revolutionary government in Cuba.

In May, 1959, a delegation of Hopis from Arizona came on to New York for the purpose of having an interview with the officials of the United Nations.

They desired to report a prophecy, which, in the
newspaper reports I have seen, sounds not unlike the
Iroquois one attributed to Deganawídah. They wanted
to inform all nations that "the day of purification"
was at hand. First, the Indians will leave the cities;
then, after the corn has been harvested, the time of the
Big War will come; but the forces of good will triumph, and "after this life has been purified, we will
have everlasting life and peace." They, too, got in
touch with Mad Bear and were invited to the Onondaga Council. "The Indians," I hear from Anderson,
"are comparing prophecies all over."

Fidel Castro, in return for the buckskin, invited the
Six Nations and the Miccosúkees to send delegations
to visit him in Cuba. They accepted and went to
Havana in July, 1958. "They rolled out the red carpet
for us," writes Mad Bear, "including police escort in
Cadillacs, bands and machete-waving campisinos." The
Iroquois nationalists are hoping that Cuba will sponsor
the admission of the League to the councils of the
United Nations.

Now, what are the causes, at the present time, of
this reawakening of Indian nationalism?

For one thing, it is a part of the world-wide reaction
on the part of the non-white races against the med-
dling and encroachments of the whites. The leaders of
these Indian movements are well aware of what is going
on in Asia and Africa. They know that they came
from the Orient—many of them, as I have said, could
be easily mistaken for Mongolians—and they know

Fidel Castro receiving Mad Bear in Cuba, in July, 1959. *Photograph courtesy of Dixie Photo Service, Miami, Florida.*

what has been happening in China. They also know that India has freed herself, that Ghana is now a free state, and that the Algerians are struggling to become one. They have sensed that the white man has been losing his hold, and, like the rest of the non-white races, they are sick of his complacency and arrogance. They find this a favorable moment for declaring their national identity because, in view of our righteous professions in relation to the Germans and Russians, they know that, for the first time in history, they are in a position to blackmail us into keeping our agreements and honoring their claims. When in November, 1957, Bertrand Russell addressed, in the English *New Statesman*, an open letter to Khrushchyóv and Eisenhower, imploring them to drop their nonsense and forget about the possibility of annihilating one another, our Secretary of State Dulles, answering for the President, replied that "the creed of the United States" was "based on the tenets of moral law"—derived from "the religious convictions that guided our forefathers in writing the documents that marked the birth of America's independence"—and that this creed "rejected war except in self-defense." The Soviets, on the other hand—quite unlike the American colonists—had "seized power by violence of an intensity and extent that shocked the civilized world. It has extended its power by violence, absorbing one nation after another by force or the threat of force." Khrushchyóv could not afford to let pass the marvellous opportunity offered him. He sent the *Statesman* a long rebuttal, in which, before getting on to the Mexican War, the Spanish colonies and Guatemala, he—or whoever does his history—retorted, "What about the Indians?" His description of our dealings with them is somewhat inaccurate, but he is near enough to the truth to be able to score a telling point in invoking their fate to support him in his statement that, "One must have a great belief in miracles to appeal to the memory of peoples and say that in the history of the United States there has not been any occasion 'when an effort has been made to spread its creed by force of arms.'" And this point has occurred to the Iroquois. It has also troubled Mrs. Roosevelt, who has devoted at least two of her columns to the complaints of the Six Nations; and it may be that—though there has always been a certain oscillation in our policy in regard to the Indians—the decision in favor of the Tuscaroras and the non-materialization of the Kinzua Dam have been due to a certain embarrassment vis-à-vis the rest of the world. For whatever the difference in scale, is there any real difference in principle between uprooting whole communities of well-to-do Russian farmers and shipping them off to the Urals, and depriving the Senecas of the use of their lands in such a way as to shatter their republican unit, and dismissing this intelligent and capable people to go and find homes where they can?

It is easy to ignore the Indians, and I am not, as I showed at the beginning of this book, myself in any position to take a self-righteous tone about them, having assured my visitor from England that there were almost no Indians left in New York State and

that the Mohawks were the same as the Mohicans—
a people, once the enemies of the Mohawks, of whom,
I believe, at the present time, only a few descendants
survive in the neighborhood of Groton, Connecticut.
I apologize to the Iroquois for this, and I want here
to try to explain why it is possible thus to disregard
the Indians and why it is difficult for people who care
about them to get other people interested in them.
The primary reason, of course, is that, having come
here a long time before us—the ethnologists talk in
terms of twenty or twenty-five thousand years—the
Indians do not fit into, and for the most part do not
want to fit into, the alien life we have brought here. It
seems quite self-evident to many of us that the "American Way of Life" is a wonderful thing and that everyone ought to want to share in it. Why can't they—like
the Germans, the Italians, the Scandinavians and everybody else—become good American citizens, enjoying
our privileges and luxuries? Wouldn't they, obviously,
be much better off? Isn't it the trouble that they are
not really up to it? This point of view has always
been a popular one. But the nature of the obstacles
it is bound to encounter is admirably shown in a
recent book—the best possible short guide to the
Indian situation—*Indians and Other Americans: Two
Ways of Life Meet*, by Harold E. Fey and D'Arcy
McNickle. One of the most serious of these obstacles
is that the Indians' relation to the land he inhabits is
entirely different from ours. The early Europeans
imagined that the Indians of the East were rovers,
who lived and hunted at random wherever they

pleased. They were mistaken: the tribes had their
separate tracts that were marked off by definite
boundaries. See, for example, the Six Nations map in
Morgan's *League of the Iroquois*, which shows how
a strip of the Iroquois territory was assigned to each
of these nations. But the fundamental difference between the European conception of property and that
of the American Indians was that Indian property
was held in common. The Indian had no idea of legal
title, of the individual ownership of land, and the
white man was incapable of thinking in any other
terms. In 1879, a General Allotment Act was introduced in Congress. The object, or ostensible object,
was to encourage the Indians to engage in farming by
breaking up the reservations. The fragments were to
be allotted, a hundred and sixty acres to heads of
families and eighty to single persons. The remainder
could be bought by the government, and the individual owners, after twenty-five years, were authorized to sell their land. A Sioux agent had reported
to the Indian Commissioner that "as long as the
Indians live in villages, they will retain many of their
old and injurious habits. Frequent feasts, heathen
ceremonies and dances, constant visiting—these will
continue as long as people live together in close
neighborhoods and villages. I trust that before another year is ended, they will generally be located
upon individual land or farms. From that date will
begin their real and permanent progress." Carl Schurz,
then Secretary of the Interior, had recommended the
allotment system: "The enjoyment and pride of the

individual ownership of property is one of the most effective civilizing agencies." The bill encountered opposition. "If I stand alone in the Senate," said a senator from Colorado, "I want to put upon the record my prophecy in this matter, that when thirty or forty years will have passed and these Indians shall have parted with their title, they will curse the hand that was raised professedly in their defense to secure this kind of legislation, and if the people who are clamoring for it understood Indian character, and Indian laws, and Indian morals, and Indian religion, they would not be here clamoring for this at all." A minority of a Committee on Indian Affairs expressed a similar opinion: "However much we may differ with the humanitarians who are riding this hobby, we are certain that they will agree with us in the proposition that it does not make a farmer out of an Indian to give him a quarter section of land. There are hundreds of thousands of white men, rich with the experiences of Anglo-Saxon civilization, who cannot be transformed into cultivators of the land by any such gift. . . . The real aim of this bill is to get at the Indian lands and open them up to settlement. The provisions for the apparent benefit of the Indian are but the pretext to get at his lands and occupy them. . . . If this were done in the name of greed, it would be bad enough; but to do it in the name of humanity, and under the cloak of an ardent desire to promote the Indian's welfare by making him like ourselves, whether he will or not, is infinitely worse." But the act was passed in 1887, and had the effect, say Fey

and McNickle, of depriving the Indians of ninety
million of their hundred and forty million acres. Few
of them had taken to farming. Even if they had been
eager to farm, they had no money to invest in equipment or livestock, and since their allotments were
held in trust, they were unable to get commercial
credit. If they did not dispose of their property, and
it was divided among their descendants, there was
soon very little for anybody left. Nor had they been
induced by the dominant race to abandon their "frequent feasts," their "heathen ceremonies and dances"
and their "constant visiting." A new bill now before
the legislature, against which, in September of '58,
an Indian congress in Montana was held to protest,
is a proposed further step in this same direction. It
has been said of it by Mrs. La Verne Madigan, executive director of the Association on American Indian
Affairs: "The question is whether the Indian tribes
are communities of people or hills of ants. They
should not have to live in perpetual fear that the
federal foot is going to squash them to death. Yet
this is the situation in which they exist under an on-
again off-again application of federal pressures that
would be considered intolerable by any white community."

It should be noted that the result of the first great
attempt on the part of the Indians to assimilate themselves was not such as to encourage them further.
Toward the end of the eighteenth century, the Iroquois's able cousins, the Cherokees, who inhabited the
Alleghanies and other regions further south, set out

to master European techniques and to live as the white men did. They exchanged their tribal lands for farm implements, spinning wheels, looms and other tools of civilization. In the twenties of the following century, the Cherokee leader Sequoya invented a syllabary for their language, and the Cherokees began getting out a newspaper called the *Cherokee Phoenix*. In 1826, the editor of this paper was able to report in Philadelphia to the First Presbyterian Church on the remarkable progress of his people in raising sheep, pigs and cattle, blacksmithing and milling, spinning and weaving, roadbuilding, ferrying and schooling. "In one district there were, last winter, upward of a thousand volumes of good books." The reward for this effort of adaptation was Andrew Jackson's Indian Removal Act of 1830—as a result of which the literate Cherokees, along with less adaptable tribes, were moved to the primitive wilderness beyond the Mississippi. Some of them took to their hills; but most of them—driven out at the point of the gun—made the journey in winter on foot, and a quarter of their number perished.

In a society of competing property-owners, it is easy to ignore or to underrate a people who do not care about this kind of prestige. To the white man who passes through a reservation—or through parts of certain reservations—it is likely to look like a slum. He will note that many houses are unpainted, and if he should happen to visit one, he might find that the rooms were littered, that the stuffing was protruding from old armchairs and that the paper was

peeling off the walls. But this would give him no true
index to the quality of the inhabitants, who might be
people of much brains and fine character. It has, in
fact, been a tradition of the *royaneh*, the families from
which chiefs are chosen, that they should not be
ostentatious. Indifference to money and belongings
was a sign of superiority. Cadwallader Colden, in
his history, speaks of the contempt of the Indians
for the traders with whom they dealt: they were far
more at home with the officers of the monarchs across
the sea; and the authors of *Indians and Other Americans* quote one of the early Indian agents as complaining that the colonies have "seldom if at all sent
proper persons" to treat with the Indians. "But the
management of them has often been left to traders,
who have no skill in public affairs, are directed only
by their own interests, and being generally the lowest
kind of people, are despised and held in great contempt by the Indians as liars, and persons regarding
nothing but their own gain." The Iroquois does not
become a farmer, and he does not become a bourgeois.
If he prospers, he lives "like a gentleman," as a white
observer said to me—though this word belongs to our
system, not theirs, and is likely to be misleading, for
though it is accurate as applied to the Iroquois in
suggesting dignity and leisure and a love of independence, it is less so in implying a place which is kept
so far as possible in good repair and a pride in interior decorating.

The most curious feature of Iroquois life, as trans-
posed into terms of the twentieth century, and one

of those that are most difficult for the white man to grasp, is the substitution of iron and steel work for the ancient male pursuits of hunting and fighting. A good deal of light has been thrown on the relation between these two kinds of activity, the substitution in the modern age of one for the other, in a paper by Dr. Morris Freilich called *Cultural Persistence Among the Modern Iroquois*.* He shows that the steelworkers travel in bands as the hunters and warriors did, leaving their women at home, and that they amuse themselves on their return—as they did in the past—by sitting together and boasting about the feats they have performed in their travels and the dangers they have overcome. Mr. Freilich believes that the foreman, or "pusher," who bosses a band of young steelworkers corresponds to the head of a party of warriors, and that the prizes, a new car or a well-stuffed wallet, that the adventurer brings back to the reservation, correspond to the captives or loot carried off from a raid on the enemy. The discrepancy between the new occupation and the old way of living and worshipping is thus largely in the eye of the white beholder; but unless one has studied the Indians, one is liable to the alternative errors of assuming, from their homes, that they are shiftless or, from their expert mechanical competence, that they ought to, and, therefore, that they must, desire to live as we do.

I have shown in various ways the impingement of the white man's gimmicks on even the stoutest of the

* *Anthropos*, Volume 53, 1958, published in Fribourg, Switzerland.

reservations; yet the Indians have never ceased to be critical of the alien civilization. Their recent interpretations of their prophecies tend to show that they are becoming skeptical as to the value of white inventions which negate human life itself. Are the Indians, they ask, really conscienceless savages and the white men enlightened Christians? I have heard some fine Bernard Shaw speeches delivered by eloquent Indians: Ray Fadden and William Rockwell (the latter a solitary Oneida, over ninety and incredibly vigorous, who possesses a one-man reservation, of which his family had been deprived by the foreclosure of a mortgage, after the rest of the Oneidas had been lured to Wisconsin, but which—by bringing suit on the valid grounds that such liens on Indian property are illegal—he finally recovered for himself). "The white man," Ray Fadden will say, "has invented an Indian in his own image: unforgiving, vindictive, treacherous. The Indian is none of these things and never was. The white man has foisted on the Indian all the worst of his own characteristics." "Does the Indian boy," demands Rockwell, "come home with a gun and shoot his father and mother and his little brothers and sisters? Did he ever amuse himself by sitting in a bar and watching a television show in which somebody else is sitting in a bar and another man comes in, and they look at one another like cats, and then 'Bang, bang, bang!—Bang, bang, bang!'?" And it is impossible not to be disgusted—when one has seen even a little of the real Indian world—by our surreptitious efforts, on the one hand, to despoil and disperse the

Indians and, on the other, our loud exploitation of literary Indian romance: the Mohawk Airlines, the Pontiac cars, the Hotels Onondaga and Iroquois, and the Seneca Cocktail Lounges. This romance—from James Fenimore Cooper to the latest galloping Western—is at least as much a myth of the whites as the double-dealing fiend of Ray Fadden, also a creation of Cooper's, in whose novels the Iroquois are the horrible Mingoes bedevilling the noble Mohicans. A scene that sticks in my mind as a synthesis of incongruities is a Seneca living room, with a handsome boy, naked to the waist, working over an airplane model while his sister, somewhat younger, was studying a school textbook called *How We Became Americans*, in which the Indians got very little attention. The lively and handsome mother—having first made the boy put his shirt on—served us an excellent dinner in the style of upstate New York, but, unlike a New York State matron, did not sit with the men and the children but served us standing up and presided over the conversation. She did not give us the conventional invitation to eat. "All I say," she announced, "is ——," some word that made everybody laugh. I was told that it meant, "Beware!" She had with Fenton—through his standing as a member of a clan and some kinship which this implied—what I had read about in anthropological works as a "joking relationship" but had never seen illustrated before. This relationship was extended to me, and the evening became a contest of repartee. Had we all "become Americans"?

But what has set off the Iroquois resurgence and

caused it to gather power is the gluttonous inroads on tribal property—such as have also been felt by the whites as an encroachment on personal property— by state and federal projects. The struggle to restrain these projects is undoubtedly at the present time one of the principle problems of American life. In a letter to his English publisher, the Russian Borís Pasternák has explained that he wanted, in *Doctor Zhivago*, to dramatize the conflict of the modern individual with the forces of the centralized state, which were becoming more formidable all over the world, and for reasons that were sometimes contradictory. Some years before these articles were written, the writer, who then lived on Cape Cod and who still spends a part of the year there, was informed that a new state highway was to run straight past his front porch in such a way as to shave off his whole front lawn. I made strong representations in Boston to the Department of Public Works and eventually averted this nuisance; but in the spring of 1958, it was suddenly announced to the inhabitants of the Cape that, at the cost of dispossession of some seven hundred families, many of whom had lived there for generations, almost the whole eastern part of Cape Cod was to be turned into a national park. The indifference or opposition to local zoning laws had partly led to this, and we had been quite prepared for the government to take steps to protect the beaches, but not, without any previous consultation, to be told we were to be turned wholesale out of our homes, whether located on beaches or not—for the park, at the Provincetown end, was to cover the whole breadth of the Cape. The resistance was prompt and determined, and a meeting at which questions were supposed to be answered but for the most part were simply evaded by Park Commissioner C. L. Wirth was anything but reassuring. We presently learned that a bill—apparently in counterattack to the local resistance—had just been presented to Congress on behalf of the Department of the Interior, of which the purpose, in the words of an editorial in the *Saturday Evening Post* of July 18, 1959, was "arbitrarily to take over sections of Cape Cod or any other area regarded by the National Park Service as suitable for a park, with scant regard to local interest. Instead of adhering to the usual practice of designating specific areas designed for park purposes, Senator [Richard] Neuberger's bill authorizes the Secretary of the Interior to take over not more than 100,000 acres distributed as he may decide among any three areas in the whole country. . . . There is no opportunity of a debate in Congress on the merits of the areas selected, because their identity would be the secret of the National Park Service until it elects to announce them. No reference is made to an effort to consult the owners of the desired property or how it would be 'procured.' " I have learned also while working on the Indians that Shrewsbury, New Jersey, the little crossroads community in which my father was born and where my grandfather preached for fifty years, which is still one of the most attractive of the old New Jersey towns—the Episcopal Church has a communion service donated by Queen Anne and a charter from George III—is to be gutted, unless the people find a device to prevent it, by another of these state highways at the expense of encroachment on the churchyard and the destruction of a seventeenth-century house; and, returning last summer to the village in New York State in which I am writing this, I found that—to the horror of many of the inhabitants—a planting of splendid elms that had made a majestic approach to Boonville on the road that leads from Utica was in process of being chopped down in order to transform this road into a four-lane highway for trucking. I should have said, when I first started out on my travels in Iroquoia, that I myself was almost as much a member of a half-obsolete minority as these even more old-fashioned Americans of twenty thousand years ago, but I have come to believe that there are many white Americans who now have something important in common with these recalcitrant Indians, that the condition of being an American, whether from A.D. or B.C., should imply a certain minimum security in the undisturbed enjoyment of our country. If it was true that one found, in Niagara Falls, a good deal of sympathy on the part of the whites for the fight of the Tuscaroras, this attitude, I was told, when they won their decision from the Federal Power Commission, turned soon into a kind of resentment: "If the Indians can stand up to the Power Authority, why can't we white voting Americans?" The Indians have actually a better case: they can appeal to the terms of their treaties. But by defending their rights as Indians, they remind us of our rights as citizens.

One cannot, of course, when one contemplates these great highways and seaways and dams, fail to be much impressed by the genius of engineering they represent, by the practical imagination, the delicate mechanical devices and the complicated computations that have gone to lay down and erect them, to start them going and to keep them running, to deepen and divert the great waterways, to light more lamps and to set more wheels turning, to enmesh all mankind, to girdle the earth. But it is well to remember the beavers. The beavers are engineers. A friend of mine in Massachusetts, who has recently retired to the country, imported a pair of beavers, which were furnished him by the State Division of Fisheries and Game, and put them to live in a little stream that runs through his rather wild place. These animals proceeded immediately to construct an enormous dam, and thus flooded a whole area of woodland. The trees are now broken-off sticks that prick dismally out of the beaver pond, in the middle of which humps an igloo bristling with gray dead twigs; the managerial offices are here, the housing for the personnel. All around this, the forest has been devastated. The stumps end in pyramidal spikes, produced by symmetrical chiselling; the trunks lie rotting on the ground, with the bark partly or wholly gnawed off. The beavers are indifferent to landscape, to the convenience of human beings, whom they fearlessly swim up to and stare at, and whom they try to frighten away by insolently slapping their tails.

They build burrows as well as lodges, to take refuge in if the lodge should be threatened. They plan and put through canals and they clear away the brush on the edges of these in order to transport the branches which they anchor underwater for their winter store. When anything goes wrong with the dam, they immediately swim out to repair it, each assigning itself a specific task. They are untiring and, if not interfered with, can go on with their operations along infinite networks of streams and through infinite generations. The descendants of my friend's beaver couple have now built a whole new series of dams and lodges. When they started on a stream in which he did not want them, he had to destroy one of their dams eleven times—taking a pickaxe to it: their mud construction is almost as tough as masonry—before its so expert builders, who had trusted their own calculations in regard to water level and current, were convinced that they had made an error. Lewis Morgan, who, following his book on *The League of the Iroquois*, wrote one on *The American Beaver and His Works*, believed that the activity of beavers was to some extent unnecessary, gratuitous. They compulsively keep on building and digging, cannot be happy if they are not doing this. Mr. Merle Deardorff of Warren, Pennsylvania, whose studies I have cited earlier and who has always, in the matter of the Kinzua Dam, been strongly sympathetic with the Indians, has told me that a colonel of Engineers who had been sent to look over the site once said to him: "You and I may never live to see that dam. But in the long run nothing under Heaven can prevent an engineer from building it. You can dam so much water for so little money!" This is the blind gift of building, the will to build. But my friend, when his beavers are going too far, is able to call a halt to their operations. He has twice summoned the Fisheries and Game people to take some of the beavers away. Unlike the Seneca Indians if the Kinzua project goes through, he can avoid having his whole property flooded. One is coming more and more to feel, as our bureaucrats and engineers seem to be getting more and more out of hand, that the problem for all the rest of us is to provide some reliable means of checking on the desirability of what they propose to do, and, if necessary, as in the case of the beavers, of having them removed from the premises.

9. THE LITTLE WATER CEREMONY

The Little Water Company is the most important of the Iroquois medicine societies: the most sacred and the most secret and the one that has been most rigorously cultivated. The members of this society are the guardians of a miraculous medicine which has the power to revive the dying, and they must sing to it three or four times a year in order to keep up its strength—a ceremony which, like the Dark Dance described above, must always be performed in the dark. The members of this society are either people who have been cured by the medicine or people who have had a dream involving some part of the ceremony. They are likely to be men of high standing, and they ought, one would think, to have good voices. There is a tradition that they are able, without oral communication, to fix upon the dates for the ceremony, and they are supposed to need no rehearsals. They may not sing or hum the songs except when performing the ceremony. Non-members are rarely admitted to the room in which this takes place, but if the members approve, they may listen in an adjoining room or outside the house. Many Indians have never heard this ceremony. I was told by an old man at Tonawanda that, though his brother had been head of the society, he had never been allowed to attend and had never been able even to get his brother to "tell him what it was all about." In his case, it is probable that the reason for this was his having become a Christian.

I was fortunate enough, however, to be given an opportunity of hearing this rite in the Tonawanda Seneca reservation—again through the kindness and in the company of Fenton—and we were even invited to sit with the singers. As in the case of the Dark Dance, the Little Water Ceremony consists mainly of an elaborate series of song sequences, and since these, as with the Dark Dance, are based on a legend, I must begin by telling the story.

The theme of the Little Water legend is the familiar one of death and resurrection. There was once a young hunter—a chief—who was greatly respected by the animals on account of the kindness he showed them. He never killed a deer that was swimming or a doe that had a fawn, or an animal that he took unawares or that was tired from long pursuit. For the predatory birds and animals he would always first kill a deer and skin it and cut it open and cry, "Hear, all you meat-eaters. This is for you." He would always leave some honey for the bears and some corn in the fields for the crows. The tripes of the game he killed he threw into the lakes and streams for the fish and the water animals. One day, when cut off from his party, he was captured and scalped by the

Cherokees. When they had gone, the Wolf smelled
blood, and he came up and licked the bloody head.
But when he recognized the Good Hunter, he howled
for the rest of the animals, who all came and gathered
around and mourned for their lost friend. The Bear
felt the body with his paws and on the chest found a
spot that was warm. The birds had come, too, and
they all held a council, while the Bear kept him warm
in his arms, as to how they could bring the young
hunter to life. The only dissenting voice was that of
the Turkey Buzzard, who said, "Let's wait till he gets
ripe and eat him." And they compounded a powerful
medicine, to which each one contributed a "life-
spark"—in some versions a bit of the brain, in others
a bit of the heart. But the mixture of all these ingredients made an essence so concentrated that it
could all be contained in an acorn shell, and it is
called for this reason the Little Water.

Now the Owl said, "A live man must have a scalp,"
and who was to go for the scalp? In certain of the
tellings of the story, a long discussion takes place.
One animal after another is decided unfit. The quadrupeds will never do: what is needed is a clever bird.
The Dew Eagle is sometimes chosen. He is the ranking bird of the Iroquois, who carries a pool of dew
on his back and, when rain fails, can spill it as mist.
One variant makes it the Hummingbird, who moves
quickly and is almost invisible. But it is more likely
to be the Giant Crow (Gáh-ga-go-wa), the messenger for all the birds, who plays a prominent rôle
in the ceremony. He flies to the Cherokee village,

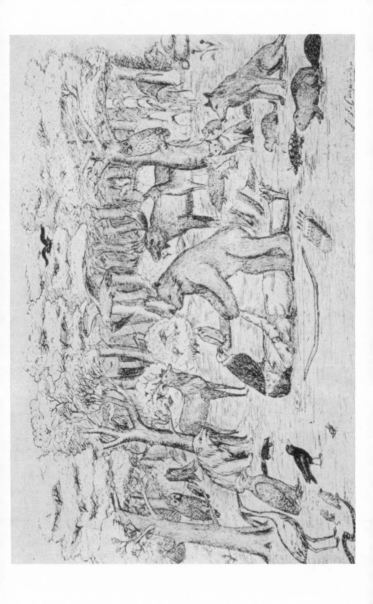

The Good Hunter revived by the animals in the legend on which the Little Water Ceremony is based. A drawing by Jesse Cornplanter of Tonawanda, which appears as an illustration in *Seneca Myths and Folk-Tales* by Arthur C. Parker.

and there he sees the good hunter's scalp, which has been stretched on a hoop and hung up to dry in the smoke that comes out of the smoke-hole. He swoops down and snatches it. The Cherokees see him and shoot their arrows at him, but the Crow flies so high that they cannot reach him.

When he has brought the scalp back to the council, they find it is too much dried out to be worn by a living man. The Great Crow has to vomit on it and the Dew Eagle sprinkle on it some drops of his dew before it is supple and moist enough to be made to grow back on the hunter's head. He has already been given the medicine, and he feels himself coming to life. As he lies with his eyes still closed, he realizes that he is now able to understand the language of the animals and birds. They are singing a wonderful song, and he listens to it and finds later on that he is able to remember every word. They tell him to form a company and to sing it when their help is needed. He asks how they make the medicine, and they say that they cannot tell him because he is not a virgin. But someone will be given the secret, and they will notify this person by singing their song. The Bear helps the youth to his feet, and when he opens his eyes, there is nobody there: only a circle of tracks. It is dawn. He goes back to his people.

We met the Little Water singers at about ten o'clock on the night of June 6, 1959. The hours of singing must coïncide with the duration of the events of the story, so one has to sit up all night. The cere-

mony took place in an ample kitchen. No one may
smoke cigarettes in the room, and no one may be
present who has been drinking liquor; no menstruating
woman may enter the house. Such impurities would
spoil the medicine. It is possible for women to be
"bundle-holders"—that is, guardians of the sacred
powder; but on this occasion none was present. The
lady of the house sometimes entered the kitchen, before the proceedings began, to attend to operations on
the stove, but she always withdrew and, when the ceremony started—with doors closed and lights extinguished—she sat, with her young son and another
woman (entertained, in this case, by no television),
in a lighted adjacent room. On the other hand, the
doors were not locked, with a sentinel posted outside,
as, according to Arthur C. Parker, had formerly been
the custom.

The Senecas of Tonawanda are, as a group, perhaps the most self-confident and the proudest in the
whole Iroquois world. Their dwellings range from
pretty modern cottages to log-cabins with plastered
cracks, and both kinds seem quite sound and well-kept.
The man who presides at the Little Water ceremony
—whose English name is Corbett Sundown—is a chief
whose hereditary title is So-gánt-dzo-wa, He Has a
Large Forehead, and one of the dominating personal-
ities at Tonawanda. He struck me as being more like
the kind of Indian with whom the first settlers dealt
than anyone else I had met: good-looking with trenchant features, speaking English with a strong accent,
giving an impression of formidable strength in reserve.

Chief Sundown likes to tell funny stories, and his laughter is somewhat harsh. (The Indians are extremely humorous, but as a rule they do not smile or laugh until one of their deadpan jokes makes *you* laugh, when the tone of the conversation may become quite jovial.) Corbett Sundown is both a foreman in a gypsum plant and a guardian of ancient tradition. In Tonawanda, the fires of nationalism do not seem to burn so fiercely as they do on certain other of the reservations; but, though we found Sundown rather noncommittal, it was evident that he was fully informed about everything that was going on in Iroquoia. He had sent a message to Fenton inviting him to attend the ceremony, but I had to be approved and invited before Fenton could bring me in, so we first went to his house to see him. My previous requests to be allowed to hear the ceremony had not met with any success, and he now told me that they did not want people who came simply out of curiosity, and that especially they did not want journalists who knew nothing about Indian life and who printed preposterous stories. There was a television show going on in the room next to that in which we sat, and the head of a young boy presently peered in at the door to see who the visitors were, then at once disappeared again. "That's *his* culture," said Corbett Sundown. "He grew up with it." I wondered what the result would be of growing up, in such an *echt* Indian household as Sundown's apparently was, on a diet of white rubbish. It was evident that TV was like the air he breathed. First he watched on his back from the bed, then he

listened on his face on a rug. He left the table to go
back to it while we were still eating supper. For of
course we were not allowed to leave without sharing
the Sundowns' supper—the only meal I had with the
Indians that included a distinctively Indian dish
(except for succotash, which we borrowed from
them): something called Indian "cornbread," which,
however, does not resemble our bread and which I
took at first for some sort of meatloaf. It is gray and
has kidney beans embedded in it; they fry it in thick
slices.

In the kitchen of the other house where the ceremony was to be performed, the conversation was
mostly in Seneca, with an occasional exchange in
English with us. I noticed that the time was always
given in English: "eleven o'clock," etc. There was a
good deal of kidding and joking, with Corbett Sundown, as it were, sparking off the laughs. Their
voices are low and their speech is rapid compared to
those of other upstate New Yorkers. They are said
to complain of our loudness. Whenever the door was
opened, a swarm of mosquitoes came in, and these
provoked a good deal of mirth. When I was slapping
my ankles and the top of my head, a round-faced
bespectacled chief remarked with a quiet grin, "If
you don't bother them, they'll leave you alone."
Fenton told me that the mosquitoes at Tonawanda had
always been famous for ferocity. One of the Senecas
had said that the Tonawanda mosquitos were tri-
motored. There was a legend about their origin. There
had at first been a single huge mosquito. One day she

Chief Sundown (Sogántjowah) of Tonawanda, standing on the right. In the middle is the late Jesse Cornplanter, the author of *Legends of the Longhouse* and the executor of the drawing of the Good Hunter in the previous illustration. On the left is Chief Sundown's young son, whose interest in television has been mentioned in the text. This photograph was made for the centennial—1857-1957—of the purchase of the Tonawanda Reservation by the Tonawanda Indians.

chased a man, who ran for his life and then dodged behind a tree. The proboscis of the monster was thrust into the tree, and, swollen with blood, she exploded. From the myriad drops of her blood sprang the Tonawanda breed of mosquitoes, smaller but equally fierce. This set off a man from Canada—the only Indian present who wore a tie—to give us another version, in which the mosquito was shot with an arrow, and, evidently an experienced storyteller, he went on to other tales. An Indian had met a bear, and getting a tree between him and it, had seized the front paws of the bear on either side of the tree. But then he could do nothing more: he had to stand there holding the bear. At length his brother came by with another man, and he called out for them to help him. "Have you had your breakfast yet?" asked the brother of his companion. The companion answered yes. "Then *you* help him: I haven't had mine."—In Canada, a Member of Parliament was eating at a lunch-counter beside an Indian. The Indian ate a stack of pancakes. "I wish I had your appetite," said the Member of Parliament. "I never have any appetite." "Take it," said the Indian. "Why don't you take it?" "What do you mean?" said the Member of Parliament. "You've taken my land, you've taken my freedom, you've taken my women," said the Indian. "You might as well take my appetite, too."

The materials for the ceremony and the feast were brought in. The soup was in a copper washboiler; the pork for it was set on the stove. There were two or three baskets of fresh strawberries and some cans of frozen ones. Chief Sundown removed the stems of the former, and poured them all into two white enamelled pails, already partly filled with water, so that they floated in a kind of syrup. The rattles were carried in a big white bag. They are pale yellow polished gourds—some very large, some small—with dried cherrystones inside. Three reed flutes were laid on the table. The medicine, in two modern boxes, one of them a tin tea-caddy, was set on the same table and covered with a sheet of white muslin. This muslin is a part of the "quantity of goods of the value of $10,000" provided for in the Pickering Treaty of 1794, which the Iroquois still collect from the federal government. Everybody, including ourselves, brought in a small package of Indian tobacco, which, as one entered, was handed to Sundown. This tobacco is mixed in a single receptacle, and little piles of it—set down counterclockwise—are carefully placed on the table, two rows of four each, which represent the eight clans of the Senecas, to show that the medicine has been given for all. The singers sat on two long benches against two walls of the kitchen that met at a right angle. There were only ten Indians present (the number of the singers is not fixed). In the kitchen were a large wood stove, a washing machine and a white modern sink. On a shelf stood a big box of Corn Flakes.

At a quarter past eleven, the preliminaries to the ceremony began. Chief Sundown arose and, closing his eyes, with his hands held down and clasped, made a twenty-minute speech in Seneca—with many repetitions, I was told—announcing what they were going to do. Two friends from afar had come to help them. Then the food and the musical instruments were all placed on the stove or beside it, to be blessed to the use of the ceremony; the piles of tobacco were picked up from the table in the same order in which they had been laid; and Chief Sundown, taking off one of the stove-lids, began dropping tobacco in pinches into the red-burning fire below, invoking, as he did so, the Divinity and His deputies, the Sun, Moon, Stars, Winds, etc.:

"Now I give you incense,
You, the Great Darkness!
You, our great-grand-parents, here tonight—
We offer you incense!
We assemble at certain times in the year
That this may be done.
   (We trust that all believe in this medicine,
   For all are invited to partake of this medicine.). . .
   Now we offer you this incense!
Some have had ill luck
Endeavoring to give a human being.*
We hope you will take hold
And help your grandchildren,
Nor be discouraged in us!
   Now we act as we offer you incense!
You love it the most of all offerings!
With it you will hear us better
And not tire of our talking,

* In childbearing.

But love us with all power
Beyond all treasures
Or spreading your words through the air!
   All men travelling under the great heavens,
You have invited your grandchildren and all na-
     tions!
   O you that make the noise,
You the great Thunderer!
Your grandchildren wish to thank you!
All your grandchildren have asked me
To offer this incense upon the mountain to you! . . .
   O you the Manager of All Things!
We ask you to help us,
To help us make this medicine strong!
You are the Creator,
The Most High,
The Best Friend of men!
We ask you to help us!
We implore your favor!
   I have spoken."

Then the rest of the tobacco was put into pipes,
and they smoked for a few minutes in silence. Then
the strawberry pails were passed in a ritualistic order,
the guests being served last. This was done after each
intermission, just before the new sequence was begun.
Everyone drinks from a ladle; and they jokingly
called out a word—"Nyon, nyon" (pronounced as
in French *bon*)—which I did not understand but
which reminded me of the traditional *"Gor'ko,
gor'ko!"* that the guests cry at Russian wedding
parties. This, it seems, is the word for "You're wel-

come." The point is that—somewhat in the fashion
that the English have abbreviated, "Thank you," to
" 'Kyou"—the Senecas have averted it altogether by
saying "You're welcome" first. The preliminary cries
of this word eliminate the monotonous interchange.
I had noticed that I was the only person present who
said "Thank you" when I was offered the syrup.

Now the door to the next room was closed, the
switch in the wall was turned off, and the ceremony
proper began. The room with its Corn Flakes had
vanished: you were at once in a different world. The
single beat of a rattle is heard in the sudden blackness
like the striking of a gigantic match, and it is answered by other such flashes that make rippings of
sound as startling as a large-scale electric spark. Then
the first of the two chief singers cries "*Wee yoh!*"
and the second "*Yoh wee!*," and the first of them now
sets the rhythm for the rattles, which is picked up
by the rest of the company. In this section the tempo
is uniform, and it reminds one of the rapid jogging
that is heard by the passenger on an express train. The
rhythm is kept up, without raggedness or flagging,
for a little less than an hour. Arthur Parker says that
the pace is 150 a minute; but I do not know whether
this applies to the section I am now describing or to
the even faster passages in the later ones. The songs
themselves are in slower time. Their structure has
something in common with that of old English and
Scottish ballads, as well as their nonsense refrains—
like the English, "Benorio, benory"—and the wist-
fulness of their accent, as of human beings alone with

nature, singing in unpeopled spaces. The first singer gives the couplet, and this is repeated by the second; then all take it up in a powerful chorus. A man and a woman are searching for the magical Little Water that has brought the Good Hunter to life but the receipt for compounding which, because he was not a virgin, the animals could not teach him. Now their song has been heard, and the man and the woman are obeying its summons to search. The first line of every couplet always applies to the woman—since the woman, among the Iroquois, is always given first place—and the second line to the man:

"She went to the village.
He went to the village."

—to the fields, to the little spring, to the edge of the wood, etc. In the climactic final couplet, they go to the top of a hill, and there they are left "standing under the clouds."

In the second section, the rhythms of the rattles are different. While the first and second singers are introducing the couplets, the rattles are going so fast that they seem to weave a kind of veil or screen— a scratching almost visible on the darkness—that hangs before the lyric voices; but when the chorus takes up the theme, this changes to a slow heavy beat that has something of the pound of a march. The shift is extremely effective. When it occurs, this accompaniment of the rattles—contrary to our convention— does not quite coincide with the song and the chorus but always overlaps a little. The big shimmer of the solo begins before the pound of the chorus has ended: in a moment, you are given notice, a fresh song will be springing up; and in the same way the lusty thump will commence before the song has quite finished. In this section, the animals assemble: "The She-Owl," and then "the He-Owl," "came bringing tobacco and joined the song." And presently these creatures begin to speak, as they are mentioned pair by pair in the couplets. They are mimicked by one or more singers—who have had their parts assigned them—as the arrival of each is announced. The effect of this is startling and eerie. The Gáhgagowa caws—the first half of his name is evidently onomatopoetic; the Bear and the Panther roar; the Owl has a soft four-note hoot: "Wu-wu, Wu-wu." There are many archaic words in the ritual that nobody now understands. Besides the Giant Crow, the Great Eagle, the Dew Eagle, the Great Phoebe, the Great Woodpecker and a bird which, after a moment's thought, had been identified for us by Sundown as the Kingbird, there are birds which can no longer be identified, and when one of these birds was mentioned, the cackle of a hen who has just laid an egg—followed by quiet laughter—was heard from the prehistoric darkness. A climax of animation occurs toward the end of this section. The She- and He-Wolves arrive. They are heralded as running along the rim of the hills, and afterwards through the meadows. They do not howl; since they are running, they bark like dogs. A queer kind of excitement is created here. The animals are supposed to be present, and I learn from Arthur Parker that the adepts are believed to see them. He hints at further mysteries which he is not allowed to reveal; and from reading Fenton's unpublished notes on the Little Water Ceremony, I get the impression that the singers are supposed to *become* the animals. They are forbidden to keep time with their feet—as they do in all the other ceremonies—since the quadrupeds go on pads and the tread of the birds is soundless. The men who serve the syrup are called Eagles, and the man who presides is the Giant Crow. The Wolf has also some special rôle. I did not see any animals nor did the medicine become visibly luminous, as it was formerly supposed to do when its power was renewed by the singing. I could not see that the boxes were even opened. Nor was I conscious of another phenomenon that Chief Sundown had told me to listen for. "You'll hear a woman's voice," he had said, "and there's no woman in the room." I have learned that the best first singers—who always sing the feminine lines—have a practice of outdoing the chorus by pitching each song in a sequence a little higher than the one before. If this singer starts the sequence off so high that it is sure at a later stage to get out of the range of the others, he is stopped, and they have to begin again—the worst *gaffe* that can be committed except for a singer's forgetting the words. (I noticed, in an intermission, that the first singer, who was younger than the others, was studying his lines in a notebook.)

It was delightful to go out in these intermissions. One was here in the cool June night of the green Tonawanda woodland. There was a fragrance of something blooming. The back lawn, where the grass had been cut, was revealed by a bulb with a reflector behind it that directed the light from the top of the house. The peelings of asbestos shingling, in imitation of brick, that were hanging away from this wall contrasted with the beauty of the landscape and the music that had been liberated inside the house. The Indians talked softly and smoked a little. The hoot of a real owl was heard; a mudhen croaked from nearby Salt Creek; a nighthawk flew away through the lighted air to the forest that made the background.

The third section is the climax of the symphony. Now the medicine at last is found. The questers have discovered that the marvellous song emanates from the top of a mountain—the mountain, I suppose, that the man and the woman have ascended at the end of the first sequence. But it ought to be explained that this couple do not appear in all versions of the ceremony, which differs somewhat in the different reservations. There is a version in which it is simply a man; and the account I shall give here of the search is taken from a telling of the *legend*—not always consistent with the songs—in which the searchers are two young men. These questers set out in the dark, and they are to endure a whole set of ordeals, to surmount a whole series of obstacles. At the start they are trapped in a "windfall," a place where the trees have been blown down, and they must break their way out of this. They feel that there are presences about them, that the animals are guiding them to the source of the song. Next they must plod through a swamp. Then they have to cross a ravine; then they hear the roaring of a cataract and are confronted with another ravine through which a swift river runs. One of the young men is "almost afraid"; but they go down and swim across it, though the waters are terribly cold. A mountain now rises before them, so steep that they think they can never climb it. The less hardy of the searchers proposes a rest, but the other says they have to go on, and when he has spoken, they hear a voice that sings "Follow me, follow me!", and a light comes flying over them. This is the Whippoorwill, whose song is the "flourish of the flute" mentioned to me by Nicodemus Bailey. Each of the sequences is opened and closed by this cry, but it is only in this third part, I think, that the flute intervenes in the narrative. It plays a rôle like the bird in *Siegfried* that will guide the hero to the Ring. With effort, the young men scale the mountain, and at the top they find a great stalk of corn growing out of the barren rock, and from this stalk comes the song that has drawn them. They are told by the winged light to burn a tobacco offering and then to cut the root of the corn. When they do so, it bleeds human blood, but immediately the wound heals. They are now told by the voices of the animals how to collect the ingredients of the medicine, how to mix it and how to apply it.

This section is more complicated than the others, and it is said to be difficult to sing. In each of the first two sequences, the songs all follow a pattern; but in the third, they begin on unexpected notes and follow unfamiliar courses. This is magic, a force beyond nature is tearing itself free. There is a passage of re-iteration that entirely departs from the ballad stanzas and that sounds like some sort of litany. A great structure is raised by the rattles that is neither the big shimmer, the express train nor the grand triumphal march. And a paean is let loose: it fills the room with its volume. One finds oneself surrounded, almost stupefied, as if the space between the four walls had become one of the tubes of a pipe organ and as if one were sitting inside it, almost drowned in a sustained diapason. How strange when the lights are turned on—strange, apparently, for the singers, too, who sit blinking and dazed at first, having to bring themselves up short in this kitchen, in this new electric-lighted world—to find oneself there in the room with these ten men who work in the daytime in the gypsum mines and plants of the neighboring town of Akron, dressed in their unceremonious clothes: an assortment of physical types, some handsome, some not so handsome, some young and some old, some fat and some lean, some sallow, one almost black, some with spectacles, some with their teeth gone, who have just given body in the darkness to a creation which absorbed and transcended them all. A car had driven up to the house while the singing was going on; its headlights had glared toward the window. I saw the profile against it of a man turning round to look; but the singing was not interrupted, and the driver, when he heard it, withdrew.

This sequence, through which is expressed the whole mystery and virtue of the Little Water, seems hard for even the well-informed outsider to follow, though the first two parts, apparently, for a student of Seneca, are plain enough sailing. The reports on it are rather scrappy and mutually inconsistent. Neither Parker

nor Jesse Cornplanter, who has also touched on the
Little Water, throws any light at all on its central
episode. My description of this part of the quest is
based upon the version of the legend given by Arthur
Parker. In our earlier conversation with Chief Sundown, William Fenton had quoted songs from the
first two sections, but said he could not remember the
third. Sundown did nothing to help him out: he said
simply, "Everything has a meaning. I'm not very
good on songs." We questioned the second singer in
the intermission that followed this section. He brought
out some of the keywords in Seneca but his command
of English was limited. "He goes to the swamp. . .
He goes to the swamp . . ." he made an attempt to
explain. "He [I do not know who this was] told us
what everything meant." I learn from another source
that a swamp is the place in which the searchers find
saxifrage, the one plant included in the medicine. I do
not know whether the saxifrage is a variant on the
singing stalk of corn.

The singers had worked hard over this complicated
section. One man declared that he was soaked with
sweat. I should think they must all have been. But the
next part is relatively relaxing. The music is the same
as in the second sequence. The animals are thanked
pair by pair, and they make their appropriate ac-
knowledgments. The mood is one of calm jubilation.

This usually ends the ceremony; but on this occasion they sang a fifth sequence, which is used in the
treatment of patients. In the old days the medicine
powder was carried along in warfare to revivify the
badly wounded. Today it is only applied in cases of

accident or illness that are regarded as more or less desperate. At the bedside, three pinches of the powder are dropped in a cup of water so as to make the points of a triangle. (The water must have been dipped from the stream in the direction in which it is running.) If the powder sinks to the bottom, the patient must be given up; if the water is clouded, the results are doubtful; if it floats, the chances are good. The treatment goes on four days. The medicine man takes some of the water in his mouth and sprays it on the part afflicted, and the medicine songs are sung. Then the patient is protected by a white screen, and given nothing but white food to eat: white of chicken and white of egg —if possible, from a white fowl. I was told that a doctor who for many years had been attending a Seneca community would say, when he heard of an accident, "They won't call me in for four days, and by that time his leg will be all swollen and purple." After the doctor had set the leg, the Indians would claim that the medicine had healed it. The fifth sequence we heard was the ritual intended for broken bones, and, instead of being enlivened by animal cries, it was lacerated by shrieks and groans supposed to be coming from the patient.

We left—being extremely sleepy—without taking part in the final feast, at which the members, cawing like crows, eat the stew in the manner indicated by the verb which has already been mentioned in connection with the ceremony of the Dark Dance.

But there is more to the Little Water Ceremony than the effort to renew the medicine. To have heard it is to understand its importance as a builder of morale, and why it has to be performed by a small group of men in a darkened room. The members of this medicine society really constitute a kind of élite, and they are making an affirmation of the will of the Iroquois people, of their vitality, their force to persist. These adepts have mastered the principle of life, they can summon it by the ceremony itself. Through this they surpass themselves, they prove to themselves their power. Ten men in a darkened kitchen, with an audience of four or five of whom the celebrants are hardly aware, make a core from which radiates conviction, of which the stoutness may sustain their fellows.

I knew that the Little Water—with its theme of near-death and resuscitation—was supposed to end just at daybreak. "It is brightening. Dawn is approaching. The morning star is already up," says one version of the Good Hunter legend of the hour when the hunter goes home. And I had wondered how precisely they would time it. When the lights were turned on, it was half past four. I had certainly at one point observed, glancing out of the torrent of sound, that the windows were becoming less dim; but when I thanked Corbett Sundown, I wished him goodnight. "Not goodnight, good morning," he said, and he wished us a safe journey home. To Fenton he said, "You can tell your wife that you were up all night with us." And when we went out of the house to our car, I found that it was indeed dawn. The birds were now tuning up, the sun was just topping the forest and the woodland of the roadside was already quite green in the first soft and misty daylight.

APPENDIX

Letters from Edmund Wilson Concerning
Apologies to the Iroquois, 1957–1965

To WILLIAM SHAWN   December 3, 1957
The New Yorker   Wellfleet

. . . Please send me a letter explaining that I am writing about the Iroquois Indians for *The New Yorker*, and whatever assistance, etc. Nobody asked me for my credentials except Standing Arrow, who has none himself, having been repudiated by his clan; but I think it might be as well for me to have some—especially since I shall next time be traveling with [William N.] Fenton and want to be able to make it clear that I am not a New York State official . . .

To JOHN DOS PASSOS   November 19, 1958

. . . There is lots that I'd like to talk to you about but it can't be handled in a letter. I'm still entangled in the Civil War, which, as Liebling at *The New Yorker* says, is

like the Tar Baby in *Uncle Remus.* I've also taken on the
Iroquois Indians, who are having themselves a nationalist movement against the United States. Mad Bear, the
Tuscarora leader, is the first person in history who has
succeeded in stopping Robert Moses, as you must have
been seeing in the papers. Investigating these Indian situations has taken me into the big power projects, the St.
Lawrence Seaway, the proposed Kinzua Dam, and other
developments in New York State, and it is appalling to
see how much this country is getting to be run by engineers, bureacrats, and the Armed Forces . . .

To Van Wyck Brooks   December 18, 1957
                                               Wellfleet

. . . By the way, I have been rereading your chapter on
Parkman and find—page 178 of the old edition—that
you speak of the Mohawks and the Iroquois as if they
were different tribes. *Iroquois* is the collective name for
the Confederacy of the Six Nations, of which the Mohawks were one. I am particularly up on this because I
have discovered, to my great surprise, that I am surrounded at Talcottville by an Iroquois national movement—not unlike Scottish nationalism and Zionism—
with a revival of the old religion and claims for territory
of their own. They have some legitimate grievances because they are losing their property in their reservations
on account of the St. Lawrence Seaway. I went over
there in October and found some very strange things
going on and am going again at the end of January, when
the Iroquois celebrate their New Year, and will eventually write something about it . . .

To Roger W. Straus, Jr., 1958

I had wanted to talk to you about Fenton before you saw him. He is the country's greatest authority on the Iroquois Indians—brilliant and quite free from anthropological jargon. He grew up among the Indians in the southwestern [part of] New York and knows them intimately in a personal way.

To William N. Fenton   October 29, 1957
                                              Wellfleet

Dear Dr. Fenton: Thank you very much for your helpful information and the Iroquois literature. I was able to catch a plane immediately, so went on to Boston.

It would be immensely useful to me to go, as you suggested, on a tour of the reservations at the Iroquois New Year. If you can go, I hope you will take me along. I'll be better informed by that time.

By the way, I did not catch the name of the epic you said you had translated. I cannot find it in your bibliography.

Sincerely, Edmund Wilson

To Elena Wilson   January 24, 1958
                                              Salamanca, N.Y.

. . . toward evening it began to snow, we stopped off and spent the night at Geneva. Fenton talked a blue streak all the way . . . and gave me quantities of information, all very much to the point . . .

We stopped off in the late morning at the Tonawanda

Seneca reservation, where Fenton had spent two years, and called on a most extraordinary old Seneca. He had been to the old Indian college Carlisle, now discontinued, was a power in politics, played the piccolo and flute (had once played in Sousa's band), and was something of an Indian scholar. Though you never would have thought English was his native language, he spoke it with an unexpected felicity and exactitude, and seemed more like a cultivated old Russian or Oriental than like anything in upstate New York, though he had some of the old-fashioned New York turns of phrase and ways of speaking. Fenton himself comes from this part of the state and knows everybody and all about the local affairs, as well as knowing more about the Iroquois than anybody else alive. The Indians receive him as a local boy whose family have been here for generations and an authority on their own history and religions . . .

We then moved on to the Cattaraugus and Allegany reservations. These two are inhabited by the children of the 1848 revolution . . . These Senecas had revolted against the sachems and chiefs who had been selling their lands to the whites, had deposed them and set up a council, with an elected president at its head. They are organized—incorporated, I think—as the Seneca Nation . . . missed the beginning of the ceremonies, which included one of the things I most wanted to take in. This is a kind of opera or cantata, which is entirely done in the dark and lasts all night till dawn. Fenton and the old man at Tonawanda were telling me about it, singing parts of it, and making it sound wonderful—a legend of the good hunter, who was scalped by the Cherokees but then rescued by the animals, to whom he had been considerate; they brought him back his scalp and raised him from the dead . . . we might spend the last night near Tonawanda, to look in on the ceremonies there . . . Tomorrow begins a round of ceremonies. The woman who gave us the dinner told me I should have to dance in spite of my gouty foot, and that once you started dancing, it was impossible to stop. Due to the protests of the Buffalo humane society and the dying out of the special breed which used to be raised for the purpose, they no longer, I was rather relieved to find, sacrifice the white dog . . .

This country is monotonous and grim in the wintertime—gray sky and gray snow, bristling with small black woodland . . .

To ROGER W. STRAUS, JR.   February 5, 1958
                                                            Wellfleet

. . . My trip to the Indians was immensely successful— I saw most of the New Year's festival and got a pretty good understanding of the most important of the Iroquois' grievances: that one of their reservations will be completely destroyed if a flood-control dam on the Allegheny River is put through as proposed by the government. The Indians in that part of the world are fortunately rich enough to have hired a smart Washington lawyer, and there is a chance that they may succeed in saving their reservation. I'll be doing an article or articles on the overall situation of the Iroquois in the United States, and there may possibly be a small book in it . . .

To Elena Wilson   June 9, 1958
                                               Talcottville

. . . Philip Cook, the Mormon Mohawk, has asked us to
supper at St. Regis on Thursday. This will probably be
a two-day trip. The Strawberry Festival takes place, apparently, the 22nd and the Little Water Ceremony (of
the resurrected hunter) is sung the night before. Bill
Fenton has told me what to do to get admitted, and I
hope I may succeed. We shall probably, however, start
on our trip next Sunday and give it a whole week: Syracuse, Niagara Falls, then the southwestern corner of the
state, where I went with Fenton last winter . . .

To Elena Wilson   June 14, 1958
                                               Talcottville

. . . We got back last night . . . We had a very successful two-day trip. Cook is full of affection and good will
and has a kind of natural authority. All through the
evening, people kept dropping in or coming to see him
about something—an aluminum worker to get him to
find him a new house, a young man who had just graduated from Hamilton and wanted a job. The next day
we went to a place near Saranac Lake to see another
Indian expert, who has an Indian museum there but
earns his living as a schoolteacher. He is a curious character: his father was Irish, and he looks and behaves like
an Irishman—has red hair and blue eyes and a terrific
gift of gab. But, having grown up in the Mohawk reservation with his Mohawk mother, he has canalized all the
eloquence, wit, and fighting spirit which used to be de-

voted to Irish patriotism into the cause of the Six Nations. The boys in the St. Regis reservation have gone
in for having their heads shaved, in the traditional way,
leaving only a strip of hair down the middle for a scalp
lock . . .

To ELENA WILSON   June 19, 1958
                                         Salamanca

The situation at the Tuscarora reservation has been very
tense lately. I went to the house of a family in which the
father had been the head of an Indian Defense organization and one of the sons had taken part in the recent riot.
The father was rather suspicious at first—a sheriff's car
was patrolling the reservation—but then the son came
and recognized me from having seen me at the Onondaga
reservation when I was put out of the Longhouse by that
old man. Everybody in the Indian world seems to know
about this incident—it is just like the Russian grapevine.
They ended by asking us to supper, having talked for
about three hours. I then looked up the Tuscaroras' lawyer [Stanley Grossman], who came to see me at the
hotel. He turned out to be a very bright young Jew, full
of enthusiasm for the Indian cause, who believes that he,
too, can get his case before the Supreme Court and, in
any event, hold up the power project at least a year . . .

To ELENA WILSON   June 21, 1958
                                         Salamanca

. . . The evening after I wrote you last, we went to call
on the Crouses. Reuel thinks that he is like a German

burgomaster. He is also like all the husbands of clever and sought-after wives—quiet and polite. Myrtie is the Sibyl Colefax of the Allegany reservation, who entertains visiting palefaces just as Lady Colefax entertains visiting Americans . . . The next day we went to see Cornelius Seneca, the president of the Seneca Nation—very satisfactory interview . . . He said that he sometimes wondered whether he wouldn't have been happier in the Indians' primitive state. Since he wouldn't have "known any better," he wouldn't have missed the things they didn't have; and life would have been so much quieter. They only killed such animals as they needed to eat, and otherwise lived on good terms with them. It is curious that the loss of good relations with the animals seemed to be one of the things he most regretted.

. . . Then I went to call on the man who is the custodian of the sacred medicine of the Little Water Ceremony, to which I was hoping to get admitted. The Indians I had talked to about it were dubious about my succeeding. No Indian can be admitted unless he has taken the medicine and become, by having done so, a member of the fraternity, and very few people are willing to take the medicine—compounded of all those parts of animals—even in the extreme emergencies in which it supposed to be efficacious. The keeper of the Little Water told me that the ceremony had already taken place, but did not discourage me from applying in September. He said that he would have to consult his fraternity mates . . .

To Elena Wilson   June 23, 1958
                                             Talcottville

. . . The Strawberry Festival was animated but brief.
The confessions and the reciting of the Handsome Lake
code had taken place before, as, to my disappointment,
had the Little Water Ceremony. There is only one dance
—the Feather Dance, which is done in costume, with
such terrific stampings by the men that you think it will
bring down the Longhouse. Myrtie Crouse asked us afterwards to lunch . . . Excellent lunch of ham, potato
salad, some kind of beans, cole slaw, and a tremendous
strawberry shortcake. At the festival, the strawberries
are served in pails floating in strawberry syrup and offered to everyone in turn in a dipper. Then people—
especially the children—go and take as much as they like
in glasses or cups . . .

To Arthur Schlesinger, Jr.   June 24, 1958
                                             Talcottville

Dear Arthur: . . . I am sorry to be missing you at Wellfleet. I should like to hold an old-fashioned school debate
on "Resolved that the United States is an international
menace and nuisance"—you, I assume, taking the nega-
tive. I have just come back from a tour of the Iroquois
reservations, which has confirmed my worst suspicions
as to what Washington and New York State are doing to
the Indians. What has surprised me, however, is that
there are quite a few white people who hope that they
will win their cases. I think that many people nowadays
are nervous about their rights.

                                             As ever, Edmund

To Daniel Aaron   [undated, 1958]
                                   Talcottville

Dear Dan: I have had the following idea. There is going
to be a pageant at the Six Nations reservation in Canada
—near Brantford, just west of Niagara Falls—which I
want to go to: August 15–16. Would you like to come
here, say, the 14th, and drive me?—all expenses paid by
The New Yorker. I have business in the Tuscarora and
Tonawanda reservations, which would be right on our
way, and this would enable you to see quite a little of
the Iroquois . . .

                                   As ever, Edmund

To Daniel Aaron   [undated, 1958]

Dear Dan: Here is a souvenir of our trip.* Mad Bear and
Stanley Grossman were summoned to St. Regis by the
Mohawks in connection with the income-tax crisis—
which, I guess, developed after you left (the Mohawks
refuse to pay the state tax)—and had dinner with me on
their way back. I got Mad Bear to tell me the prophecy
again and took it down word for word. Hope you are
enjoying yourself.

                                   Edmund W.

* "Deganawida's prophecy as told me by Mad Bear (Wallace Anderson), August 31, 1958."

To Elizabeth Huling   November 4, 1958
                                              Wellfleet

. . . I spent most of my summer on the Iroquois Indians,
who for various reasons are having their reservations
taken away from them or ruined. They have worked up
a nationalist movement, are bringing suits against the
U.S. and the State of New York, and are threatening to
appeal to the U.N. They have taken some beatings in
the courts but have also had some rather remarkable
successes and have the glory of having been the first
people in history to stop the operations of Robert Moses.
All too long to tell about in a letter, but it will be coming
out soon in *The New Yorker* . . .

To William N. Fenton   February 28, 1959
                                              Wellfleet

Dear Bill: . . . We would be delighted to have you
March 23rd. By that time I hope to have the whole
Indian thing done and typed. I am only just getting to
the Seneca, which I keep till last for the *pièce de résistance*.
You, of course, know about the remarkable victory over
Moses of Mad Bear and Stanley Grossman. Mad Bear, I
gather, is becoming, as I thought he would, something
of a big Iroquois leader. The last news I heard from
Niagara was that he was first going to have a conference
with Mrs. Roosevelt and then advance on Washington
with four hundred Indians.

                                    Best regards, Edmund

To MARY MEIGS AND BARBARA DEMING   April 2, 1959
Wellfleet

. . . My friend Bill Fenton, the Indian authority from
Albany, spent two highly animated days with us. He
brought unpublished records of Indian music that I wish
you could have heard. The Six Nations Reserve in Ontario has declared its independence of Canada and upset
their puppet government. The Mounties were sent in to
put it back. I don't know what will happen . . .

To MARY MEIGS   April 11, 1959
Wellfleet

. . . I am just starting off on another Indian trip—to
attend the hearing, in Canada, on the Iroquois chiefs
who have proclaimed their independence and been
arrested . . .

To ELENA WILSON   May 1959
Talcottville

. . . It is a marvelous day and I feel full of energy. Mad
Bear called me up before seven. Stanley Grossman is
taking the defense of the Indian who is supposed to have
shot that trooper. He is a first cousin of my friend Papineau at Onondaga. They claim that he did not do the
shooting but was framed by the police. He himself was
shot and is in the hospital at Watertown. Grossman and
Mad Bear are presumably coming to see me the last of
the week. Fenton tells me that the state authorities have
"got their backs up" against the Indians . . .

To Robert Lowell   June 8, 1959
                                                      Wellfleet

Dear Robert: Thanks for the poem. When you come up
here again, you must engrave it below the other one. I've
just come back from two weeks at Talcottville, inter-
spersed with trips to the Indians. I finally succeeded in
hearing (it is all in the dark) the Little Water Ceremony
—wasn't I telling you about it?—which is terrific and
makes you realize how much life there is left in the Indians. I hope you are back home or in Europe. Love to
Elizabeth.

                                                      Edmund

To Mary Meigs   July 3, 1959
                                                    Talcottville

. . . I am here all alone, but productive and enjoying
myself. Besides doing the Indians, I have completely
revised the text of *Hecate County*, which I do think is my
best book. I like sitting here in this house, which seems
to be practically part of the prehistoric limestone forma-
tion, and receiving Indians, lawyers for Indians, state
officials, and local relatives. It makes me feel like Sir
William Johnson—if you know who he was . . .

I finally succeeded in hearing the Little Water Ceremony—the thing that I missed before. Fenton got me
in, and we were the only people there. It is really terrific,
quite unlike anything else I have ever heard, except the
other song cycle which they also sing in the dark, and
not even much like that. I won't describe it here because
I am writing about it at length in my book. The Iroquois

nationalist movement is now going ahead so fast that what I am writing about it can hardly keep up with it . . .

I have been reading mostly local history—Mormonism, Indians, etc.—all very queer and violent . . .

To Mary Meigs   August 4, 1959
                                                      Talcottville

. . . Last week two Canadians came to visit us in connection with Indian matters. Canada is itself nowadays developing a passionate nationalism. They feel that they have got away from England, but that they now have to contend with the United States. It was amusing to find that my guests and I were presently competing as to which group of Iroquois—ours or the Canadian ones—was the more authentic and important. Since the Iroquois sided mostly with the British at the time of the Revolution, the Canadians regard them as their loyal vassals, who defended them against the nasty Yanks. Mad Bear, the Iroquois leader, has just sent me a card from a big hotel in Cuba, where he says he is the honored guest of Castro. I don't know what this means . . .

To William Shawn   September 1959
The New Yorker   Wellfleet

Here is the whole thing. I held over Part III, hoping to get the latest news about the Kinzua Dam. It still hasn't come, so I'll have to attend to this in proof . . . The point I have omitted on pp. 284–5 is really, I think, important, but the article will read more smoothly without it.

Anyone who edits the MS or reads the proofs ought to know that the Allegany reservation, the Allegheny River, and the Alleghany Mountains are all spelled in different ways. My writing of the Indian names does not keep to a consistent usage, but I'll straighten that out in the proofs.

EW

NOTEBOOKS OF THE SIXTIES

She is a very pretty Seneca woman . . . who comes from the Allegany reservation and went to the Indian school —married an Italian psychiatrist who went to Princeton and now practices there.

To Bette Crouse Mele   August 10, 1960
                                                    Talcottville

Dear Mrs. Mele: Thank you very much for your letter. It happened to arrive when Bill Fenton was here visiting me, and he told me that he remembered your mother well, that she was a beauty, and that he was once allowed to be present when she was ill and they were performing ceremonies to cure her—he and I and a lot of other people are doing what we can to avert the Kinzua Dam. I suppose you must be related to Clifford Crouse of Quaker Bridge (I described his family in my book) and Elon Crouse of Tuscarora.

I should like very much to meet you, but I almost never get to New York—I live in Massachusetts in the winter. Do you ever get to this part of the world? . . . The little village I live in is Talcottville, Lewis County. It is about an hour's drive north of Utica. I should be very glad to see you. Or if you should come to Boston, I'll be at 12 Hilliard Street, Cambridge, this winter.

I was interested in what you say about Seneca family life. I hadn't been aware of this, but I suppose a somewhat uncomfortable situation is created by each new generation's being drawn more and more strongly toward the non-Indian world about them.

I am very much pleased that you wrote me.

Sincerely, Edmund Wilson

To Bette Crouse Mele   December 16, 1961
                                    Cambridge

Dear Mrs. Mele: I understand that Kennedy spent part of a day looking up the Kinzua Dam situation and decided that it was something that had been settled during the Eisenhower Administration and that there was nothing he could do about it. William Fenton, when I last saw him, told me that the reservation was now doomed. It is outrageous—like a lot of other things that our government has been doing.

Christmas greetings, Edmund Wilson

To Bette Crouse Mele   January 2, 1963
                                    Cambridge

. . . I was glad to have news of Quaker Bridge and the Senecas. I get their bulletin about the Kinzua situation, and it always makes me angry to think what has happened to them . . .

To BETTE CROUSE MELE   April 3, 1964
                                           Rome, Italy

. . . About taxes: The Mohawks in St. Regis not long ago forced a showdown with the tax authorities. They put up a battle but lost. They should certainly not have to pay taxes, when they refuse to be U.S. citizens. Of course, I should be very much honored to belong to the Hawk clan, but I don't think it is a good idea to bring pressure to bear for this purpose . . .

To BETTE CROUSE MELE   June 13, 1965

Dear Mrs. Mele: I am glad to hear that the baby has arrived, and I am honored that you have wanted to name him after me. But I do think it is something of a mistake to give a child so many names. I have only one myself and have always been glad not to be loaded with initials. Everybody, I imagine, will call your boy Tony and forget about the rest. After all, he may never read my books and may not like them if he does . . . My regards to your husband . . . Best wishes to you and Tony.

                                         Edmund W

In 1963 I met Edmund Wilson in Talcottville. I had written him following the *New Yorker* articles which became the book that is the best contemporary work on the Iroquois. Mr. Wilson took the Iroquois out of the libraries of archaeological and anthropological texts into the modern world. He presented us in a most sensitive fashion, as people capable of handling our own destiny in spite of the overwhelming odds against us, due to the multiple water projects in New York State at a time when the general U.S. population was not aware of Native Americans east of the Mississippi . . .

. . . I had the child named Antonio Edmund Wilson Mele so that Mr. Wilson's name would be on the Seneca rolls . . .

The Memorial ceremony for Edmund Wilson was in Wellfleet. But part of the memorial tribute to Mr. Wilson belongs to us, for the legacy of *Apologies to the Iroquois*, which made an impact on both the Indian and the non-Indian world at a critical time in Iroquois history . . .

—Bette Crouse Mele, "Edmund Wilson, 1895–1972,"
in *The Indian Historian* (Fall 1972)

To Sir Compton Mackenzie　　　　August 18, 1958
Edinburgh, Scotland

Dear Sir Compton: I have lately been interested in the nationalist movement of the Iroquois Indians in New York State. They occupy reservations their title to which and jurisdiction in which were supposed to be guaranteed to them by treaties with the federal government made after the Revolution, when they were recognized as a sovereign nation. They have recently been deprived of certain rights, and are fighting not to be put out of several of their reservations, which the New York or U.S. authorities are threatening to take for various public projects. I am going to write something about this